First World War
and Army of Occupation
War Diary
France, Belgium and Germany

51 DIVISION
152 Infantry Brigade
Princess Louise's (Argyll & Sutherland Highlanders)
1/8th Battalion
5 August 1914 - 17 March 1918

WO95/2865/2

The Naval & Military Press Ltd
www.nmarchive.com
Published in association with The National Archives

Published by

The Naval & Military Press Ltd

Unit 10 Ridgewood Industrial Park,

Uckfield, East Sussex,

TN22 5QE England

Tel: +44 (0) 1825 749494

www.naval-military-press.com

www.nmarchive.com

This diary has been reprinted in facsimile from the original. Any imperfections are inevitably reproduced and the quality may fall short of modern type and cartographic standards.

© Crown Copyright

Images reproduced by permission of The National Archives, London, England, 2015.

Contents

Document type	Place/Title	Date From	Date To
Heading	WO95/2865 8/Argyll & Sutherland Highlanders Apr'15-Mar'18		
Heading	51st Division 152nd Infy Bde 8th Bn A. & S. Hdrs Apr 1915-Mar 1918		
Miscellaneous	Training Details	04/08/1914	04/08/1914
War Diary	Dunoon	05/08/1914	16/08/1914
Miscellaneous	Appendix No. 1		
Miscellaneous	Appendix 2.		
Miscellaneous	Appendix III		
Miscellaneous	Appendix IV		
War Diary	Bedford	17/08/1914	30/11/1914
War Diary	Howbury	01/12/1914	31/12/1914
War Diary	Howbury-Bedford	01/01/1915	17/02/1915
War Diary	Bedford	03/01/1915	28/02/1915
Miscellaneous	Operation Orders by Lieut Colonel R. Campbell Commanding 1/8th (The Argyllshire) Battalion Princess Louise's (Argyll & Sutherland) Highlanders	20/03/1915	20/03/1915
War Diary	Bedford	01/03/1915	31/03/1915
Miscellaneous	Special Order 23 By Brigadier General St George Burton Commanding 1/1st Argyll & Sutherland Infantry Brigade T.F.	26/03/1915	26/03/1915
Miscellaneous	Special Order 22 By Brigadier General St George Burton Commanding 1/1st Argyll & Sutherland Infantry Brigade T.F.	26/03/1916	26/03/1916
Miscellaneous	Bde No C/B. 6	01/04/1915	01/04/1915
War Diary	Bedford	01/04/1915	30/04/1915
Heading	51st Division 1/8th A & S. H Vol I 1-31.5.15		
War Diary	Bedford	01/05/1915	01/05/1915
War Diary	Folkestone	02/05/1915	02/05/1915
War Diary	Boulogne	02/05/1915	02/05/1915
War Diary	Pont De Briques	02/05/1915	02/05/1915
War Diary	Merville	02/05/1915	02/05/1915
War Diary	Robecq	03/05/1915	14/05/1915
War Diary	Merris	14/05/1915	18/05/1915
War Diary	Vielle Chapelle	19/05/1915	19/05/1915
War Diary	Richebourg	20/05/1915	25/05/1915
War Diary	Richbourg La Couture	26/05/1915	27/05/1915
War Diary	Richebourg	28/05/1915	30/05/1915
War Diary	Locon	30/05/1915	31/05/1915
Heading	51st Division 1/8 A & S Hd Vol II 1-30.6.15		
War Diary	Locon	01/06/1915	01/06/1915
War Diary	La Tombe Wilot	01/06/1915	08/06/1915
War Diary	Festubert	09/06/1915	14/06/1915
War Diary	Locon	14/06/1915	15/06/1915
War Diary	Le Touret	16/06/1915	16/06/1915
War Diary	Locon	16/06/1915	16/06/1915
War Diary	Le Touret	17/06/1915	17/06/1915
War Diary	Festubert	18/06/1915	23/06/1915
War Diary	Le Cornet Malo	23/06/1915	25/06/1915
War Diary	Estaires	26/06/1915	30/06/1915

Heading	51st Division 1/8 A & S. H Vol III 1-31.7.15		
War Diary	Picantin	01/07/1915	09/07/1915
War Diary	La Gorgue	10/07/1915	14/07/1915
War Diary	Laventie	15/07/1915	27/07/1915
War Diary	La Houssey	28/07/1915	29/07/1915
War Diary	Bouzincourt	30/07/1915	30/07/1915
War Diary	Authille	31/07/1915	31/07/1915
Heading	51st Division War Diary of 8th Bn. Argyll & Sutherland Highrs From 1st-31st 1915 Vol IV		
War Diary	Authville	01/08/1915	13/08/1915
War Diary	Millencourt	14/08/1915	21/08/1915
War Diary	La Boisselle	21/08/1915	31/08/1915
Heading	51st Division War Diary Of 8th Argyll & Sutherland Highrs From 1.IX.15 To 30.IX.15 Vol V		
War Diary	La Boiselle	01/09/1915	01/09/1915
War Diary	Millencourt	02/09/1915	10/09/1915
War Diary	Albert	11/09/1915	18/09/1915
War Diary	Millencourt	19/09/1915	21/09/1915
War Diary	Aveluy	22/09/1915	26/09/1915
War Diary	Millencourt	27/09/1915	30/09/1915
Heading	War Diary Of Head Quarters. 152nd Inf. Bde. From 1.IX.15 To 30.IX.15		
Heading	51st Division 1/8th A & S H.Q. Vol VI Oct 15		
Heading	War Diary of 1st 8th 13th Arg. & Suth Highlanders from 1st To 31st October 1915 Volume II		
War Diary	Authville	01/10/1915	10/10/1915
War Diary	Millencourt	11/10/1915	19/10/1915
War Diary	Authville	20/10/1915	30/10/1915
War Diary	Martinsart	30/10/1915	31/10/1915
Miscellaneous	1/8th (The Argyllshire) Bn Argyll & Sutherland Highlanders	28/10/1915	28/10/1915
Miscellaneous	51st Division War Diary Of 1/8th Argyll & Sutherland Highlanders From 1st November 1915 To 30th November 1915 Vol VII		
War Diary	Martinsart	01/11/1915	07/11/1915
War Diary	Aveluy	08/11/1915	22/11/1915
War Diary	Millencourt	23/11/1915	28/11/1915
War Diary	Authville	29/11/1915	30/11/1915
Heading	War Diary Of 1/8th Argyll & Sutherland Highlanders Form 1st December 1915 To 31st December 1915 Vol VIII		
War Diary	Authville	01/12/1915	11/12/1915
War Diary	Millencourt	12/12/1915	15/12/1915
War Diary	Aveluy	16/12/1915	23/12/1915
War Diary	Millencourt	24/12/1915	28/12/1915
War Diary	Montigny	29/12/1915	29/12/1915
War Diary	Villers Bocage	30/12/1915	31/12/1915
Heading	War Diary Of 1/8th Bn. Argyll & Sutherland Highlanders From 1st January 1916 To 31st January 1916 Vol IX		
War Diary	Villers Bocage	01/01/1916	31/01/1916
Miscellaneous	51st (Highland) Division	23/01/1916	23/01/1916
Miscellaneous	51st (Highland) Divisional School		
Miscellaneous	School Programme	24/01/1916	24/01/1916
Miscellaneous	School Programme	30/01/1916	30/01/1916

Heading	War Diary Of 1/8th Bn. Argyll And Sutherland Highlanders February 1916 Vol X		
War Diary	Villers Bocage	01/02/1916	07/02/1916
War Diary	Corbie	08/02/1916	25/02/1916
War Diary	Daours	26/02/1916	29/02/1916
War Diary	In The Field	29/02/1916	29/02/1916
Heading	War Diary Of 1/8th Bn. Argyll & Sutherland Highlanders From 1st March 1916 To 31st March 1916 Vol XI		
War Diary	Mollien Au Bois	01/03/1916	05/03/1916
War Diary	Beauval	06/02/1916	08/02/1916
War Diary	Ivergny	09/03/1916	09/03/1916
War Diary	Maroeuil	10/03/1916	10/03/1916
War Diary	Labyrinthe	11/03/1916	25/03/1916
War Diary	Maroeuil	26/03/1916	30/03/1916
War Diary	Labyrinthe	31/03/1916	31/03/1916
Heading	War Diary Of 1/8th Bn. Arg. & Suth'd Highlanders From 1st April 1916 To 30th April 1916 Vol XII		
War Diary	Labyrinthe	01/04/1916	16/04/1916
War Diary	Maroeuil	17/04/1916	22/04/1916
War Diary	Labyrinthe	23/04/1916	30/04/1916
Miscellaneous	General Officer Commanding 152nd Infantry Brigade	28/04/1916	28/04/1916
Heading	War Diary Of 1/8th Battn. Argyll and Sutherland Highlanders From 1st May 1916 To 31st May 1916 Vol 13		
Miscellaneous	152nd Infantry Brigade Secret No. 134	02/06/1916	02/06/1916
War Diary	Labyrinthe	01/05/1916	11/05/1916
War Diary	Maroeuil	12/05/1916	16/05/1916
War Diary	Labyrinthe	17/05/1916	24/05/1916
War Diary	Bray	25/05/1916	31/05/1916
War Diary	In The Field	31/05/1916	31/05/1916
Heading	War Diary Of 1/8th Bn. Argyll & Sutherland Highlanders From 1st June 1916 To 30th June 1916 Vol 14		
Miscellaneous	152nd Inf. Bde. Secret No. 134	01/07/1916	01/07/1916
War Diary	Neuville St Vaast	01/06/1916	05/06/1916
War Diary	Vimy (P. Sector)	06/06/1916	12/06/1916
War Diary	Bray	13/06/1916	17/06/1916
War Diary	Vimy (P. Sector)	18/06/1916	22/06/1916
War Diary	Vimy	23/06/1916	24/06/1916
War Diary	Neuville St Vaast	25/06/1916	29/06/1916
War Diary	Vimy (P Sector)	30/06/1916	30/06/1916
Heading	152nd Brigade 51st Division 1/8th Battalion Argyle & Sutherland Highlanders July 1916		
Heading	152nd Inf. Brigade Secret No. 134 Vol 15 War Diary Of 1/8th Bn. Argyll & Sutherland Highlanders July 1916		
War Diary	Vimy Ridge P (Left 2) Sector	01/07/1916	04/07/1916
War Diary	On Line Of March	05/07/1916	05/07/1916
War Diary	Osterville	06/07/1916	10/07/1916
War Diary	Ecoivres	11/07/1916	11/07/1916
War Diary	Maroeuil	12/07/1916	14/07/1916
War Diary	Ecoivres	15/07/1916	15/07/1916
War Diary	Sus St Leger	15/07/1916	15/07/1916
War Diary	Gezaincourt	16/07/1916	21/07/1916
War Diary	Fricourt	22/07/1916	23/07/1916

War Diary	Becordel-Becourt	24/07/1916	25/07/1916
War Diary	Mametz Wood	26/07/1916	27/07/1916
War Diary	Fricourt Wood	27/07/1916	31/07/1916
Heading	152nd Brigade 51st Division 1/8th Battalion Argyle & Sutherland Highlanders August 1916		
Miscellaneous	Headquarters 152nd Inf Bde.	01/09/1916	01/09/1916
War Diary	Fricourt Wood	01/08/1916	04/08/1916
War Diary	High Wood	05/08/1916	07/08/1916
War Diary	Buire	08/08/1916	09/08/1916
War Diary	Longpre Les-Corps-Saints	10/08/1916	12/08/1916
War Diary	Blaringhem	13/08/1916	18/08/1916
War Diary	Armentiers	19/08/1916	31/08/1916
Heading	War Diary Of 1/8th Bn. Arg. & Suth'd. Highlanders From 1st September 1916 To 30th September 1916 Vol 17		
Miscellaneous	Headquarters 152nd Inf. Bde.	01/10/1916	01/10/1916
War Diary	Armentieres	01/09/1916	18/09/1916
War Diary	Bailleul	19/09/1916	30/09/1916
Heading	War Diary Of 1/8th Bn. Argyll and Sutherland Highlanders From 1st October 1916 To 31st October 1916 Vol 18		
War Diary	Gezaincourt	01/10/1916	01/10/1916
War Diary	Bois Du Warnimont	02/10/1916	03/10/1916
War Diary	Sailly Au Bois	04/10/1916	05/10/1916
War Diary	Hebuterne	06/10/1916	08/10/1916
War Diary	Bus	08/10/1916	16/10/1916
War Diary	Auchonvillers	17/10/1916	19/10/1916
War Diary	Mailly Maillet	20/10/1916	21/10/1916
War Diary	Lealvillers	22/10/1916	31/10/1916
Heading	War Diary Of 1/8th Bn. Argyll and Sutherland Highrs. November 1916 Vol 19		
War Diary	Mailly Wood	01/11/1916	05/11/1916
War Diary	Forceville	06/11/1916	14/11/1916
War Diary	Mailly Wood	14/11/1916	18/11/1916
War Diary	Trenches	19/11/1916	23/11/1916
War Diary	Forceville	24/11/1916	26/11/1916
War Diary	Senlis	27/11/1916	30/11/1916
Miscellaneous	Report On The Operation At Beaumont Hamel On The 13th November 1916	18/11/1916	18/11/1916
Miscellaneous	Casualties During Action Of 13/14 Nov 1916	30/11/1916	30/11/1916
Miscellaneous	List Of Officer Joining On	25/11/1916	25/11/1916
Heading	War Diary Of 1/8th Bn. Argyll and Sutherland Highrs. From 1st December 1916 To 31st December 1916 Vol 20		
War Diary	Senlis	01/12/1916	03/12/1916
War Diary	Ovillers Huts	04/12/1916	09/12/1916
War Diary	Courcelette	09/12/1916	15/12/1916
War Diary	Senlis	16/12/1916	21/12/1916
War Diary	Ovillers Huts	22/12/1916	27/12/1916
War Diary	Courcellette	28/12/1916	31/12/1916
Heading	152nd Inf. Bde. Secret No. 134 War Diary Of 1/8th Battn. Argyll And Sutherland Highrs. From 1st January 1917 To 31st January 1917 Vol 21		
Miscellaneous	H.Q. 152nd Inf. Bde.	31/01/1917	31/01/1917
War Diary	Ovillers	01/01/1917	01/01/1917
War Diary	Aveluy	02/01/1917	02/01/1917

War Diary	Senlis	03/01/1917	08/01/1917
War Diary	Ovillers	09/01/1917	11/01/1917
War Diary	Senlis	12/01/1917	12/01/1917
War Diary	Beauquesne	13/01/1917	13/01/1917
War Diary	Le Meillard	14/01/1917	14/01/1917
War Diary	Yvrencheux	15/01/1917	15/01/1917
War Diary	Nouvion En Ponthieu	16/01/1917	29/01/1917
War Diary	Le Plessiel	30/01/1917	31/01/1917
Heading	War Diary Of 1/8th Bn. Argyll & Sutherland Highlanders From 1st February 1917 To 28th February 1917 Vol 22		
War Diary	Le Plessiel	01/02/1917	04/02/1917
War Diary	Maison Ponthieu	05/02/1917	05/02/1917
War Diary	Noeux	06/02/1917	06/02/1917
War Diary	Oeuf	07/02/1917	07/02/1917
War Diary	Chelers	08/02/1917	08/02/1917
War Diary	Villers Brulin	09/02/1917	09/02/1917
War Diary	Maroeuil	10/02/1917	10/02/1917
War Diary	Roclincourt	11/02/1917	16/02/1917
War Diary	Ecurie	17/02/1917	26/02/1917
War Diary	Ecoivres	27/02/1917	28/02/1917
Heading	War Diary Of 1/8th Bn. Argyll And Sutherland Highlanders From 1st March 1917 To 31st March 1917 Vol 23		
War Diary	Ecoivres	01/03/1917	02/03/1917
War Diary	Roclincourt	03/03/1917	09/03/1917
War Diary	Ecoivres	10/03/1917	16/03/1917
War Diary	Roclincourt	17/03/1917	17/03/1917
War Diary	Ecoivres	18/03/1917	21/03/1917
War Diary	Agnieres	22/03/1917	22/03/1917
War Diary	Caucourt	23/03/1917	29/03/1917
War Diary	Agnieres	30/03/1917	30/03/1917
War Diary	Caucourt	31/03/1917	31/03/1917
Miscellaneous	Report On Raid Carried Out By 1/8th Bn. Argyll & Suth'd Highrs	17/03/1917	17/03/1917
Map	Second Phase Zero To Zero +2		
Map	Third Phase Zero + 2 To Zero +40		
Miscellaneous	First Phase Zero-1 To Zero		
Miscellaneous	Appendix III. Action of Vickers Guns.		
Operation(al) Order(s)	152nd Infantry Brigade Order No. 129	14/03/1917	14/03/1917
Miscellaneous	Rate of fire and ammunition		
Miscellaneous	Programme Of Raid		
Miscellaneous	Amendment No. 1 To 152nd Infantry Brigade Order No. 129		
Miscellaneous	Addenda To 152nd Inf. Bde. Order No. 129		
Miscellaneous	Addition To 152nd Infantry Brigade Order No. 129		
Operation(al) Order(s)	Operation Order No. 21 by Lieut Colonel R. Campbell Commanding 1/8th (The Argyllshire) Battn Princess Louise's (Argyll & Sutherland) Highlanders	12/03/1917	12/03/1917
Miscellaneous	Addenda To Report On Raid By 1/8th Bn. A. & S. Highrs.	18/03/1917	18/03/1917
Miscellaneous	Stares Carried By Groups		
Map	II Groups Each Under An Officer		
Miscellaneous	On His Majesty's Service.		
Heading	War Diary Of 1/8th Bn. Argyll & Sutherland Highlanders For April 1917 Vol 24		

War Diary	Agnieres & Caucourt	01/04/1917	05/04/1917
War Diary	Bois De Maroeuil	06/04/1917	08/04/1917
War Diary	Roclincourt	09/04/1917	11/04/1917
War Diary	Ecoivres	12/04/1917	13/04/1917
War Diary	ACQ.	14/04/1917	16/04/1917
War Diary	Arras.	17/04/1917	18/04/1917
War Diary	Fampoux	19/04/1917	22/04/1917
War Diary	Arras	23/04/1917	24/04/1917
War Diary	St. Nicholas	25/04/1917	26/04/1917
War Diary	ACQ.	27/04/1917	28/04/1917
War Diary	Ternas	29/04/1917	30/04/1917
Heading	War Diary Of 1/8th Bn. Argyll and Sutherland Highlanders May 1917 Vol 25		
War Diary	Ternas	01/05/1917	10/05/1917
War Diary	Arras	11/05/1917	12/05/1917
War Diary	Fampoux	12/05/1917	16/05/1917
War Diary	St. Laurent Blangy	17/05/1917	17/05/1917
War Diary	Arras	18/05/1917	30/05/1917
War Diary	Ternas	31/05/1917	31/05/1917
Miscellaneous	Operation Order By Lieut-Colonel R. Campbell D.S.O. Commanding 1/8th (The Argyllshire) Battalion Princess Louise's (Argyll & Sutherland) Highlanders	13/05/1917	13/05/1917
Miscellaneous	Operation 16th May 1917	18/05/1917	18/05/1917
Miscellaneous	1/8th Bn. Argyll & Sutherland Highlanders	13/05/1917	13/05/1917
Miscellaneous	Roll Of Officers Who Took Part In Operations 12/17th May 1917	12/05/1917	12/05/1917
Miscellaneous	WO95/2865 8 & 9 End Public Record Office		
Heading	War Diary Of 1/8th Bn. Argyll and Sutherland Highlanders June 1917 Vol 26		
War Diary	Ternas	01/06/1917	04/06/1917
War Diary	Hestrus	04/06/1917	05/06/1917
War Diary	Dennebroeucq	06/06/1917	09/06/1917
War Diary	Recques	10/06/1917	21/06/1917
War Diary	St. Momelin	22/06/1917	03/07/1917
War Diary	Vlamertinghe	04/07/1917	07/07/1917
War Diary	Yser Canal	08/07/1917	10/07/1917
War Diary	Vlamertinghe	11/07/1917	11/07/1917
War Diary	Lederzeele	12/07/1917	24/07/1917
War Diary	Proven A. 30. Sector	24/07/1917	30/07/1917
War Diary	N. Of Yser Canal	31/07/1917	31/07/1917
Operation(al) Order(s)	Operation Order No. 43 by Lieut Colonel R. Campbell Commanding 1/8th (The Argyllshire) Battn Princess Louise's (Argyll & Sutherland) Highlanders	25/07/1917	25/07/1917
War Diary	Yser Canal	01/08/1917	01/08/1917
War Diary	A. 30 Central	02/08/1917	04/08/1917
War Diary	Siege Camp	05/08/1917	08/08/1917
War Diary	St. Janster Biezen	09/08/1917	29/08/1917
War Diary	Essex Farm	30/08/1917	02/09/1917
War Diary	Langemarck Line	03/09/1917	06/09/1917
War Diary	Dirty Bucket Camp	07/09/1917	19/09/1917
War Diary	Varna Farm	20/09/1917	20/09/1917
War Diary	Snipe House	20/09/1917	22/09/1917
War Diary	Dirty Bucket Camp.	23/09/1917	24/09/1917
War Diary	Siege Camp.	25/09/1917	30/09/1917
Heading	War Diary October 1917 8th Arg & Suth Hrs. Vol 30		

Heading	1/8th Battn. Argyll & Sutherland Highlander War Diary October 1917 Volume III Sheets 46,47,48		
War Diary	Achiet-Le-Petit	01/10/1917	05/10/1917
War Diary	Boisleux Au Mont	06/10/1917	16/10/1917
War Diary	Heninel	17/10/1917	31/10/1917
Heading	152nd Brigade 51st Division 1/8th Battalion Argyle & Sutherland Highlanders November 1917		
War Diary	Warlus	01/11/1917	17/11/1917
War Diary	Rocquigny	18/11/1917	18/11/1917
War Diary	Metz-En-Couture	19/11/1917	24/11/1917
War Diary	Flesquires	25/11/1917	25/11/1917
War Diary	Ytres	26/11/1917	26/11/1917
War Diary	Aveluy	26/11/1917	26/11/1917
War Diary	Bouzincourt	26/11/1917	30/11/1917
Miscellaneous	Headquarters 152nd Inf. Brigade	28/11/1917	28/11/1917
Miscellaneous	Operation On 21st Nov. 1917	21/11/1917	21/11/1917
Miscellaneous	Operation On 23rd November 1917	23/11/1917	23/11/1917
Miscellaneous	Signal Communications		
Miscellaneous	Casualties		
War Diary	Barastre	01/12/1917	01/12/1917
War Diary	Barastre & Fremicourt	02/12/1917	02/12/1917
War Diary	Fremicourt	03/12/1917	04/12/1917
War Diary	Louverval	05/12/1917	09/12/1917
War Diary	Louverval Fremicourt	10/12/1917	13/12/1917
War Diary	Fremicourt	11/12/1917	13/12/1917
War Diary	Fremicourt Bancourt	14/12/1917	14/12/1917
War Diary	Bancourt	14/12/1917	26/12/1917
War Diary	Demicourt	26/12/1917	29/12/1917
War Diary	Fremicourt	30/12/1917	31/12/1917
Heading	War Diary Of 1/8th Bn. Arg. & Suth'd Highrs. From 1st To 31st Jan. 1918 Vol 33		
Heading	February 1918 War Diary Of 8th A. & S. H. Vol 34		
War Diary	Fremicourt	01/01/1918	07/01/1918
War Diary	Doignies	08/01/1918	15/01/1918
War Diary	Fremicourt (Middlesex Camp)	16/01/1918	17/01/1918
War Diary	Achiet-Le-Petit	18/01/1918	31/01/1918
Map	Map		
War Diary	Buchanan Camp	01/02/1918	01/02/1918
War Diary	Achiet-Le-Petit	01/02/1918	04/02/1918
War Diary	Achiet-Le-Petit & Languevoisin	05/02/1918	07/02/1918
War Diary	Languevoisin & Vaux	07/02/1918	11/02/1918
War Diary	Pontruet	12/02/1918	19/02/1918
War Diary	Pontruet & Marteville	20/02/1918	28/02/1918
Miscellaneous	A Form Messages And Signals		
War Diary	Marteville Huts	01/03/1918	02/03/1918
War Diary	Beauvois	03/03/1918	10/03/1918
War Diary	Fresnoy	11/03/1918	17/03/1918

2

WO95/2865

8/Argyll & Sutherland Highlanders

Apr '15 – Mar '18

51ST DIVISION
152ND INFY BDE

~~T~~ 8TH BN A. & S. HDRS

APR 1915 - ~~JAN~~ MAR 1918

Latter part of March is missing !!! (21st onwards)
L. H. M.

TO 15 DIV 45 BDE

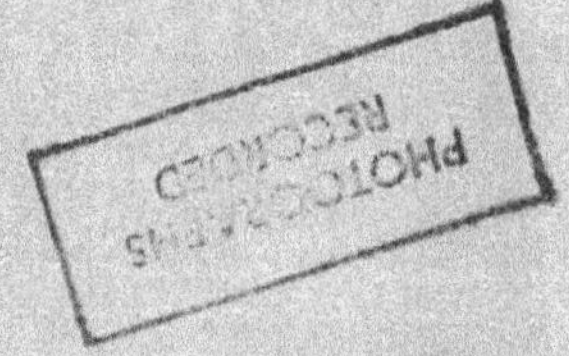

Highlanders

$\frac{152}{51}$

Training Details

4.8.14 30.4.15

X1-9

Sheet one

Instructions regarding War Diaries and Intelligence Summaries are contained in F. S. Regs., Part II. and the Staff Manual respectively. Title pages will be prepared in manuscript.

WAR DIARY
or
~~INTELLIGENCE SUMMARY~~
(Erase heading not required.)

Army Form C. 2118.

Hour, Date, Place	Summary of Events and Information	Remarks and References to Appendices
5.30 p.m. 4/8/14 Dunoon.	Order to mobilize received by wire.	Notices to join were completed and posted by an officer at 3.22 a.m. 5/8/14 App.
5/8/14. Dunoon	nil	
6/8/14. Dunoon	10 a.m. Took over billets. Battalion assembled at Head Quarters in accordance with mobilisation scheme.	No hitch in carrying arrangement Appendix II
7/8/14. Dunoon	mobilising	
8/8/14		
9/8/14		
10/8/14		
11/8/14	Brigadier informed mobilization complete except for Ordnance Stores	Ordnance Stores for [illegible] [illegible] from Ordnance Depot should be despatched first.
12/8/14	Embarkation of 1st & 2nd line transport. This was completed to time under supervision of entire Battalion Staff.	This also worked without hitch.
13/8/14 Dunoon Dunblane	Battalion embarked at Dunoon and disembarked with 1st & 2nd line transport complete at GOUROCK and entrained for DUNBLANE at scheduled hours. Arrived at DUNBLANE. And occupation of Billets.	
14/8/14 Dunblane	In billets at DUNBLANE	Latrine accommodation insufficient for raw troops; no screens provided.
15/8/14 Stirling	march to STIRLING by ½ battalions and entrain at 6 & 8 p.m. ← for BEDFORD	
16/8/14 [illegible]	Arrived at BEDFORD at 11.30 a.m. and 12.45 p.m. and [illegible] billets in vicinity of [illegible] [illegible] Road.	Latrine accommodation inadequate at first. An outbreak of [illegible] [illegible] occasioned [illegible].

Appendix No. 1

1. The notices were only got out by the time 3.22 a.m. by volunteers from the local company. The want of sufficient trained clerks in the Orderly Room — annually commented upon in Battalion Confidential (Report) — necessitated this and the same want has been the cause of enormous strain being thrown upon Officers & N.C.Os already over-engaged in other duties and which continue to the present moment. A Perm. Staff Sgt. with a Regtl. Ord. Rm training is essential. And two National Reservists with some training available on receipt of the precautionary wire should be appointed.

2. Owing to the scattered situation of the 8th Arg. & Suth. Highrs. a clerk — National Reservist or Pensioner — available on Mobilizn should be appointed for duty in Gr. Ars Depy.

3. War Establishments and Mobilization Tables are too technical for civilian or Territorial Officers employed on Horse Purchasing duties. Either separate Tables or explanatory equivalents should be issued for many items of equipment.

Appendix 2.

Owing to the want of definite instructions regarding the formation of a Depôt the work of Mobilization was unduly hampered by the great influx of recruits and candidates for commissions. A depôt consisting of a personnel according to requirement, i.e., a Commandant with an officer to act as Adjutant and Quartermaster, 1 Permanent Staff Sergt. 1 Qr. Mr. Sergt. and at least 8 N.C.Os, all to be supernumerary to establishment should form the Depôt at the place of Mobilization at a different building.

All training equipment was left at the Depôt and the want of it during training has been irreparable.

Appendix III

<u>Training.</u>

Physical Training. This only improved men under 30 years of age. Older men only got strained and lost other instruction through reporting sick.

Trews should be issued to kilted Battalions for wear during physical training, or shorts.

On completion of mobilization the Officers and N.C.Os should be given a three weeks course of instruction apart from the men altogether to fit them to act as instructors which at present they are not able to do. The men could be exercised in Route marching under Battn arrangements and thoroughly instructed in Hygiene, both personal and in regard to their quarters by the Medical Officer during this period.

5

Appendix IV

Permanent Staff

The Permanent Staff appointed has been found on mobilization to be totally inadequate to the training and administrative requirements.

Sheet two

WAR DIARY

or

~~INTELLIGENCE SUMMARY~~

(Erase heading not required.)

Army Form C. 2118.

6

Instructions regarding War Diaries and Intelligence Summaries are contained in F. S. Regs., Part II. and the Staff Manual respectively. Title pages will be prepared in manuscript.

Hour, Date, Place	Summary of Events and Information	Remarks and References to Appendices
17/8/14 BEDFORD.	Training	Appendix 3 & 4
[illegible]/8/14	"	
[illegible]4/8/14	"	
[illegible]0/8/14	"	
[illegible]1/8/14	"	
[illegible]/8/14	"	
[illegible]/8/14	"	
[illegible]4/8/14	"	
[illegible]5/8/14	"	
[illegible]6/8/14	"	
[illegible]/8/14	Inspection of ... Brigade by G.O.C. in C. Central Force.	
[illegible]/8/14	Training	

8th Cavl. Bde

Third Sheet

Instructions regarding War Diaries and Intelligence Summaries are contained in F. S. Regs., Part II, and the Staff Manual respectively. Title pages will be prepared in manuscript.

WAR DIARY
or
~~INTELLIGENCE SUMMARY~~
(Erase heading not required.)

Army Form C. 2118.

Hour, Date, Place	Summary of Events and Information	Remarks and References to Appendices
30/[illegible] BELFORT	Sunday Church service conducted by a Minister C of S [illegible]	
31/[illegible]	Inspection by G.O.C. 1st Army	
1/[illegible]	Training	
2	[illegible] of H.Q. to [illegible] Road	Order [illegible]
3	Training	
4	[illegible]	
5		
6	Sunday	
7	[illegible] Training [illegible] of [illegible] and T. [illegible]	[illegible] [illegible]
8	Training	
9	[illegible] Training	
10	Training	
11	Training [illegible]	[illegible]

8th Beds Fourth Sheet

Army Form C. 2118.

WAR DIARY
or
INTELLIGENCE SUMMARY
(Erase heading not required.)

Instructions regarding War Diaries and Intelligence Summaries are contained in F. S. Regs., Part II. and the Staff Manual respectively. Title pages will be prepared in manuscript.

Hour, Date, Place	Summary of Events and Information	Remarks and References to Appendices
BEDFORD	Company training. Further outbreak of Scarlet Fever in C. Coy	Inoculation continued
	Training under new scheme	
	C. Coy to isolation camp Third Sheet	Lectures on [illegible] by CO to Coy Comdrs on training all the week
	Company training. Study drill [illegible]	
	Training of Officers commenced	
	Brigade Route March	
	Sunday	
	Company training in area commenced	Inoculation continued
	Continued throughout week	
	Sunday	
	Company training – confined to Section training [illegible] other continued	

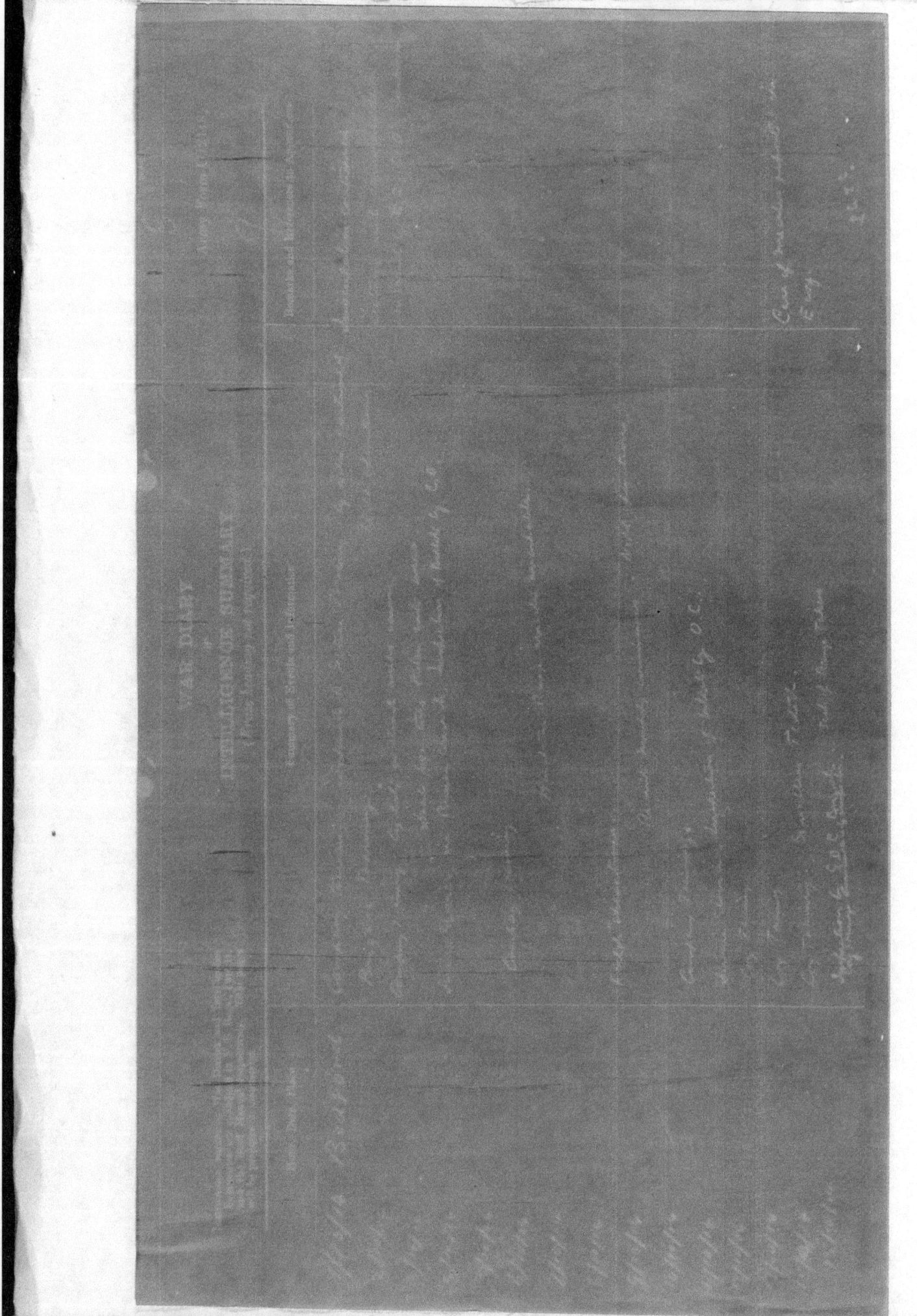

Army Form C. 2118.

WAR DIARY
or
INTELLIGENCE SUMMARY
(Erase heading not required.)

Hour, Date, Place	Summary of Events and Information	Remarks and References to Appendices
[illegible]	[illegible]	[illegible]

Instructions regarding War Diaries and Intelligence Summaries are contained in F. S. Regs., Part II. and the Staff Manual respectively. Title pages will be prepared in manuscript.

WAR DIARY
or
INTELLIGENCE SUMMARY
(Erase heading not required.)

6th Sheet

Army Form C. 2118.

10

Hour, Date, Place		Summary of Events and Information	Remarks and References to Appendices
16/10/14	Bedford	Coy Training. Recruits musketry. and drills	
17/10/14		Coy Training.	
18/10/14	"	Divine Service. Inspection by C.O. of billets.	
19/10/14	"	Coy Training Recruits training and Miniature Range	S Coy returned from Isolation Camp.
20/10/14	"	Coy Training. Recruits training and Miniature Range	
21/10/14	"	Coy Training Recruits training and Miniature Range	
22/10/14	"	Review of Highland Division by H.M. The King.	28 officers 990 other ranks on Parade.
23/10/14	"	Company training	
24/10/14	"	Company training.	E Coy to Segregation Camp
25/10/14	"	Divine Service Inspection of billets by C.O.	
26/10/14	"	Company marches by ½ batt" Recruits training	
27/10/14	"	" "	
28/10/14	"	Practice moove. Coy at training Recalled "	5)
29/10/14	"	Company marches 2nd ½ batt" Recruits training	[illegible]
30/10/14		" "	
31/10/14			

8/ A. T. N. 7th Sheet

(2 Sheets. 1st Sheet)

Instructions regarding War Diaries and Intelligence Summaries are contained in F. S. Regs., Part II. and the Staff Manual respectively. Title pages will be prepared in manuscript.

WAR DIARY
or
~~INTELLIGENCE SUMMARY~~
(Erase heading not required.)

Army Form C. 2118.

11

Hour, Date, Place		Summary of Events and Information	Remarks and References to Appendices
November 1	BEDFORD	Sunday. Divine Service [illegible]	
2		Divisional exercise in vicinity of CLAPHAM. Siting of trenches [illegible]	
3		Musketry commenced Table B. Part II. Appendix IV. at COPLE Range	
4		Battalion training [illegible]	[illegible] at Cople Range
5		— do — Route march	— do —
6		— do — [illegible] instruction	— do —
7		— do — — do — Battalion ordered to proceed to BIRMINGHAM on 9th November 1914	— do —
8		Sunday. Move to BIRMINGHAM cancelled. Divine Service	[illegible]
9		Musketry training — B. and [illegible]	— do —
10		— do — — do — [illegible] ground [illegible]	[illegible]
11		Musketry [illegible] Table B. Part II. Appendix IV. at COPLE Range	
12		— do — — do — — do —	
13		— do — — do — — do —	
14		— do — — do — — do —	[illegible]
15		— do — — do — — do —	
16		— do — — do — [illegible] Appendix [illegible] at COPLE	
17		— do — — do — — do —	
18		— do — — do — — do —	

Instructions regarding War Diaries and Intelligence Summaries are contained in F. S. Regs., Part II. and the Staff Manual respectively. Title pages will be prepared in manuscript.

8/A. [illegible] N

WAR DIARY
or
INTELLIGENCE SUMMARY
(Erase heading not required.)

8th Sheet

(2 Sheets – 2nd Sheet)

Army Form C. 2118.

12

Hour, Date, Place		Summary of Events and Information	Remarks and References to Appendices
Nov. 19th	BEDFORD	Battalion Musketry Practice at COPLE Range – Appx I Part III, Table B to R	Recruit Training
6 pm		Paraded at 6 pm for Insp. by Brigadier ready for Emergency move	
" 20	"	Musketry practice at COPLE Range – Appx I Part III Table B & R	"
" 21	"	——— do ——— ——— do ———	"
" 22	"	——— do ——— ——— do ———	Draft of [illegible] for [illegible]
" 23	"	Training. [illegible] HOWBURY whilst Musketry at COPLE	Several other ranks [illegible]
" 24	"	Moved to Camp at HOWBURY PARK 3 miles E of BEDFORD	Regular Adjutant Capt [illegible] to join Exped. Force [illegible] Adjutant of 6th Bn. GORDONS
" 25	"	Training and Recruits Musketry Training at COPLE Range	
" 26	"	Digging Trenches – Musketry at COPLE cancelled	Lectures daily at 6.30 pm by C.O. on Customs of War and more particularly on [illegible]
" 27	"	Siting and digging trenches near GT BARFORD	
" 28			
" 29		Divine Service, Inspection of Camp by Commanding Officer	
" 30		Battalion Training – Digging Trenches	

[illegible signature] Capt & Adjt. [illegible]

7th Sheet

Instructions regarding War Diaries and Intelligence Summaries are contained in F. S. Regs., Part II. and the Staff Manual respectively. Title pages will be prepared in manuscript.

WAR DIARY
or
INTELLIGENCE SUMMARY
(Erase heading not required.)

Army Form C. 2118.

13

Hour, Date, Place	Summary of Events and Information	Remarks and References to Appendices
December 1. NEWBURY.	Battalion Training – Entrenching. Recruit Training	Lectures daily by C.O. and other Officers to all ranks.
" 2 "	" " " " "	
" 3 "	" " " " "	
" 4 "	" " " " " Night Operations	
" 5 "	" " " " "	
" 6 "	Sunday – Camp Inspection	
" 7 "	Interior Economy and Drill } To improve Interior Economy	
" 8 "	" " " " }	
" 9 "	" " " " } Drill and Discipline	
" 10 "	" " " " }	
" 11 "	" " " " } Recruits Musketry – Standard Tests	Cross Country Running by companies
" 12 "	" " " " } " "	
" 13 "	Sunday " " "	
" 14 "	Battalion Training – ~~[illegible]~~ Training of additional M. G. Sections commenced.	
" 15 "	Battalion Training – M. G. Training – Recruit Training	
" 16 "	Battalion Training – Attack on an entrenched position.	Death of No. 1205 Cpl. E. McColl B Coy (Benderloch) & No. 1542 Pte. R. McPherson. C Coy. (Taira) Both from measles.
" 17. "	— do — Entrenching.	

10th Sheet

Army Form C. 2118.

WAR DIARY
or
~~INTELLIGENCE SUMMARY~~
(Erase heading not required.)

Instructions regarding War Diaries and Intelligence Summaries are contained in F. S. Regs., Part II. and the Staff Manual respectively. Title pages will be prepared in manuscript.

14

Hour, Date, Place	Summary of Events and Information	Remarks and References to Appendices
December 18th HOWBURY	Battalion Training – Night Operations	
" 19th "	— do — – Route march – 14 miles	
" 20th "	Sunday – Camp Inspection.	
" 21st "	Battalion Training – Entrenching	
" 22nd "	Battalion Training – Route march. Entrenching & Revetting [Brigade Training cancelled owing to ~~[illegible]~~	adaption of 4 Coy. organization for Training purposes.
" 23rd "	— do — Emergency move practice	
" 24th "	— do — Inspection by Brigade Commander in Emergency move order.	
" 25th "	Battalion Training	
" 26th "	Sunday — do — Camp Inspection.	
" 27th "		
" 28th "	Brigade Training.	
" 29th "	— do —	
" 30th "	— do — Route march with 1st Line Transport and Train.	
" 31st "	— do —	

Archd. Jackson Capt. & Adjt.
1/7 A. & S. Hghrs

[illegible] / 4th [illegible] H.

11th [illegible]

Army Form C.2118

WAR DIARY or ~~Intelligence~~ Summary.

15

Hour, Date, & Place.	Summary of Events and Information,	REMARKS and references to Appendices.
[illegible]RY – BEDFORD	Transferred into billets in BEDFORD. White [illegible] billeted in furnished houses.	[illegible] at [illegible] left standing owing to wet weather.
[illegible] BEDFORD	Sunday – Divine Service. Inspection of billets. Death of No. 926 Pte D. JOHNSTONE	"A" Coy [illegible]
[illegible]	[illegible] Training – Emergency [illegible] Practice – By Road.	
[illegible]	– do – Route March in Division. [illegible] Discipline.	
[illegible]	– do – [illegible] Drill & Interior Economy	
7th	– do – Attack on a position	
[illegible]	– do – Battalion Drill & Interior Economy. Entrainment in [illegible] train practised.	[illegible] Entrainment & Detrainment took 45 minutes.
9th	– do – [illegible] marching on [illegible] roads.	
[illegible]	Sunday – Divine service – Inspection of billets	
11th	[illegible] Training – Retreat.	
12th	– do – Battalion Drill & Interior Economy	
13th	– do – Flank March	
14th	– do – Entrainment [illegible] in [illegible] train [illegible] 70 minutes.	
[illegible]	– do – [illegible] operations	
16th	– do – Emergency [illegible] Practice – By Road.	
17th	Sunday – Divine service. Inspection of billets. Death of No. [illegible] Pte [illegible] "A" Coy at TAMWORTH	

[illegible signature]
[illegible] Major
7th [illegible]

Army Form C 2118

12th Sheet 16

WAR DIARY
or
~~Intelligence~~ Summary.

Hour, Date, & Place.	Summary of Events and Information,	REMARKS and references to Appendices.
January 1915 BEDFORD	Company Recruit Cyclists M.G. Section & Signallers Training. Death of No. 1314 Pte H. Macdonald	H Coy at Kimbolton Rd Isolation Hosp. [illegible] from Measles - Broncho-Pneu
[illegible]	— do —	
[illegible]	Company & Battalion Training	
[illegible]	— do —	
[illegible]	— do —	
[illegible]	— do —	
[illegible]	[illegible]	[illegible]
[illegible]	Company & Battalion Training	
[illegible]	— do —	[illegible]
[illegible]	— do —	[illegible]
[illegible]	[illegible]	[illegible]
[illegible]	Company & Battalion Training	[illegible]
[illegible]	— do —	
[illegible]	[illegible]	

[illegible] Capt. & Adjt.
[illegible]

1/8th Bn Arg & Suth Highrs

13th Sheet

WAR DIARY
OF
~~INTELLIGENCE SUMMARY~~
(Erase heading not required)

Army Form C. 2118.

17

Hour, Date, Place			Summary of Events and Information	Remarks and References to Appendices
February	1st	BEDFORD	Company Training	
	2nd	"	Divisional Training - Route march & Inspectn by G.O.C.-in-C. Central Force.	
	3rd	"	Company Training. Party of Recruits proceeded to ATHERSTONE for musketry	{Designation of Battalion changed to 1/8th Battn
	4th	"	Company Training - Route march with Service Transport.	
	5th	"	— do —	
	6th	"	— do —	
	7th	"	Sunday Divine Service & Inspn. of Billets	
	8th	"	Company Training	(Inspection on 3rd duly of R&S Bde by H.R.H. Princess Louise.)
	9th	"	— do —	
	10th	"	— do —	
	11th	"	— do — Route march with Service Transport.	
	12th	"	— do —	
	13th	"	— do — No 914 Pte. A Sinclair, A Coy. died at Leicester Gen. Hospt.	
	14th	"	Sunday - Divine Service & Inspn. of Billets	
	15th	"	Company Training	
	16th	"	— do —	

[signature] Capt & Adjt
1/8th A. & S. Highrs

1/8th Arg. & Suth. Highrs

11th Sheet

WAR DIARY

(Erase heading not required)

Army Form C. 2118.

18

Hour, Date, Place			Summary of Events and Information	Remarks and References to Appendices
February	17th	BEDFORD	Company Training	
"	18th	"	Battalion Route March with Service Transport — 20 miles	
"	19th	"	Company Training	
"	20th	"	— do —	
"	21st	"	Sunday: Divine Service. Inspection of Billets	
"	22nd	"	Company Training	
"	23rd	"	— do —	
"	24th	"	Brigade Training. Route March & occupation of Defensive position.	
"	25th	"	Company Training	
"	26th	"	— do —	
"	27th	"	— do —	
"	28th	"	Sunday — Divine Service. Inspection of Clothing & Billets	

[illegible] Capt. & Adjt.
1/8th Arg. & Suth. Highrs

BATTALION ORDERS

by

Lieut, Colonel J. Campbell Commanding 1/8th(The Argyllshire) Battalion Princess Louise's Argyll & Sutherland Highlanders.

Bedford, Saturday, 20th. March, 1915.

SPECIAL ORDER.

The Commanding Officer announces, with the deepest regret, to the Battalion that he has received private information that Captain F. [illegible]. L. Campbell, Younger of Jura, has died from wounds received in action at Neuve Chapelle.

Captain Campbell had spent most of his military career in active service. He was through nearly all the South African Campaign, and thereafter spent two long periods of duty in Nigeria, where at that time, the Imperial Forces lived perman--ently under active service conditions and were constantly engaged in military operations, in which, though the forces employed were few in number, the enemy was numerous, brave and active.

By these experiences his character, naturally bold and energetic, was moulded into that swift, determined, stern type of soldier which should be the model for all ranks to aim at.

His services to this Battalion are too well known to need mention here.

The Commanding Officer mourns his loss sincerely, but rejoices that he died on the field of honour and is certain that all ranks will share his feelings.

The pipes will not play when marching to and from Divine Service to-morrow.

[illegible]

Capt. & Adjutant,
1/8th. A. & S. Highlanders.

1/8th Arg & Suth Highrs

Instructions regarding War Diaries and Intelligence Summaries are contained in F. S. Regs., Part II. and the Staff Manual respectively. Title pages will be prepared in manuscript.

WAR DIARY

or

~~INTELLIGENCE SUMMARY.~~

(*Erase heading not required.*)

Army Form C. 2118.

15th Sheet

20

Hour, Date, Place		Summary of Events and Information	Remarks and references to Appendices
March 1st	BEDFORD	Company Training – Musketry (Trained Soldiers)	
2nd	"	— do —	
3rd	"	— do — Musketry (Trained Soldiers)	
4th	"	— do — — do (— do — & Recruits)	
5th	"	— do — — do — (— do — — do —)	
6th	"	— do — — do — (— do — — do —)	
7th	"	Sunday – Divine Service. Musketry (Trained Soldiers)	
8th	"	Company Training	
9th	"	Battalion — " — – Interior Economy	
10th	"	Divisional Exercises	
11th	"	Battalion Training	
12th	"	— do — at STAGSDEN — Entrenching & Obstacles.	
13th	"	— do —	
14th	"	Sunday – Divine Service. Inspection of Billets & Clothing	
15th	"	Musketry – Individual & Collective Field Practices	
16th	"	Divisional Exercise	[signature]

(13989) W4141—463. 400,000. 9/14. H.&J.Ltd. Forms/C. 2118/10.

1/8th Argyll & Sutherland Highlanders

Instructions regarding War Diaries and Intelligence Summaries are contained in F. S. Regs., Part II. and the Staff Manual respectively. Title pages will be prepared in manuscript.

WAR DIARY
or
~~INTELLIGENCE SUMMARY.~~
(Erase heading not required.)

Army Form C. 2118.
16th Sheet

21

Hour, Date, Place	Summary of Events and Information	Remarks and references to Appendices
March 17th BEDFORD	Musketry - Individual & Collective Field Practices	
18th "	Company Training & Recruits Musketry	
19th "	Battalion — " — & Bayonet Fighting	Capt. Campbell (1/8th of Tain) died 19-3-15 of wounds received at Neuve Chapelle on 10/3/15
20th "	Battalion Training - Forced Marching. Marched 1 mile without timing,	then marched 11 miles in 2 hours & 57 minutes including 20
21st "	Divine Service - Inspection of Billets & Kits.	minutes halt.
22nd "	Company Training, Bayonet Fighting & Surmounting Obstacles on 22/3/15	21 N.C.O.s & 61 Ptes. (Total 82) [illegible] proceeded to Dunoon on transfer to 2/8th
23rd "	— do — — do —	
24th "	— do — — do — — do —	
25th "	— do — — do — Musketry - Fire Direction practice	for Officers & N.C.O.s.
26th "	— do — — do — & Surmounting Obstacles	
27th "	— do — — do —	
28th "	Divine Service - Inspection of Billets and Equipment	
29th "	Company Training, Bayonet Fighting and Physical Training	
30th "	Divisional Exercise	
31st "	Company Training, Bayonet Fighting and Physical Training	[signature]

[signature]

Lieut. Colonel
Commanding 8th Bn. Arg. & Suth. Highrs.

(73989) W4141—463. 400,000. 9/14. H.&J.Ltd. Forms/C. 2118/10.

SPECIAL ORDER

BY

Brigadier General St. George Burton, Commanding,

1/1st. ARGYLL & SUTHERLAND INFANTRY BRIGADE. T.F.

Headquarters,
6 Glebe Road,
BEDFORD.

Friday, 26th March, 1915.

....

The death of Captain Campbell, Younger of Jura from wounds received at Neuve Chapelle is reported.

It is with a deep sense of regret shared by all ranks that the Brigade Commander makes this announcement.

The 8th Argyllshire Highlanders in recalling with admiration the valuable services of the late Captain Campbell, mourns the loss of a gallant comrade and brother Highlander.

(Sgd.) H. A. Thomson,
Major, Brigade Major.
1/1st A. & S. Infantry Brigade.T.F.

22

SPECIAL ORDER

BY

Brigadier General St. George Burton, Commanding,

1/1st. ARGYLL & SUTHERLAND INFANTRY BRIGADE. T.F.

Headquarters,
6 Glebe Road,
BEDFORD.

Friday, 26th March, 1915.

The death of Captain Campbell, Younger of Jura from wounds received at Neuve Chapelle is reported.

It is with a deep sence of regret shared by all ranks that the Brigade Commander makes this announcement.

The 8th Argyllshire Highlanders in recalling with admiration the valuable services of the late Captain Campbell, mourns the loss of a gallant comrade and brother Highlander.

(Sgd.) N. A. Thomson,
Major, Brigade Major.
1/1st A. & S. Infantry Brigade. T.F.

Certified true Copy

Bedford
29-3-15

[signature] Capt. & Adjt.
1/8th Arg. & Suth. Highrs.

Bde No C/B. 6

C/2/11
1-4-15
8/A.V.P. H

24

O.C. 1/8 A.V.P. H

1. Your diary will in future be ~~treated~~ as a confidential document – and not sent in open and unaddressed

In view of this you will adopt the covering form laid down para (4). Section 140, F.S.R. II

2. Generally your diary affords no information for future reference with a view to effecting improvements. in the organization etc & administration

An improvement in this respect is called for.

3. Where lined in blue your letter of 1-4-15

This paragraph to be withdrawn – you have adopted a tone I disapprove of.

(Sd) St.G. Barton B.G.
Comdg. A.V.P. Bde.

3/4/15.

1/8th Bn Arg & Suth'd Highlanders

WAR DIARY ~~or~~ INTELLIGENCE SUMMARY.

Army Form C. 2118.

Instructions regarding War Diaries and Intelligence Summaries are contained in F. S. Regs., Part II. and the Staff Manual respectively. Title pages will be prepared in manuscript.

~~(Erase heading not required.)~~

17th Sheet

26

Hour, Date, Place	Summary of Events and Information	Remarks and references to Appendices
1-4-1915 BEDFORD	Company Training, Bayonet Fighting	
2-4-1915	Good Friday – No Training	
3-4-1915	Company Training, Bayonet Fighting.	
4-4-1915	Sunday – Divine Service Inspection of Equipment	
5-4-1915	Company Training Bayonet Fighting – Highland Games	
6-4-1915	Divisional Operations	
7-4-1915	Company Training Physical Training & Bayonet Fighting. Night Operations	
8-4-1915	Company Training, Physical Training & Bayonet Fighting.	
9-4-1915	—— do —— —— do ——	
10-4-1915	—— do —— —— do ——	
11-4-1915	Sunday – Divine Service Inspection of Equipment	
12-4-1915	Company Training, Physical Training & Bayonet Fighting	
13-4-1915	—— do —— —— do —— Received order to prepare for service overseas.	
14-4-1915	Physical Training & Bayonet Fighting. Inspection of arms Equipment etc	
15-4-1915	—— do —— —— do —— Transferred to 1st High Ld Bde & inspected by Brig Genl Ross CB	
16-4-1915	Inspection of arms, equipment etc continued. Medical Inspection. Inoculation.	
17-4-1915	Inspection of Imperial Service personnel, Arms, equipment etc by C.O.	
18-4-1915	Sunday – Divine Service. Inspections continued. Draft of 226 men received from 2/8th Bn	Draft of 3 Officers & 214 N.C.Os & men received from 2/8th Bn Arg Highrs

[signature] Capt & Adjt

(73989) W4141—463. 400,000. 9/14. H.&J.Ltd. Forms/C. 2118/10.

Instructions regarding War Diaries and Intelligence Summaries are contained in F.S. Regs., Part II. and the Staff Manual respectively. Title pages will be prepared in manuscript.

1/8th Arg & Suth Highrs

WAR DIARY

or

~~INTELLIGENCE SUMMARY.~~

~~(Erase heading not required.)~~

Army Form C. 2118.

25 18th Sheet

Hour, Date, Place	Summary of Events and Information	Remarks and references to Appendices
19-4-1915 BEDFORD	Inspections continued. Drafts inoculated.	
20-4-1915 "	— do — Musketry for Draft commenced	
21-4-1915 "	— do — — do — continued	
22-4-1915 "	— do — — do —	
23-4-1915 "	— do — — do —	
24-4-1915 "	— do — — do — Battn with completed 1st Line Transport inspected by G.O.C. 1st Highland Inf. Bde	
25-4-1915 "	Sunday - Divine Service.	
26-4-1915 "	Inspections continued. Musketry of Draft finished	
27-4-1915 "	Brigade Route March with 1st Line Transport complete. All equipment in accordance with Mobilization Store Table now complete except for a few small articles.	
28-4-1915	Company Training	
29-4-1915	Company & Battalion Training. 1 officer and ~~103~~ 117 men (Home Service Details) proceeded to Scottish	
30-4-1915	Advanced party of 3 officers, and 104 men with 73 horses, 23 vehicles and 9 bicycles entrained at Bedford [illegible] Siding for SOUTHAMPTON at 5.20 a.m. en route for HAVRE	

[signature] Capt & Adjt.

[signature] Lieut Col Comdg 1/8th Arg & Suth Highrs

(73989) W4141—463. 400,000. 9/14. H.&J.Ltd. Forms/C. 2118/10.

Gil.

51st Division

121/5556

1/8th A. & S. H.

Vol I 1 – 31. 5. 15.

X. 10

Instructions regarding War Diaries and Intelligence Summaries are contained in F. S. Regs., Part II. and the Staff Manual respectively. Title pages will be prepared in manuscript.

1/8th Bn Arg. & Suth. Highlanders

1915

WAR DIARY

~~or~~

~~INTELLIGENCE~~ ~~SUMMARY~~.

~~(Erase heading not required.)~~

Army Form C. 2118.

Sheet No. 19

Place	Date	Hour	Summary of Events and Information	Remarks and references to Appendices
	May			
BEDFORD	1st	p.m. 7.42	Headquarters & C & D Coys under Lt. Col. J Campbell entrained AMPTHILL ROAD SIDING	
"	"	p.m. 8.15	A & B Coys under Capt. G. M Duncan entrained AMPTHILL ROAD SIDING	
FOLKESTONE	2nd	am. 12.40	Headqrs. & 'C' & D Coys. embarked H.M.H.T. 'ONWARD'	
"	"	am. 1.15	A & B Coys embarked H.M.H.T. 'ONWARD'.	
BOULOGNE	"	a.m. 2.50	Whole Bn arrived BOULOGNE, disembarked and marched to Rest Camp, distance 2 miles arriving 4 a.m.	
"	"	am. 10.0	Battalion marched to PONT DE BRIQUES Railway Station – distance 4 miles and entrained in train bringing advanced party and transport. Battalion now complete.	
PONT DE BRIQUES	~~2nd~~	12 Noon	Journey commenced – via BOULOGNE, CALAIS, ST. OMER, HAZEBROUCK.	
MERVILLE	2nd	6 pm.	Arrived and detrained	
"	"	6.45 pm.	Marched via CALONNE and ROBECQ to hamlet 1 to 2 kilometres South of AIRE CANAL on ROBECQ – LILLERS Rd. arriving about 9 pm. Battalion billeted in barns and farm houses.	
ROBECQ	3rd	–	Training in vicinity of billets	
"	4th	–	— do —	
"	5th	A.M. 6.30	Brigade Route march – Route – ROBECQ – BUSNES – L'ECLEME – ROBECQ.	
"	6th	–	Training in vicinity of billets, Respirators issued. 1 per officer & man	
"	7th	–	— do — Gas Sprayers issued – 1 for Battalion	

[signature] Capt. & Adjt.

1/8th Bn Arg. & Suth. Highrs

WAR DIARY
or
INTELLIGENCE SUMMARY.
(Erase heading not required.)

Army Form C. 2118.

Sheet No. 20

Instructions regarding War Diaries and Intelligence Summaries are contained in F. S. Regs., Part II. and the Staff Manual respectively. Title pages will be prepared in manuscript.

Place	Date	Hour	Summary of Events and Information	Remarks and references to Appendices
	May.			
ROBECQ	8th	–	Training in vicinity of billets.	
"	9th	9.30 am.	Sunday – Divine Service. Ordered to be in state of readiness to move at 2 hours notice.	
"	10th	–	Training in vicinity of billets — do —	
"	11th	–	— do — — do —	
"	12th	–	— do — — do —	
"	13th	–	— do — — do —	
"	14th	9. am	Marched in Brigade via MERVILLE and VIEUX BERQUIN.	
MERRIS	14th	2.30 pm	Took over billets in MERRIS vacated by Canadian cavalry.	
"	15th	–	Training in vicinity of billets	
"	16th	9.30 am	Sunday – Divine Service. Ordered to be in state of readiness to move at 2 hours notice.	
"	17th	–	Training in vicinity of billets. Part of 9th Division marched through billeting area. 10th Bn A. & S. H. included in 9th Dvn.	
"	18th	–	— do —	
"	18th	6.30 pm	Marched in Brigade via VIEUX BERQUIN, NEUF BERQUIN, and LA GORGUE to VIELLE CHAPELLE	
VIELLE CHAPELLE	19th	2.30 am	Billeted in Barns in vicinity of town.	
"		2.30 pm.	3 platoons, one each of B. C. & D. Coys. proceeded to trenches occupied by 1 Bn LIVERPOOL Regt. West and SOUTH WEST of RICHEBOURG L'AVOUE	

1577 Wt. W10791/1773 500,000 1/15 D. D. & L. A.D.S.S./Forms/C. 2118.

[signature] Capt & Adjt

1/8th Arg. & Suth. Highrs

WAR DIARY
or
INTELLIGENCE SUMMARY.
(*Erase heading not required.*)

Army Form C. 2118.

No. 21 Sheet

Instructions regarding War Diaries and Intelligence Summaries are contained in F. S. Regs., Part II. and the Staff Manual respectively. Title pages will be prepared in manuscript.

Place	Date	Hour	Summary of Events and Information	Remarks and references to Appendices
VIELLE CHAPELLE	May 19th	pm. 5.30	Remainder of Battalion marched to vicinity of RICHEBOURG L'AVOUE. 9 platoons went into support and Reserve trenches – (3 platoons already in fire trench). One Company remained in Reserve with Battn H.Q. at RUE DES BERCEAUX.	
RICHEBOURG	20th	-	Battalion remained in trenches. No change in distribution. Captain A. CAMPBELL wounded, & 1 man	Casualty List for month of May appended.
"	21st	10 pm.	Battalion evacuated trenches which were taken over by 6th Bn Seaforth Highlanders, and proceeded to neighbourhood of RICHBOURG ST. VAAST where billeted in dug-outs and barns. Bn H.Q. remained at RUE DES BERCEAUX.	
	22nd	-	Battalion furnished working parties for repair and construction of trenches and burial of numerous dead of Northampton Regt, Liverpools, R. Sussex, K.R. Rifles, Black Watch & Gurkhas lying on RICHEBOURG battlefield.	
"	23rd	a.m. 11.15	By German shell fire (N.E) 8 men killed outright, 3 died of wounds & 21 wounded. One shell which struck a house caused most of the casualties. Working parties for construction & repair of trenches & burial parties sent out as usual. 10 of N.C.Os & men killed or died of wounds were buried at 6 pm at West end of RUE DES BERCEAUX.	
"	24th		Furnished working and burying parties during daytime and at night.	
	25th		——— do ———	
RICHEBOURG LA COUTURE	26th		Moved into new area between RICHEBOURG ST. VAAST and LA COUTURE. Companies located chiefly in Defence trenches and Dug-outs. Working and burying parties furnished. During period 21-5-15 to 27-5-15 229 British and 12 German dead were buried by	

1577 Wt. W10791/1773 500,000 1/15 D. D. & L. A.D.S.S./Forms/C. 2118.

1/8th Arg. & Suth. Highrs

Instructions regarding War Diaries and Intelligence Summaries are contained in F. S. Regs., Part II. and the Staff Manual respectively. Title pages will be prepared in manuscript.

WAR DIARY
or
INTELLIGENCE SUMMARY.

(Erase heading not required.)

Army Form C. 2118.

22nd Sheet

Place	Date	Hour	Summary of Events and Information	Remarks and references to Appendices
RICHEBOURG LA COUTURE	26th	–	parties of this Battalion. 2 wounded Germans also brought in.	
	27th	–	Working parties for collection of arms, equipment & stores furnished	
RICHEBOURG –do–	28th	9.30 pm	Trenches W. and S.W of RICHEBOURG L'AVOUE taken over from 6th Bn Arg. & Suth. Highrs. 4 platoons in firing line, 4 in support & 8 in Reserve trenches. Quiet night.	
–do–	29th	–	Heavy shell fire (H.E.) between 9 and 11 am. No casualties. Remainder of day quiet.	
–do–	"	9.0 pm	Change over of Platoons in fire trench with those in support. 1 platoon re-inforced fire trench from Reserves.	
–do–	30th	8.0 AM	Platoons in support re-inforced by one platoon from Reserves.	
–do– LOCON	"	10 pm.	Battalion relieved by 9th Gurkhas and marched to billets near LOCON. Lieutenant J.C. LAUDER and 1 Sergeant wounded.	
"	31st	1.30 AM	Marched into new billets. Rest and clean up.	

[illegible] Capt. & Adjt.

[signature] Lieut. Col.
Comdg. 1/8 Arg. & Suth. Highrs.

51st Division

121/5921.

1/8 A & S Hrs
Vol II 1 — 30. 6. 15.

X.11

Instructions regarding War Diaries and Intelligence Summaries are contained in F. S. Regs., Part II. and the Staff Manual respectively. Title pages will be prepared in manuscript.

1915

1/8th Arg. & Suth. Highrs

WAR DIARY or ~~INTELLIGENCE SUMMARY.~~

(Erase heading not required.)

Confidential No 134

152nd Inf Bde

Army Form C. 2118.

23rd Sheet

Place	Date	Hour	Summary of Events and Information	Remarks and references to Appendices
LOCON	1-6-15	2 pm	Marched to new billets and lined both sides of road in town of LOCON during passage of Mr Asquith. The Premier was accompanied by Gen. Sir Douglas Haig and Lieut. Gen. Sir H. Rawlinson.	
A TOMBE WILOT	1-6-15	4 30 pm	Arrived new billets.	
	2-6-15		Rested in billets	
	3-6-15		Company training in vicinity of billets.	
	4-6-15			
	5-6-15		Furnished working parties daily for improvement of new line of trenches taken over by Brigade in vicinity of FESTUBERT	
	6-6-15			
	7-6-15			
	8-6-15	6 pm	Marched via LOCON and LE TOURET to new trench line in neighbourhood of FESTUBERT and took over Reserve trenches from 1/6th A & S H who moved up into fire and support trenches. Captain G. McDuncan and five men wounded	
FESTUBERT	9-6-15		In occupation of Reserve trenches. 2 men wounded, 1 man died of wounds.	
	10-6-15		— do — — do. — 1 man wounded	
	10-6-15	10 pm	Relieved 1/6th A & S H in fire trenches.	
	11-6-15		In occupation of fire trenches. 1 NCO & 2 men killed 1 man wounded & missing (believed killed) 10 men wounded	[signature] Adjt

1577 Wt. W10791/1773 500,000 1/15 D. D. & L. A.D.S.S./Forms/C. 2118.

Instructions regarding War Diaries and Intelligence Summaries are contained in F. S. Regs., Part II. and the Staff Manual respectively. Title pages will be prepared in manuscript.

WAR DIARY
~~or~~
~~INTELLIGENCE SUMMARY.~~
(Erase heading not required.)

1/8th Arg. & Suth. Highrs

Army Form C. 2118.

24th Sheet

Place	Date	Hour	Summary of Events and Information	Remarks and references to Appendices
FESTUBERT	12.6.15		In occupation of fire trenches 1 NCO & 3 men killed 8 men wounded	
	13.6.15		In occupation of fire trenches 1 NCO & 5 men wounded	
	14.6.15	1 am.	Relieved by 1/6th Seaforth Highrs. and marched to billets near LOCON 1 man wounded	
LOCON	14.6.15	6 pm	Machine Gun section moved back into fire trenches at FESTUBERT	
	15.6.15	6 pm	Moved to breastwork crossing RUE DES CHAVATTES near village of LE TOURET and remained at first in Divisional General Reserve and afterwards about 11 pm as Brigade Reserve to 154th Bde during attack on hostile trenches at FESTUBERT. Lieut. H.B. Phillimore & 2nd Lt. A. Frazer Campbell severely wounded. (1 man killed 1 NCO wounded & missing)	2 men wounded
LE TOURET	16.6.15	6 am	Marched back to billets at LOCON. Lieut. H.B. Phillimore died of wounds.	
LOCON	16.6.15	4 pm	Returned to breastworks at LE TOURET as Divisional General Reserve for new attack on FESTUBERT trenches. Sent out working and carrying parties to fire trenches.	
LE TOURET	17.6.15	8 pm	Relieved 1/6th A & S H in occupation of Reserve trenches in vicinity of FESTUBERT. 3 men wounded	
FESTUBERT	18.6.15		In occupation of Reserve trenches. 1 NCO & 3 men wounded	
	19.6.15 20.6.15		Provided working parties for improvement of fire and communication trenches. Practically every officer, NCO and man employed nightly	
	20.6.15	10 pm	Relieved 1/6th A & S H in fire trenches	
	21.6.15		In occupation of fire trenches. 1 man died of wounds. 2 men wounded	[illegible] Capt Adjt

1577 Wt. W10791/1773 500,000 1/15 D. D. & L. A.D.S.S./Forms/C. 2118.

Instructions regarding War Diaries and Intelligence Summaries are contained in F. S. Regs., Part II. and the Staff Manual respectively. Title pages will be prepared in manuscript.

WAR DIARY ~~or INTELLIGENCE SUMMARY.~~

1/8th Arg. & Suth. Highrs

(Erase heading not required.)

Army Form C. 2118.

25th Sheet

Place	Date	Hour	Summary of Events and Information	Remarks and references to Appendices
FESTUBERT	22.6.15		In occupation of Fire trenches. 1 man wounded	
	23.6.15	1 am	Relieved in Fire trenches by 4th Black Watch and marched to Billets at LE CORNET MALO.	
LE CORNET MALO		3 pm.	Officers & Sergeants attended a demonstration of method of using asphyxiating gas.	
	24.6.15	10 am	Divine Service. Training in vicinity of Billets	
	25.6.15		Training in vicinity of Billets.	
		8 pm	Marched to new billets at ESTAIRES via LESTREM and LA GORGUE	
ESTAIRES	26.6.15	11 pm	Training in vicinity of Billets.	
	27.6.15	9.30 am	Divine Service	
	27.6.15	7 pm	Marched via LAVENTIE to FAUQUISSART and took over trenches from 2/S.R & 2/W.Y Regts.	
	28.6.15		In occupation of fire trenches	
	29.6.15		In occupation of fire trenches 5 men wounded.	
	30.6.15		In occupation of fire trenches. Mine exploded at 3 am and destroyed about 50 yds of enemys parapet. Considerable damage done. 4 NCOs & 7 men wounded	

N. Lockie Capt Adjt.

J. Humphrey [?] Lieut Col.
Comdg. 1/8th Arg. & Suth. Highrs

1577 Wt. W10791/1773 500,000 1/15 D. D. & L. A.D.S.S./Forms/C. 2118.

51st Division

121
6358

1/8 A & S. Hrs

Vol III

Incl. 1 - 31 - 7 - 15

X. 12

Instructions regarding War Diaries and Intelligence Summaries are contained in F. S. Regs., Part II. and the Staff Manual respectively. Title pages will be prepared in manuscript.

1/8th Arg. & Suth. Highrs

WAR DIARY ~~or~~ ~~INTELLIGENCE SUMMARY.~~

(Erase heading not required.)

Army Form C. 2118.

26th Sheet

Place	Date	Hour	Summary of Events and Information	Remarks and references to Appendices
	July			
PICANTIN	1st.	–	In occupation of fire Trenches. 2 men wounded	
"	2nd	–	— do — 1 man killed, 3 men wounded	
"	3rd	2 A.M.	Battalion Headqrs. shelled out of farm on Rue Tilleloy. Orderly Room Sgt. killed & 8 men wounded.	
"	"	11 p.m.	Companies relieved by 6th Argylls in fire Trenches, & took over No. 17, 18, & 19 Posts in Reserve.	
"	4th	–	In occupation of Bde. Reserve Posts & billets	
"	5th	–	— do — No. 19 Post taken over by 8th Division. 1 man wounded	
"	6th	–	— do — working parties employed by day & night.	
"	7th	–	— do — — do — 1 man wounded	
"	8th	–	— do — — do — 1 man wounded	
"	9th	–	Relieved by 154th Bde. 51st (Highland) Division. & marched to new billets on LA BASSEE Rd.	
LA GORGUE	10th	–	Furnished working parties for work on Divisional Trench line.	
"	11th	–	— do —	
"	12th	–	— do —	
"	13th	–	— do —	
"	14th	–	— do —	
LAVENTIE	15th	–	Took over Battn in Reserve, Right section, duties at 9.15 pm. Battn billeted in LAVENTIE	[signature] Capt.

Instructions regarding War Diaries and Intelligence Summaries are contained in F. S. Regs., Part II. and the Staff Manual respectively. Title pages will be prepared in manuscript.

1/8th A. S. Highrs

WAR DIARY
or
~~INTELLIGENCE SUMMARY.~~
(Erase heading not required.)

27th Sheet

Army Form C. 2118.

Place	Date	Hour	Summary of Events and Information	Remarks and references to Appendices
	July			
LAVENTIE	16th	–	In Reserve billets – furnished working parties – 238 N.C.Os & men. 1 man killed	
"	17th	–	— do — — do — ~~1 man wounded~~ M.	
"	18	–	— do — — do — 1 man wounded	
"	19	–	— do — — do — 1 man wounded	
"	20th	–	— do — — do — 2 men wounded	
"	21st	–	— do — — do — 1 man wounded	
"	22nd	10pm	Marched via ESTAIRES & MERVILLE to billets near Forest of Nieppe.	
"	23rd	–	Company Training in Rest billets.	
"	24th	–		
"	25th	–		
"	26th	–		M.
"	27th	3.30 am	Entrained at LA GORGUE and proceeded by troop train to CORBIE, arriving there at 5 pm. marched to Billets at LA HOUSSEY arriving at 7 pm.	
LA HOUSSEY	28th	-	Company training at Billets. At 4.30 pm inspected by Lieut Genl C.C. Monro on joining Xth Corps. 3rd Army	
	29th	5.30 pm	Marched to BOUZINCOURT arriving at 10-45 pm.	
BOUZINCOURT	30	-	Marched at 11-30 pm to take over trenches from 1/116th Regt of French Infantry. Arrived at AUTHILLE at 1.20 am	W.

1577 Wt. W10791/1773 500,000 1/15 D. D. & L. A.D.S.S./Forms/C. 2118.

Instructions regarding War Diaries and Intelligence Summaries are contained in F. S. Regs., Part II. and the Staff Manual respectively. Title pages will be prepared in manuscript.

WAR DIARY
or
INTELLIGENCE SUMMARY.
(Erase heading not required.)

Army Form C. 2118.

Place	Date	Hour	Summary of Events and Information	Remarks and references to Appendices
AUTHILLE	31st	3am	Completed relief of Right sector of Brigade line occupying trenches on Hill 141.	[illegible] Capt. for Adjt.
			[signature] Captain A/Adjutant [signature] Lieut. Colonel Cmndg 1/8th A & S Hghrs	

1577 Wt. W10791/1773 500,000 1/15 D. D. & L. A.D.S.S./Forms/C. 2118.

51st Division

X 13

CONFIDENTIAL
No 134
152 INF. BDE.

Confidential

121
6737

War Diary

of

8th Bn. Argyll & Sutherland Hrs

from 1st – 31st Aug 1915

Vol IV

Instructions regarding War Diaries and Intelligence Summaries are contained in F. S. Regs., Part II. and the Staff Manual respectively. Title pages will be prepared in manuscript.

1/8th Bn. A & S Highrs

WAR DIARY
or
~~INTELLIGENCE SUMMARY.~~

(Erase heading not required.)

29th Sheet.

Army Form C. 2118.

Place	Date	Hour	Summary of Events and Information	Remarks and references to Appendices
	AUGUST			
AUTHUILLE	1st	–	In occupation of Fire Trenches. Reinforcement of 3 Officers 2nd Lts A. Mackinnon, D.B. Adam & W.M. Sladden, joined. 3 Officers & 47 men of North Irish Horse attached to Bn & were attached to 'D' Coy to hold left sector of Battalion line.	
do	2nd	–	In occupation of Fire Trenches: Captain D.M. Campbell & 1 NCO wounded	
do	3rd	–	In occupation of Fire Trenches 2nd Lt W. Chalmers joined from Base.	
do	4th	–	In occupation of Fire Trenches. 10th Bn Essex Regt commenced Course of Instruction in Trench duties	
do	5th	–	In occupation of Fire Trenches	
do	6th	–	In occupation of Fire Trenches	
do	7th	–		
do	8th	–		
do	9th	–		
do	10th	–	Lt Col J. Campbell went on leave, Major H. Brown to command Battn.	
do	11	–	In occupation of Fire Trenches Rev Mr Reid wounded. 1 man killed.	
do	12	–	In occupation of Fire Trenches	
do	13	12 mn	Relieved from Fire Trenches by 13th Hussars, 3rd Skinners Horse & 18th Lancers, Indian Cavalry Corps, (3rd Indian Cavalry Divn)	
MILLENCOURT	14	2.30am	Battalion reached Billets	
do	15		Divine Service. Working party for 2nd line defences, 4 Off. & 150 men	

1577 Wt. W10791/1773 500,000 1/15 D. D. & L. A.D.S.S./Forms/C. 2118.

N. [illegible] Capt

Instructions regarding War Diaries and Intelligence Summaries are contained in F. S. Regs., Part II. and the Staff Manual respectively. Title pages will be prepared in manuscript.

1/8th A & S H. 30th Sheet.

WAR DIARY
or
INTELLIGENCE SUMMARY.
(*Erase heading not required.*)

Army Form C. 2118.

Place	Date	Hour	Summary of Events and Information	Remarks and references to Appendices
	AUGUST			
MILLENCOURT	16		Battalion drill parades. Officers Musketry Class. Working party of 4 off + 156 men for 2nd line defences	
do	17		do. do. do do	
do	18		do do do do	
do	19	4pm	Battn inspected by Brigadier Comdg 152nd Infy Bde. Working party of 8 off & 312 men for 2nd line defences	
do	20		Battn drill parades Officers Musketry class do do.	
do	21	9am	Adjutants Parade, 11 am Officers + NCOs Parade	
LA BOISSELLE		11pm	Battalion relieved 7th Roy. Highlanders in trenches at LA BOISSELLE, E 3 sector.	
do	22	-	Battalion in occupation of fire trenches	
do	23	-	1 NCO killed.	
do	24	-	Col Campbell from leave resumed command	
do	25	-	2 men killed	
do	26	-	2 men wounded. Reinforcement of 22 Ptes from England	
do	27	-		
do	28	-		
do	29	-		
do	30	-		
do	31	-	1 man killed	

[illegible signature] Lieut. Colonel
Comdg 1/8th Bn. Argyll & Sutherland Highrs

51st Division X 14

121
7049

CONFIDENTIAL
No. 134
152 INF. BDE.

War Diary

of 8th Argyll & Sutherland Hyrs.

from 1.IX.15 to 30.IX.15

Vol V

P

to 22/10/15

Instructions regarding War Diaries and Intelligence Summaries are contained in F. S. Regs., Part II. and the Staff Manual respectively. Title pages will be prepared in manuscript.

1/8th Bn Arg. Suth. Highrs

WAR DIARY

~~or INTELLIGENCE SUMMARY.~~

(*Erase heading not required.*)

Volume II

Sheet No. 1

Army Form C. 2118.

Place	Date	Hour	Summary of Events and Information	Remarks and references to Appendices
	Sept. 1915			
LA BOISELLE	1	10 p.m.	Battalion relieved in Trenches by 7th Black Watch & marched to billets at MILLENCOURT arriving there at 12 midnight. 2 men wounded	
MILLENCOURT	2		Rest billets. Cleaning up. Battn Grocery Bar opened.	
"	3		Rest billets. N.C.Os & Employed men, drill parades} 9 officers & 374 N.C.Os & men working parties on 2nd line defences.	
"	4		—do— —do— 9 " & 312 —do— —do—	
"	5		—do— Divine Service 9 " 312 —do— —do— Major H.B.D. BAIRD, D.S.O. 12th Cavalry assumed command in succession to Lt Col J. Campbell invalided to England.	
"	6		—do— N.C.Os & all available men, drill parades} 4 " 156 —do— —do—	
"	7		—do— Practice Test – alarm. Battalion turned out complete with 1st Line Transport in 35 minutes. 10 officers & 416 men working parties	
"	8		—do— N.C.Os & men available – drill parades 7 officers & 312 N.C.Os & men working parties	
"	9		—do— —do— 7 " & 312 —do— —do—	
"	10		—do— Cleaning up.	
ALBERT	11	6.10 p.m.	Marched to ALBERT and took over duties of Battn in Bde. Reserve from 5th Gordon Highrs. 3 Coys billeted in ALBERT 1 Coy. at BECOURT Chateau	
"	12		Furnished working parties of 1 officer & 50 men every 4 hours throughout the day and night for clearing mine heads in E.2 & E.3 Sectors (Dhollu & Ilot Sections) also parties for carrying stores for Tunnelling Company. Small parties also employed in improving drainage of Communication trenches under Battalion Drainage Officer and in making tracks for telephone wires under Brigade Signal Officer. 2 men wounded at BECOURT	
"	13			
"	14			
"	15		2 men Killed & 4 men wounded by Trench mortar bomb while on working party at Dhollu Trench	[signature], Capt. & Adjt.

1577 Wt. W10791/1773 500,000 1/15 D. D. & L. A.D.S.S./Forms/C. 2118.

Instructions regarding War Diaries and Intelligence Summaries are contained in F. S. Regs., Part II. and the Staff Manual respectively. Title pages will be prepared in manuscript.

1/8th Bn Arg. & Suth. Highrs

WAR DIARY
or
~~INTELLIGENCE SUMMARY.~~

(*Erase heading not required.*)

Volume II

Sheet No. 8

Army Form C. 2118.

Place	Date	Hour	Summary of Events and Information	Remarks and references to Appendices
	Sept 1915			
ALBERT	16th		Furnished daily working parties in E.2 & E.3 Sectors. 3 men wounded by shell fire.	
"	17th		— do —	
"	18th	10 p.m.	3 Coys at ALBERT relieved by 8th Suffolk Regt. & 1 Coy. at BECOURT by East Kent Regt. {Marched to billets at MILLENCOURT arriving there about 11 p.m.	
MILLENCOURT	19th		In billets. Cleaning up.	
"	20th		Route march via BAZIEUX and HENENCOURT – 9 miles. Marched past General Sir C.C. MUNRO Comdg. 3rd Army. Lt. Gen. MORLAND Comdg. X Corps & Maj. Genl. ALLASON Comdg. 51st. Dvn. also present.	
"	20th		The Army Commander expressed himself as being pleased with the turn-out and soldierly bearing of the men.	
"	21st	5.15 pm	Marched to AVELUY & took over 7.1 Sector from 1/8th Liverpool Regt.	
AVELUY	22nd		In trenches – 7.1 Sector, near AVELUY. Lieut. N. A. MUNRO killed by bomb while attempting to capture a German flag, set up between the German & British lines. His body was recovered by 4 N.C.Os. 2 of whom – Cpl. Sneddon & L/Cpl. Graham were recommended for D.C.M. by C.O. Cpl. Sneddon promoted Sgt. & L/Cpls Graham, McLellan & McVicar promoted Cpl. for devotion to duty. L/C. Graham wounded.	
"	23rd		In trenches at AVELUY – 7.1 Sector. 1 Sgt. wounded.	
"	24th		— do — 3 men wounded.	
"	25th		— do — A rousing cheer was given at 6.30 pm. by the Battalion & Battalions in adjacent sectors on which the Germans opened a heavy M.G. & Rifle fire & appeared much alarmed.	
"	26th	5.30 am	The cheering was repeated at 5.30 am. & artillery co-operated by spraying hostile parapets with shrapnel but Germans did not reply. 2 men wounded.	
"		9.0 pm	Relieved in trenches by 1/8th LIVERPOOL Regt. and marched to MILLENCOURT arriving about 11 p.m.	
MILLENCOURT	27th		Rest billets. Cleaning up. Hot baths opened to Bn at MILLENCOURT. Baths for 16 men per hour available.	
"	28th		— do — Drill parades under O.C. Coys & Adjutant. {Inspected in field near billets by Maj. Genl. Harper C.B., D.S.O new Commander of 51st (Hd) DIVISION	

1577 Wt. W10791/1773 500,000 1/15 D. D. & L. A.D.S.S./Forms/C. 2118.

[illegible] Col.

Instructions regarding War Diaries and Intelligence Summaries are contained in F. S. Regs., Part II. and the Staff Manual respectively. Title pages will be prepared in manuscript.

1/8 A. & S. Highrs

WAR DIARY
or
~~INTELLIGENCE~~ SUMMARY.
(Erase heading not required.)

Volume II
Sheet 3

Army Form C. 2118.

Place	Date	Hour	Summary of Events and Information	Remarks and references to Appendices
	Sept 1915			
MILLENCOURT	29th		Rest Billets. Drill parades under O.C. Coys and Adjutant.	
"	30th	6.0 pm.	Marched via ALBERT & AVELUY to trenches at AUTHUILLE previously occupied by Battn in	
"	"		July & August & took over from 6th Bn. Black Watch.	

30/9/1915

D Baird Major
Comdg. 1/8th Bn. Arg. & Suth. Highrs

A.L. capt. & adjt.

1577 Wt. W10791/1773 500,000 1/15 D. D. & L. A.D.S.S./Forms/C. 2118.

War Diary

of

Head Quarters.

152nd Inf. Bde

from 1.IX.15 to 30.IX.15.

51st Division

121
7384

1/8th A & S Hrs
Vol VI
Oct 15

X.15

CONFIDENTIAL
No. 134
152nd INF. BDE.

Confidential

War Diary

of

1st 8th 13th Arg. & Suth. Highlanders

from 1st to 31st October, 1915.

Volume II

Instructions regarding War Diaries and Intelligence Summaries are contained in F. S. Regs., Part II. and the Staff Manual respectively. Title pages will be prepared in manuscript.

CONFIDENTIAL
No. 134
152nd INF. BDE.

Volume II
Sheet No. 4

Army Form C. 2118.

1/8th Bn. Arg. & Suth'd H'rs WAR DIARY ~~or INTELLIGENCE SUMMARY.~~

(Erase heading not required.)

Place	Date	Hour	Summary of Events and Information	Remarks and references to Appendices
	1915 Octr.			
AUTHUILLE	1st		In trenches G1 sector, AUTHUILLE.	
"	2nd		do 3 men wounded	
"	3rd		do	
"	4th		do 1 man killed	
"	5th		do 1 man wounded	
"	6th		do	
"	7th		do Hot water Baths in village of AUTHUILLE used by Battn. in parties of 4.	
"	8th		do	
"	9th		do Special order issued by GOC 152nd Bde on excellent state of trenches occupied by 8th	
"	10th	9 pm	Relieved in trenches by 1/6th Black Watch. Marched via ALBERT to MILLENCOURT arriving about 11·30 pm. 2 men wounded.	
MILLENCOURT	11th		Rest billets, cleaning up. ~~261 all ranks on working parties.~~	
"	12th		Rest Billets. 261 all ranks on working parties. All others Drill parades under Adjutant	
"	13th		Rest Billets. Drill parades under Coy. Commanders and Adjutant	
"	14th		Route march via HENENCOURT - SENLIS - WARLOY, BAZIEUX, BRESLE, LAVIEVILLE.	
"	15th		Rest Billets 261 all ranks on working parties Drill parades under Adjutant. Tactical exercise with Bombers.	
"	16th		Rest Billets. Battn. engaged in Tactical exercise against flagged position	[initials]

1577 Wt. W10791/1773 500,000 1/15 D. D. & L. A.D.S.S./Forms/C. 2118.

CONFIDENTIAL
No. 134

Volume II
Sheet No 5

Instructions regarding War Diaries and Intelligence Summaries are contained in F. S. Regs., Part II. and the Staff Manual respectively. Title pages will be prepared in manuscript.

1/8th Bn A & S Hrs. **WAR DIARY** 152nd INF. BDE.

~~or~~

~~INTELLIGENCE~~ **SUMMARY.**

(*Erase heading not required.*)

Army Form C. 2118.

Place	Date	Hour	Summary of Events and Information	Remarks and references to Appendices
	1915 Oct.			
MILLENCOURT	17th		Rest billets. 261 all ranks on working parties. 4.45 pm Divine Service.	
"	18th		Rest Billets. ROUTE MARCH, via MILLENCOURT, LAVIEVILLE, ALBERT-AMIENS ROAD - BAZIEUX - HENENCOURT.	
"	19th		Rest Billets. 261 all ranks on working parties. Drill Parades under Adjutant	
AUTHUILLE	20th	5.30pm	Marched to AUTHUILLE via BOUZINCOURT and NEW ROAD and took over G1 sector of trenches from 6th Black Watch at 8 pm.	
"	21st		In trenches G1 sector	
"	22nd		do. 1 NCO killed.	
"	23rd		do 2 men wounded	
"	24th		do 3 men wounded.	
"	25th		do	
"	26th		do	
"	27th		do 1 man died of wounds received on 24th	
"	28th		do	
"	29th		do Battn carried out fire scheme concluding by cheering lustily - Enemy gave no response. 2 men wounded.	Copy of fire Scheme orders attached.
"	30th	7.15pm	Battn relieved in fire trenches by 1/5th Gordons & in support by one company 1/6th Black Watch. Marched via BOIS d'AVELUY to MARTINSART taking over Billets there as Battalion in	[signature]

Instructions regarding War Diaries and Intelligence Summaries are contained in F. S. Regs., Part II. and the Staff Manual respectively. Title pages will be prepared in manuscript.

1/8th Bn Arg & Suth Hrs

CONFIDENTIAL
No. 134
152nd INF. BDE.

WAR DIARY
~~or~~
~~INTELLIGENCE~~ SUMMARY.

(*Erase heading not required.*)

Volume II
Sheet No 6.

Army Form C. 2118.

Place	Date	Hour	Summary of Events and Information	Remarks and references to Appendices
	1915 Oct			
	30th		Divisional Reserve	
MARTINSART	31st		In Reserve Billets. 3 pm Divine Service by half Battns.	N. Locke Capt & Adjt

31/10/15. F. L. Brown Major for Lieut Colonel
Comdg 1/8 Bn A & S Highrs

1577 Wt. W10791/1773 500,000 1/15 D. D. & L. A.D.S.S./Forms/C. 2118.

CONFIDENTIAL
No. 134
152nd INF. BDE.

1/8th (THE ARGYLLSHIRE) Bn ARGYLL & SUTHERLAND HIGHLANDERS.

FIRE SCHEME.
for
Friday 29th October 1915.

Copy No 12.

In the Field 28/10/15.

1. The following fire scheme will be carried out during Evening Stand to on Friday 29th Oct 1915, by the ARGYLLSHIRE HIGHLANDERS with the following objects:-
   (a) Practice in rapidly manning fire positions and opening sudden bursts of controlled fire.
   (b) Practice in intercommunication between the whole length of the G.1. Sector fire trench, supports and Battalion Headquarters.
   (c) Co-operation of M.G. and rifle fire with perhaps in addition some artillery.
   (d) Fostering the offensive spirit of all ranks of the Argyllshire Highlanders, annoying the enemy and inflicting loss on him.
   (e) Reinforcing various points of the fire positions by the Company in support.

2. The scheme will be carried out as follows:-

At 5.45 p.m. on 29th instant 5 rounds of platoon fire in rapid bursts will be opened by the Companies in the fire trenches as follows:-

"C" Company.
No 9 Platoon on 408 (R.31.C.3.5.)
No 10 ") enfilade fire on 411 (R.31.C.3.0.)
No 11 ") and the German trenches S.E. of this point at ranges 600-1000 yds.

"A" Company.
No 1 Platoon at 407 (R.31.C.4.7.)
No 2 " " 405 (R.31.A.5.3.)
No 3 " " " "
No 4 " " " "

N.B. Immediately after they have fired this burst of 5 rounds Platoons Nos. 1, 2 & 3 will take cover in their dugouts, to practice what they would do on hostile artillery bombardment against their part of the fire trenches.

"D" Company.
No 13 Platoon at 406 (R.31.A.6.5.)
No 14 ") ranges 400-800 yds at THIEPVAL
No 15 ") CHATEAU, the German trenches running
No 16 ") towards the same from 405 (R.31.A.5.3.) each section to be given a different point to fire at and a different range.

The M.G's will co-operate as follows:-
No 1 Gun) at 411 (R.31.C.3.0.) the German trenches
No 2 ") S.E. of same, range 500 & 700 yds.
No 3 " at 405 (R.31.A.5.3.) range 450 yds.
No 4 " at German re-entrant S.E. by S of THIEPVAL CHATEAU, range 600 yds.

Each gun will fire 50 rounds, opening fire immediately the Platoon beside it gets the order to commence firing. Night firing apparatus or screens to hide flashes to be used.

At 5.30 p.m. "B" Company will move 3 platoons to reinforce 14, 15 & 16 platoons & 1 platoon to take the place of No 11 platoon which will reinforce No 9 platoon.

At 5.50 p.m. The whole of the Battalion with the exception of 2, 3 & 4 platoons will cheer lustily.

At 5.52 p.m. The M.G's will fire another burst of 50 rounds on the targets they have been already firing on.

At 6.0 p.m. The whole Battalion will occupy artillery bombardment positions, with the exception of the M.G's who will be ready to co-operate with our

CONFIDENTIAL
No. 134
152nd INF. BDE.

1/8th (THE ARGYLLSHIRE) Bn ARGYLL & SUTHERLAND HIGHLANDERS.

FIRE SCHEME (Continued)

artillery should they be required to fire.

N.B. During each phase Company Commanders will notify to Battalion Headquarters and to the O.C. who will be in observation at point 145 the result of their fire.
Watches will be synchronized at 12 noon.

Capt & Adjt.
1/8th Bn Arg & Suth Highrs.

Issued at 10.0 a.m.
Copy No 1 to 152nd Infantry Brigade.
" " 2 " "A" Coy.
" " 3 " "B" "
" " 4 " "C" "
" " 5 " "D" "
" " 6 " M.G. Officer.
" " 7 " F.O.O.
" " 8 " O.C. 5th Seaforths.
" " 9 " O.C. 8th Scottish Rifles.
" " 10)
" " 11) Retained.
" " 12)

51st Division X.16

CONFIDENTIAL
No. 134
152nd INF. BDE.

121/7636

W A R   D I A R Y

of

1/8TH. ARGYLL &. SUTHERLAND HIGHLANDERS

FROM 1ST. NOVMEBR, 1915.
TO 30TH. NOVEMBER, 1915.

Vol VII

1/8th Battn Arg & Suthd Highlanders **WAR DIARY** Volume II

Army Form C. 2118.

Instructions regarding War Diaries and Intelligence Summaries are contained in F. S. Regs., Part II. and the Staff Manual respectively. Title pages will be prepared in manuscript.

~~or INTELLIGENCE SUMMARY~~. Sheet No 1.

(Erase heading not required.)

Place	Date	Hour	Summary of Events and Information	Remarks and references to Appendices
	1915 Nov.			
MARTINSART	1		Battalion in Divisional Reserve Billets 250 All ranks on work parties in trenches. ~~1 man died of wounds~~	
do	2		do do 215 do do	
do	3		do do 215 do do	
do	4		do do 215 do do	
do	5		do do Route march to ENGLEBELMER. 220 on work parties in trenches	
do	6		do do. 220 all ranks on work parties in trenches. Remainder at Tactical exercise	
do	7	11am	Divine Service. At 5pm Battn relieved 2/5 Lancashire Fusiliers in AVELUY as Brigade Reserve to 71 sector.	1 man wounded
AVELUY	8		Battn in Brigade Reserve billets. All available officers, NCOs & men employed on work parties in trenches	
do	9		do do do do 2 men wounded	
do	10		do do do do	
do	11		do do do do	
do	12		do do do do	
do	13		do do do do	
do	14		do do 50 men on work party. At 4 pm. Relieved 1/6th Argylls in firing line of 71 sector, Suffolk Regt on right, 6th Seaf Hrs on left 1 NCO & 3 men wounded	
AVELUY				
do	15		In trenches 71 sector. Slight fall of snow	

1577 Wt. W10791/1773 500,000 1/15 D. D. & L. A.D.S.S./Forms/C. 2118.

1/8th Bn Arg & Suthd Highrs

WAR DIARY

~~or~~

~~INTELLIGENCE~~ ~~SUMMARY~~.

(Erase heading not required.)

Volume II

Sheet No 8

Army Form C. 2118.

Instructions regarding War Diaries and Intelligence Summaries are contained in F. S. Regs., Part II. and the Staff Manual respectively. Title pages will be prepared in manuscript.

Place	Date	Hour	Summary of Events and Information	Remarks and references to Appendices
	1915 Nov			
AVELUY	16		In trenches F1 sector Heavy fall of snow 1 man wounded, ~~1 man died of wounds~~	
do	17		do	
do	18		do	
do	19		do	
do	20		do 1 man killed, 1 wounded.	
do	21		do	
do.	22		do Relieved at 6.15 pm by 1/4th Gordon Highlanders & marched to Rest Billets at MILLENCOURT arriving about 8.30 p.m.	
MILLENCOURT	23		Rest billets, cleaning up	
do	24		Rest Billets	
do	25		do. 9 am Route march with tactical exercise. Route via LAVIEVILLE, BAIZIEUX, HENENCOURT. 1 man wounded, ~~[illegible]~~	
do	26		do.	
do.	27		do. 374 all ranks on work parties in different trench sectors. 2 men wounded	
do	28		do. 4 pm Battn marched to AUTHUILLE and relieved 1/4th N. Lancs. Regt & 1/6th Scottish Rifles in G1 sector. relief completed at 7.30 pm. 4th Black Watch on right, 6th Argylls on left	
AUTHUILLE	29		In fire trenches G1 sector 2 men wounded	
do	30		do do	

1577 Wt. W10791/1773 500,000 1/15 D. D. & L. A.D.S.S./Forms/C. 2118.

D Bain Lieut. Colonel
Comdg 1/8th Bn A. & S. Highlanders

30-11-15.

X.17

CONFIDENTIAL
No. 134
152nd INF. BDE.

W A R   D I A R Y

OF

1/8TH. ARGYLL & SUTHERLAND HIGHLANDERS

51st

From 1st. December, 1915

To 31st. December, 1915.

....

Vol VIII

Instructions regarding War Diaries and Intelligence Summaries are contained in F. S. Regs., Part II. and the Staff Manual respectively. Title pages will be prepared in manuscript.

1/8th Batt^n Arg. & Suth^d High^rs

WAR DIARY or ~~INTELLIGENCE SUMMARY.~~

(Erase heading not required.)

Volume II

Sheet No. 9

Army Form C. 2118.

CONFIDENTIAL
No. 134
152nd INF. BDE.

Place	Date	Hour	Summary of Events and Information	Remarks and references to Appendices
	1915 Dec^r			
AUTHUILLE	1.		In fire trenches G1. sector	
do	2		do. do. 2 officers & 4 NCOs. 16th H. L. I. attached for instruction	
do	3		do do. 2 Platoons 16th H. L. I. attached for instruction	
do	4		do do. 4 men wounded 1 of whom died this date.	
do	5		do do. 2 Platoons 16th H. L. I. attached for instruction 1 man wounded.	
do	6		do do 1 Coy 16th H. L. I. attached for instruction	
do	7		do do	
do	8		do do	
do	9		do do 1 man wounded.	
do	10		do do.	
do	11	7/pm	Relieved by 1/6th Black Watch and returned to MILLENCOURT Rest Billets	
MILLENCOURT	12		Rest billets	
do	13		do	
do	14		do 6 officers and 325 other ranks on Work parties	
do	15		do Route march Sergeants Mess inaugurated	
AVELUY	16	4.45/pm	Moved into Brigade Reserve in AVELUY DEFENCES, relieving 2 Coys, 1/6th Sco. Rifles and 2 Coys 2/5th Lanc Fus.	

1577 Wt. W10791/1773 500,000 1/15 D. D. & L. A.D.S.S./Forms/C. 2118.

1/8th Battn Arg & Suth Highrs

Instructions regarding War Diaries and Intelligence Summaries are contained in F. S. Regs., Part II. and the Staff Manual respectively. Title pages will be prepared in manuscript.

WAR DIARY
~~or~~
~~INTELLIGENCE SUMMARY.~~

(Erase heading not required.)

Volume II

Sheet No 10.

Army Form C. 2118.

CONFIDENTIAL No. 134 152nd INF. BDE.

Place	Date	Hour	Summary of Events and Information	Remarks and references to Appendices
	1915 Decr			
AVELUY	17		In Brigade Reserve. All NCOs & men on work parties. Draft of 40 other ranks arrived from Base.	
do	18		do do	
do	19		do do	
do	20		do do 1 NCO killed & 3 men wounded while on work party.	
do	21		do do	
do	22		do do.	
do	23	5.30pm	Relieved by 15th H. L. I. and moved to MILLENCOURT Rest billets	
MILLENCOURT	24		Rest billets. Cleaning and interior economy. 10pm Divisional Brass Band played in village.	
do	25		Christmas Day, observed as a holiday. Inter platoon football matches	
do	26		Rest Billets. Divine service followed by Route march	
do	27		Rest Billets Route march	
do	28		Rest Billets, Drill parades	
MONTIGNY	29	9am	Marched from MILLENCOURT to MONTIGNY en route to Divisional Rest Area. Arrived MONTIGNY 11-50am. During march Battalion was inspected by Corps Commander.	
VILLERS BOCAGE	30	9.30 am	Marched from MONTIGNY arriving at VILLERS BOCAGE at 11 40am. Took over BILLETS to be occupied during rest period.	
do	31		Rest Billets. Battalion at drill.	

In the Field
31.12.15

D Baird Lieut Colonel
Commanding 1/8th Bn A & S Hrs

1577 Wt. W10791/1773 500,000 1/15 D. D. & L. A.D.S.S./Forms/C. 2118.

CONFIDENTIAL
No. 134
152nd INF. BDE.

X. 18

WAR DIARY.

of

1/8th Bn. Argyll & Sutherland Highlanders .

From

1st January 1916.

to

31st January 1916 .

Vol IX

1/8th Bn Arg. & Suth'd High'rs

Instructions regarding War Diaries and Intelligence Summaries are contained in F. S. Regs., Part II. and the Staff Manual respectively. Title pages will be prepared in manuscript.

WAR DIARY

~~or~~

~~INTELLIGENCE SUMMARY.~~

(Erase heading not required.)

Volume II

Sheet No. 11.

Army Form C. 2118.

Place	Date	Hour	Summary of Events and Information	Remarks and references to Appendices
	1916 Jany			
VILLERS	1		Rest billets. 10 am Batt'n Route march. Afternoon devoted to Inter half Batt'n Football match.	
BOCAGE	2		" Batt'n left 10th Corps & joined 13th Corps. No church parade owing to heavy rain	
"	3		" Batt'n training, Drill.	
"	4		" do. do.	
"	5		" do. Route march.	
"	6		" do Drill.	
"	7		" do Drill	
"	8		" do Route march	
"	9		" Church Parade	
"	10		" Batt'n training. Obstacle course completed. New Pattern censor stamp taken into use.	
"	11		" do. Draft of 46 other ranks arrived.	
"	12		" do. practising trench attack. Visit of C.in.C (informal.)	
"	13		" do Route march. Regimental Baths opened.	
"	14		" do Drill.	
"	15		" do. Route march. "B" Coy 4 off 116 other ranks proceeded on detachment to BEAUVAL	
"	16		" Church Parade. Maxim Gun section, 2 officers 35 other ranks left to form part of Brigade Machine Gun company. Reinforcement of 4 officers arrived	[signature]

1/8th Bn. Arg. & Suth. Highrs.

WAR DIARY ~~or INTELLIGENCE SUMMARY~~.

(Erase heading not required.)

Volume II

Sheet No. 12.

Army Form C. 2118.

Instructions regarding War Diaries and Intelligence Summaries are contained in F. S. Regs., Part II. and the Staff Manual respectively. Title pages will be prepared in manuscript.

Place	Date	Hour	Summary of Events and Information	Remarks and references to Appendices
VILLERS BOCAGE	1916 Jan. 17		Rest Billets: Battalion training. drill. Lewis Guns received & section formed under Lieut. Hood.	
	18		do do Routemarch	
	19		do do. Drill.	
	20		do. do. Routemarch	
	21		do. Brigade Tactical Exercise. Reinforcement of 78 other ranks arrived.	
	22		do. Battn training: 1½ coys at Divisional Grenadier Exercise.	
	23		do. Church Parade. Divisional School of instruction for officers & NCOs under Battn arrangements assembled	I
	24		do. Battn training: Drill.	
	25		do do Routemarch.	
	26		do. Brigade Tactical Exercise. 1 man wounded. accidental	
	27		do. Battn training: drill.	
	28		do. do. do.	
	29		do do. Practise trench attack.	
	30		do Church Parade	
	31		do. Battn training. drill. "B" Coy returned from BEAUVAL	

In the Field 31.1.16

D Baird Lieut. Colonel
Comdg. 1/8th Bn. A & S. Highrs.

A Rocker Major
[illegible]

1577 Wt. W10791/1773 500,000 1/15 D. D. & L. A.D.S.S./Forms/C. 2118.

Volume II, Appendix I.

51st (Highland) Division.

School of Instruction for Officers & NCOs

Commandant, & Chief Instructor.

Lieut. Colonel H.B.D. Baird, DSO 1/8th A.&S. H'rs

Adjutant.

Captain W. F. Macdonald, 1/8th Bn A&S H'rs

Assistant Instructor

2nd Lieut. A. Macdonald, 2nd (Att'd 1/8th) Bn A&S H'rs

Sergeant Major

C.S.M. N. Boyd. 1/8th Bn A&S H'rs

School assembled at VILLERS BOCAGE, 23rd Jany 1916

1st Class, dispersed, 5th Feby 1916.

Composition: 19 officers
40 NCOs

Units sending Students.

152nd Inf Bde.

1/5th Seaforth Highlanders
1/6th Seaforth Highlanders
1/6th A. & S. High'rs
1/8th A. & S. High'rs

153rd Infy Bde.

1/6th Royal Highlanders
1/7th Royal Highlanders
1/5th Gordon Highlanders
1/4th Gordon Highlanders.

154th Infy Bde.

1/4th Royal Highlanders
1/5th Royal Highlanders
1/4th Seaforth Highlanders
1/4th Cameron Highlanders.

Divisional Troops.

1/8th Royal Scots
1/6th Scottish Rifles.
Brigade Trench Mortar Battery.

And. Jockin [signature] Major
Adjt 1/8 A.&S.H.

51st (Highland) Divisional School.

Instructions to Officers.

---

1. The Officers and N.C.Os. of the Highland Division attending this School will be attached to the 1st/8th Argyllshire Highlanders for rations and discipline.

2. Officers will be made Honorary Members of the 1st/8th Argyllshire Highlanders' Battalion Mess. The N.C.Os. will have the use of a special mess which will be run for them under the School Sergeant Major.

3. Officers should bring camp kits with them if they have them, and also the following, beside full marching order: Sam Browne belt, field glasses, prismatic compasses, pistols, A.B. 153 and Infantry Training and F.S. Regulations, and F.S. pocket book, if they have them. Officers will bring one pair of trews with them for wearing at dinner.

4. Officers' servants will be prepared to wait at table in turn.

5. Officers and N.C.Os. will bring cleaning material with them for polishing buttons, cleaning belts, etc.

6. On arrival at VILLERS BOCAGE on the afternoon of Sunday, 23rd January, Officers and N.C.Os. will report themselves to Captain Fergus McDonald, 1st/8th Argyllshire Highlanders, School Adjutant, at the Battalion Orderly Room.

7. Officers will be rationed from 23rd January. N.C.Os. and officers' servants will be rationed from 24th January.

[illegible] Major
Adjt. 1/8 A.&S.H.

SCHOOL PROGRAMME.

Day	Lecture	Morning work	Afternoon Work	Lecture.
24.1.16 (Monday)	8-8.45 a.m. Lecture by C.O. Explanation of object of School and method of working it.	9-12 Squad & Communicating Drill.	2-4 Personal interview with C.O.	5.30 - 6.30 by C.O. Discipline and esprit de corps, Duty of Officers and N.C.O's.
25.1.16 (Tues.)	Lecture by C.O. Protection on march and Advance [illegible] Guards.	9.30 - 1.30 p.m. Battalion Route March. Class to form 2 platoons [illegible] with advanced guard.	3.30 - 4.30 p.m. Drill & deportment. Class will attend battalion guard-mounting parade.	by M.O. Care of men. Inspection of feet Sanitation in billets.
26.1.16 (Wed.)	Lecture by C.O. Protection while halted. Outposts.	Outpost scheme	Inspection of model billet and Squad & Communicating Drill.	on Musketry by Bn. Sergt.-Major.
27.1.16 (Thurs.	Lecture by C.O. Reconnaissance and writing of reports.	School parades for drill with Battalion under Adjutant for 1½ hours. 10.30 - 12. Tactical Scheme (reconnoitring)	2-3. Fire Control under Regt.S.M. 3-4. Use of prismatic compass & map reading.	by C.O. Military crimes & punishments.
28.1.16 (Fri.)	The trench Attack.	Battalion Trench Attack. Class participates.	2-3 p.m. Squad & Communicating Drill and Obstacle Course. 3-4 p.m. Reconnaissance for night march. 5-7 p.m. Night march.	
29.1.16 (Sat.)	Lecture by C.O. Communication reports, messages &c	Battalion route march involving advance and flank guard. School forms part of flank guard.	2.30 - 4.30 Packing & Loading Transport, Saddling Horses. Care of horses, etc.	Lecture by M.O. Gas, and Trench Feet.

[signature] Major
A.A.G.

G.693.

SCHOOL PROGRAMME.

Day	Lecture	Morning Work	Afternoon Work	Lecture
Sunday 30.1.16.	Church Parade.		Half holiday.	
Monday 31.1.16	Lecture 8-8.45 a.m. Trench Routine duties.	9-10 a.m. Map Reading. Use of Compass. 10-12. Use of ground, selection of position, field of fire &c.	2-3 p.m. Tube helmet practice. 3-4 p.m. Extended order drill Signals and intercommunication.	5.30 - 6.30 Lecture by C. The Attack.
Tuesday 1.2.16.	Lecture by Adj. Duties of Officers & N.C.O's on the march, in billets, care of men.	9.30 - 1.30 Route March with battalion deploying for attack. School to form hostile opposition.	3 - 4 p.m. Musketry and fire orders under Bn. Sergt.Major.	5.30 - 6.30 Lecture by Lt.Tang,R.E., Field Engineering.
Wed. 2.2.16	Lecture by Grenadier Offr. Use of Grenadiers.	9-10. Grenade attack. 10-12. Field Engineering.	2-4 p.m. Tactical Scheme.	Lecture by M.G.Officer. Machine Guns in trench warfare and open fighting.
Thursday 3.2.16	Lecture by 2nd in command How to keep men fit & contented in billets.	9-12 a.m. Topography, simple sketch of position and report.	2-3 p.m. Inspection of Bn. Institutes. 3-4 p.m. Instruction in simple use of machine gun.	Lecture by Major Artillery.
Friday 4.2.16.	Composition of our Army in France, Esprit de Corps of O.B.E.F., etc. Discipline, etc.	9.30 - 1.30 Route March, involving advance and flank guard. School forms one platoon of each.	3 - 4.30 p.m. Visit to Aerodrome. Description of aeroplanes.	Lecture by C.O. or Officer 7th Division. Trench discipline & routine
Sat'day. 5.2.16	The Officer and N.C.O. in the attack. The offensive spirit	Battalion Trench Attack. School participates.	2-3 p.m. Final Lecture by C.O.	School disperses.

And Locke Major
adj. 7/A.P.A.

X 19

CONFIDENTIAL
No. 134
152nd INF. BDE.

W A R D I A R Y

of

1/8th Bn. Argyll and Sutherland Highlanders.

FEBRUARY, 1916.

Vol X

1/8th Bn. Arg. & Suthd. Highlanders

WAR DIARY
or
~~INTELLIGENCE SUMMARY~~.

Volume II.

Sheet No. 13

Army Form C. 2118.

Instructions regarding War Diaries and Intelligence Summaries are contained in F. S. Regs., Part II. and the Staff Manual respectively. Title pages will be prepared in manuscript.

(Erase heading not required.)

Place	Date	Hour	Summary of Events and Information	Remarks and references to Appendices
	1916 Feby			
ILLERS BOCAGE	1		Battn in rest billets. Battalion training. Route march.	
do	2		do. Company training & training of specialists	
do	3		do. Company training. Senior officers at Brigade exercise	
do	4		do Company training & training of specialists	
do	5		do Battalion training. Attack practice. Divisional School dispersed.	
do	6		do. Divine Service	
do	7		do. Cleaning of Billets and area.	
CORBIE	8		Battn. marched at 8.45 am with Brigade to new billets in CORBIE arriving there at 1.30 pm	
do	9		Battn in rest billets. Cleaning and inspection of billets	
do	10		do. Company and specialist training	
do	11		do do. do.	
do	12		do. Battalion route march.	
do	13		do. Divine Service	
do	14		do. Company and specialist training.	
do	15		do do do.	
do.	16		do. Battalion Route march and attack practice.	

1577 Wt. W10791/1773 500,000 1/15 D. D. & L. A.D.S.S./Forms/C. 2118.

1/8th Bn Arg. & Suthd Highrs

WAR DIARY ~~or INTELLIGENCE SUMMARY.~~

(*Erase heading not required.*)

Volume II

Sheet No. 14

Army Form C. 2118.

Instructions regarding War Diaries and Intelligence Summaries are contained in F. S. Regs., Part II. and the Staff Manual respectively. Title pages will be prepared in manuscript.

Place	Date	Hour	Summary of Events and Information	Remarks and references to Appendices
	1916 Feby			
CORBIE	17		Battn in Rest Billets. Company and specialist training.	
do	18		do. do. Major A Mackie relinquished appt as Adjt on promotion 2nd Lt A Macdonald, 1/8 A&SH, to be Adjutant	
do	19		do. Bathing and interior economy.	
do	20		do. Divine Service	
do	21		do Company and specialist training 1 off & 31 OR. to HEILLY for duty.	
do	22		do Company and specialist training	
do	23		do. Battalion Route march	
do	24		do. Bathing, Inspection of Arms by Bde Armrs 50 OR. arrived from Base	
do	25		do. Company & specialist training. 3 off 103 OR. to LONGPRE for work. His Grace the Duke of Argyll Hon Colonel of Battn arrived.	
DAOURS	26		Battn marched at 11 am to new billets at DAOURS arriving 12.30 pm. The Hon Colonel marched with Battn	
do	27		All available NCOs & men working with Engineers constructing railway.	
do	28		Battn returned to CORBIE at 9 am. Detachments from HEILLY and LONGPRE returned. Hon Colonel The Duke of Argyll left battalion.	
do	29		Battn marched with Brigade to MOLLIEN au BOIS, arriving 3.30 pm.	

In the Field.
29.2.16

D Baird Lieut. Colonel
~~Comdg~~ 1/8th Bn A&SHrs

1577 Wt. W10791/1773 500,000 1/15 D. D. & L. A.D.S.S./Forms/C. 2118.

57

Vol XI

X.20

CONFIDENTIAL
No. 134
152nd INF. BDE.

W A R D I A R Y .

of

1/8th Bn. Argyll & Sutherland Highlanders.

From

1st March, 1916 .

To

31st March, 1916 .

Instructions regarding War Diaries and Intelligence Summaries are contained in F. S. Regs., Part II. and the Staff Manual respectively. Title pages will be prepared in manuscript.

1/8th Bn Arg. & Suthd High^rs WAR DIARY ~~or~~ ~~INTELLIGENCE SUMMARY~~. (Erase heading not required.)

Volume II

Sheet No 15.

Army Form C. 2118.

CONFIDENTIAL No. 134 152nd INF. BDE.

Place	Date	Hour	Summary of Events and Information	Remarks and references to Appendices
	1916 March			
MOLLIEN au BOIS	1		Battalion resting.	
do	2		Battalion resting. Company training	
do	3		do. Route march	
do	4		do. No training owing to heavy snowstorm. 8 Reinforcements arrived.	
do	5		do Divine Service	
BEAUVAL	6	9.30 am	Battalion marched with Brigade to BEAUVAL arriving 2.30 pm. 1st advance party to reconnoitre trenches.	
do	7		Battalion resting. Company training. 2nd advance party to reconnoitre trenches.	
do.	8		Battalion resting. Company training	
IVERGNY	9	8.40am	Battalion marched with Brigade to IVERGNY arriving 1.25 pm	
MAROEUIL	10	11.30am	Battalion marched with Brigade to MAROEUIL arriving 7.30 pm. Coy commanders and specialist officers to trenches	
LABYRINTHE	11	6.30/pm	Battalion proceed to trenches and at 11.35 pm completed relief of 3rd Battn 78th French Regiment of Infantry	
do			in left sub sector of LABYRINTHE (Chef de Battn Capt Teilhac) other sub sectors relieved by	
do			Right, 5th Seaforths, Centre, 6th Seaforths, Battn in Reserve, 6th A&SH. Battalion sub sector	
do			held by A & B front line, C & D in support. Transport & QMrs stores remained at MAROEUIL.	
do			154th Bde on right of 152nd Bde. 153rd Bde on left. 5th Gordon High^rs on left on 8th A&SH	
do.	12		Battalion in trenches. 2 other ranks wounded	

1/8th Bn A & S Hrs

Instructions regarding War Diaries and Intelligence Summaries are contained in F. S. Regs., Part II. and the Staff Manual respectively. Title pages will be prepared in manuscript.

WAR DIARY

~~or~~

~~INTELLIGENCE SUMMARY.~~

(Erase heading not required.)

Volume II

Sheet No 16

CONFIDENTIAL No. 134

152nd INF. BDE.

Army Form C. 2118.

Place	Date	Hour	Summary of Events and Information	Remarks and references to Appendices
	1916 March			
LABYRINTHE	13		Battalion in trenches. 3 other ranks wounded	
do	14		do	
do	15		do 4 other ranks wounded	
do	16		do C & D Coys relieved A & B in fire trenches 2.15pm	
do	17		do B Coy relieved 1 Coy 6th Seaf. Highrs in fire trenches 2.15pm	
do	18		do 3 other ranks wounded.	
do	19	6.35 ~~[illegible]~~pm	do Battn relieved in fire trenches by 6th A & S H & moved to reserve trenches as Brigade Reserve 2 other ranks killed 3 other ranks wounded.	
do	20		Battn in Reserve trenches. All available officers and other ranks on working parties.	
do	21		do do	
do	22		do do	
do	23		do do	
do	24		do do	
do	25	5.20pm	Battn relieved in Reserve trenches by 5th Seaforth Highrs and moved to MAROEUIL as Divnl. Reserve	
MAROEUIL	26		Battn in Billets as Divisional Reserve.	
do	27		do. A Coy relieved 1 Coy 5th Seaforths in firing line. 3pm	

1577 Wt. W10791/1773 500,000 1/15 D. D. & L. A.D.S.S./Forms/C. 2118.

1/8 Bn A & S Hrs

Army Form C. 2118.

Instructions regarding War Diaries and Intelligence Summaries are contained in F. S. Regs., Part II. and the Staff Manual respectively. Title pages will be prepared in manuscript.

WAR DIARY
or
~~INTELLIGENCE SUMMARY.~~

(Erase heading not required.)

Volume II

Sheet No 17

CONFIDENTIAL No. 134

152nd INF. BDE.

Place	Date	Hour	Summary of Events and Information	Remarks and references to Appendices
	1916 March			
MAROEUIL	28		Battn in Billets as Divisional Reserve. "A" Coy returned at 6pm.	
do	29		do do	
do	30		do do. Reinforcement of 3 officers 197 other ranks arrived from 1/9th Bn A & S Hrs & distributed to companies.	
LABYRINTHE	31	1pm	Battn moved to trenches and relieved 6th A & S H in M2 sector. C & D in firing line A & B in support. 6th Seaforth Highrs in M1 sector. 5th Seaforths relieved Bn in MAROEUIL. 6th A & S H to Bde Reserve trenches. Relief complete 5-10pm. 1 other ranks wounded	

In the Field
31/3/16.

J. L. Brown Major
Commanding 1/8th Bn A & S Hs

1577 Wt. W10791/1773 500,000 1/15 D. D. & L. A.D.S.S./Forms/C. 2118.

51

Vol XII

mis I

CONFIDENTIAL X . 21
No. 134
152nd INF. BDE.

W A R D I A R Y

of

1/8th Bn. Arg. & Suth'd. Highlanders.

From

1st April, 1916.

To

30th April, 1916.

1/8th Bn. Arg & Suth^d Highrs

WAR DIARY
~~or~~
~~INTELLIGENCE SUMMARY.~~
(*Erase heading not required.*)

Volume II

Sheet No. 18

Army Form C. 2118.

Instructions regarding War Diaries and Intelligence Summaries are contained in F. S. Regs., Part II. and the Staff Manual respectively. Title pages will be prepared in manuscript.

Place	Date	Hour	Summary of Events and Information	Remarks and references to Appendices
	1916 April			
LABYRINTHE	1		Battalion in trenches MB sector — 1 NCO killed 2 men wounded	
"	2		do. — 2 wounded	
"	3		do	
"	4		do — A & B to fire trenches C & D Coys to support trenches. Lt Maclaren wounded, 1 NCO killed.	
"	5		do — Captain J.K. Maclachlan wounded, 1 man killed 1 wounded	
"	6	12.10pm	Battn relieved in fire trenches (less A Coy) by 6th A & SH & moved to Bde Reserve trenches. A Coy remained in line	
"	7		Battn in Bde Reserve trenches	
"	8		do. 'A' Coy relieved & moved into support trenches	
"	9		do — 1 man killed.	
"	10	5pm	Battn relieved 6th A & S Highrs in fire trenches, D & B in firing line A & C in support	
"	11		Battn in fire trenches — 1 NCO killed 1 wounded	
"	12		do. — 4 wounded	
"	13		do — 1 wounded	
"	14		do A & C relieved B & D Coys	
"	15		do. — 3 wounded	

1577 Wt. W10791/1773 500,000 1/15 D. D. & L. A.D.S.S./Forms/C. 2118.

1/8th Bn Arg & Suth'd Highlanders **WAR DIARY** ~~or INTELLIGENCE SUMMARY.~~ Volume II

(Erase heading not required.)

Sheet No. 19

Army Form C. 2118.

Instructions regarding War Diaries and Intelligence Summaries are contained in F. S. Regs., Part II. and the Staff Manual respectively. Title pages will be prepared in manuscript.

Place	Date	Hour	Summary of Events and Information	Remarks and references to Appendices
	1916 April			
LABYRINTHE	16	6pm	Battn relieved by 1/8th A & SH moving on relief to MAROEUIL as Divisional Reserve.	
MAROEUIL	17		Battn in Divisional Reserve. Found work parties of 200 all ranks.	
do	18		do do do	
do	19		do do do	
do	20		do do do	
do	21		do do do	
do	22	6pm	Battn Relieved 6th A & SH in fire trenches M2 sub sector B & D Coys in firing line A & C in support	
LABYRINTHE	23		Battn in fire trenches — 2 wounded	
do	24		do C Coy relieved B Coy. — 1 wounded	
do	25		do A Coy relieved D Coy — 1 wounded	
do	26		do — 4 wounded	
do	27		do. Battn subjected to heavy Artillery & Trench Mortar bombardment — 5 killed 8 wounded	
do	28		do 2.13 am Mine exploded by enemy on battn front followed by an intense bombardment during which enemy attacked and were repulsed 5.15pm Battn relieved by 6th A & SHrs and moved into Bde Reserve, ½ D Coy to MAROEUIL — 4 killed 1 missing (believed buried) 14 wounded	I
do	29		Battn in Bde Reserve trenches. — 1 wounded	

1577 Wt. W10791/1773 500,000 1/15 D. D. & L. A.D.S.S./Forms/C. 2118.

1/8th Bn. A & S Highrs.

Volume II

Sheet 20

WAR DIARY

~~or~~

~~INTELLIGENCE SUMMARY.~~

(Erase heading not required.)

Army Form C. 2118.

Instructions regarding War Diaries and Intelligence Summaries are contained in F. S. Regs., Part II. and the Staff Manual respectively. Title pages will be prepared in manuscript.

Place	Date	Hour	Summary of Events and Information	Remarks and references to Appendices
LABYRINTHE	1916 April 30		Battalion in Bde Reserve trenches.	

In the Field 30-4-16

D Baird Lieut Colonel
~~Cmdg~~ 1/8th Bn A & S Highrs

1577 Wt. W10791/1773 500,000 1/15 D. D. & L. A.D.S.S./Forms/C. 2118.

Appendix I

General Officer Commanding,

152nd Infantry Brigade.

Sir,

I have the honour to report on the action of the Battalion under my command, early this morning, 28th April, when the enemy made an attack against my Sub-sector; at 2.30 a.m. the Germans sprung a mine at the eastern end of the sap (A.16.c.7.7), and immediately after this opened a very heavy artillery and trench mortar bombardment on my firing, my support line and the communicatio from the latter to the former. I immediately sent up rocket signals for artillery co-operation, which was responded to at once, our guns opening fire before I had sent up the fifth rocket. My right advanced Company immediately manned their fire positions on the parapet of the fire trench, and my left advanced company whose fire trench was very exposed to the enfilading barrage of the enemy, kept three platoons in their shelters and manned the centre fire positions of the Company with the fourth platoon.

The Lewis Guns of the Battalion immediately after the explosion of the mine, occupied their gun emplacements on the parapets of the fire trenches, and opened fire on the enemy's trenches and the craters at 765 (A.16.a.8.1.) D''' (A.16.a.8.0.) and 762 (A.16.c.7.9.)

The explosion of the mine blew in the saps between 277 (A.16.c.7.7.) and the fire trench near M.34, and also the sap leading from R to r, for some thirty yards north and south of r', (the junction of Sap 277 and Sap from R -- r.)

The bombing post at r, whose duty was to patrol sap R.277 at intervals during the night, were buried by the trench falling in on them. Three men were buried up to the neck, and two were killed (one has been recovered).

The bombing post at r, whose duty at night was to patrol saps 763 and 762 (A.16.c.7.9.) and (A.16.c.8.8.) had their covered approach cut off between them and the rest of the battalion.

A few minutes after the mine exploded, the Germans advanced in three parties against my right Company, and opened heavy gun and rifle fire from their trenches and the eastern sides of the craters against my whole front. My left Company immediately reinforced the whole of its firing line with the remainder of its platoons, and opened three rounds rapid on the enemy, and after that maintained controlled fire against the hostile trenches (which from the rifle flashes were strongly held) until the hostile fire slackened. In this the two left and the two centre Lewis Guns co-operated.

The German attack was delivered by three parties, who advanced as follows:- A party of four rushed into the sap north of R and came down towards R. The leading man was killed, and rest climbed over the parapet at R, and ran off after throwing a few hand grenades into the trench, killing one man. The second party advanced from the north end of the mine crater just formed, and attacked the bombing post between R -- r', and drove them, with the exception of two men at r, out of the trench to the fire trench M.34. The third German party, consisting of 9 men, advanced simultaneously with/

with the second attack down saps 762 and 763, and attacked the two men posted at r from two sides. The bayonet man was killed and the bomber (No.3191, Pte.R.Baker, "C" Coy.) held his ground, killed one German, wounded another, and dispersed the remainder, who, taking the wounded man with them, retired hastily up sap 763 pursued by Pte.Baker. In the meantime the remainder of Pte.Baker bombing party were re-formed in the firing trench, and moved across and drove back the Germans out of the r' -- r. sap they had entered, in co-operation with the fire of the platoons and the right company in the fire trench and the two right Lewis Guns.

The three men who had been buried up to their necks in saps between 277, were in the meantime caught hold of by some of the enemy, who tried to pull them and dig them out of the sap. When the attack retook r -- r' trench, these Germans departed with the others, taking the ~~shoulder~~ shoulder titles of the buriedmen from them. Before their departure they debated amongst themselves as to whether they would kill my men, and were persuaded by one of them not to, and they promised to return to-night and get hold of them. This mercy is surprising, as the enemy were Bavarians.

Shortly after the German was shot at R, one of my officers came back from the firing line and reported to me the Germans had broken through in my right Company.

I had under my command of two support Companies, enough men to furnish five weak platoons, as my support Companies were supplying large working parties near the front line. I immediately sent one platoon to BAIRD STREET to support my left Company, one platoon to 774 to support my right Company, and ordered a platoon to move via Point 500 to the left of the Seaforth fire trench, and from there towards R. to establish touch with the right of my right Company, and counter-attack if necessary in order to seize R.

I collected the Battalion staff and orderlies, and some men of the R.E. and 5th Sherwood Foresters fatigue parties, and posted these at the junction of VICTOIRE AVENUE and the supportline, and then ~~only~~ had only two platoons under my hand, which I did not consider sufficient to counter-attack with if, as had been reported to me, my right was really broken. I therefore, finding my direct communication with the CHEMIN CREUX was broken, telephoned to the Brigade Headquarters and asked for a message to be sent from there to the Company of the 6th Argylls, which I understood was at my disposition for tactical purposes, to move this Company up to my support line. This Company did not arrive in my support line, as I understand an order from the Brigade was sent to cancel my order. Telephonic communication between my Headquarters and my advanced Company headquarters was broken shortly after the mine was exploded, but I established communication first of all by runners, and twenty minutes after the wires were cut my Signalling Sergeant and another signaller had laid out a fresh line of wire to both Company headquarters. The runners and signallers carried out their duties in a most gallant manner under this intense artillery and trench mortar bombardment. I established liason with the Battalion on my left within five minutes of the mine exploding, and with the left of the Seaforths half an hour after the mine exploded. The telephonic communications between my Headquarters and the Seaforth Headquarters were broken immediately after the bombardment commenced. I was not aware that any mines had been sprung in front of the 6th Seaforths until I observed the craters opposite that sub-sector myself

The conduct of the Officers and men of the Battalion could not have been better. All ranks showed the greatest keenness to engage the enemy, and the coolness and disregard for personal safety ofthe Officers and men of the Argyllshire Highlanders was most marked.

After a personal reconnaisance of the situation I posted battalion snipers at R. 762 crater, 763 and r', and under cover of these and posts at d''', organised work parties to clear the trench filled with wire from d''' to r (thus establishing covered approach to saps 762 and 763 and to expedite the saps that had fallen in round r'. I also organised a party to clear the trench that was blocked between 762 and the new crater, in order to be able to consolidate the southern edge of the new crater to-night and to establish plates ~~txx~~ there.

It is of the utmost importance that we should maintain ourselves on ~~tx~~ the south edge of the new crater, as it will:
(1) Prevent the enemy from dominating our saps and fire trenches from his side of the crater.
(2) it will permit us to enfilade his main fire trench from his salient at 279 and to the south.

The R.E. have made a reconnaisance for this purpose, and will carry out this work to-night

I will forward in another letter the names of the officers and men whose conduct is deserving of reward.

I am, Sir,

Your obedient Servant,

(Sgd) D Baird Lieut. Colonel,
Comdg: 1/8th Bn. Argyll & Suth'd Highrs.

28-4-1916.

Certified true copy
A Macdonald Lieut
Adjt 1/8 Bn A&SHrs

W A R D I A R Y

of

1/8th Battn. Argyll and Sutherland Highlanders.

****

FROM

1st May, 1916.

TO

31st May, 1916.

****

152nd Infantry Brigade SECRET No.134.

Headquarters,

152nd Infantry Brigade.

I send herewith War Diary for month of May, 1916, for Battalion under my Command.

D Baird Lieut. Colonel,

Commanding 1/8th Bn. Arg & Suth'd Highrs.

2nd June, 1916.

1/8th Bn Arg Suth. Highrs

WAR DIARY
or
~~INTELLIGENCE SUMMARY~~.
(Erase heading not required.)

Volume II

Sheet No. 21.

Army Form C. 2118.

Instructions regarding War Diaries and Intelligence Summaries are contained in F. S. Regs., Part II. and the Staff Manual respectively. Title pages will be prepared in manuscript.

Place	Date	Hour	Summary of Events and Information	Remarks and references to Appendices
	1916 May			
LABYRINTHE	1		Battalion in Brigade Reserve.	
do	2		do	
do	3		do — 1 man (attached RE) mine gassed.	
do	4	4.50pm	Battalion relieved 1/6th A&SH in M2 sub-sector. — 1 man killed 2 men wounded.	
do	5		Battalion in Fire trenches — 1 man killed 2 men wounded	
do	6		do — 1 man wounded	
do	7		do	
do	8		do	
do	9		do	
do	10		do	
do	11	5.40pm	Battalion relieved by 1/6th A&SH and moved to Divisional Reserve at MAROEUIL.	
MAROEUIL	12		Battalion in Divisional Reserve, Work parties, Bathing and cleaning.	
do	13		do Specialist & company training. Reinforcts, 50 other ranks arrived	
do	14		do Divine Service 6pm	
do	15		do Specialist & company training, Work parties	
do	16		do do do	

1577 Wt. W10791/1773 500,000 1/15 D. D. & L. A.D.S.S./Forms/C. 2118.

1/8th Bn Arg & Suth^d High^s

WAR DIARY
or
~~INTELLIGENCE SUMMARY.~~
(*Erase heading not required.*)

Volume II
Sheet No 22.

Army Form C. 2118.

Instructions regarding War Diaries and Intelligence Summaries are contained in F. S. Regs., Part II. and the Staff Manual respectively. Title pages will be prepared in manuscript.

Place	Date	Hour	Summary of Events and Information	Remarks and references to Appendices
	1916 May			
LABYRINTHE	17	6 pm	Battalion relieved 1/6th A&SH in fire trenches, M2 subsector.	
do	18		Battalion in fire trenches	
do	19		do. 1 man wounded.	
do	20		do 1 officer (Lt C.E. Graham) & 9 other ranks wounded.	
do	21		do 3 other ranks wounded	
do	22		do 4 other ranks wounded	
do	23		do 2 Platoons 4th A&SH took over right portion of line 10 other ranks wounded	
do	24	6.15 pm	1 officer (2Lt J Graham Campbell wounded) Battn relieved in firing line by 2 coys 4th Gordon Highrs and in support line by 1 Coy 6th Royal Highrs and on relief marched to BRAY. Battn housed in Huts. 1 man wounded. 152nd Inf Bde now in rest billets.	
BRAY	25		Battalion in Rest Billets. Baths and cleaning up 200 other ranks work parties.	
do	26		do Company & Specialist training do	
do	27		do do do	
do	28		do Divine Service do.	
do	29		do. do	
do	30		do Company Route march. Specialist training. 100 other ranks work parties	
do.	31		do. Specialist training. Baths. 200 other ranks, work parties.	

In the Field
31.5.16

D Baird Lieut. Colonel
Comdg 1/8th Bn A&S High^rs

1577 Wt. W10791/1773 500,000 1/15 D. D. & L. A.D.S.S./Forms/C. 2118.

152nd Inf. Brigade SECRET No. 134.

X.23

Vol 14

W A R D I A R Y.

of

1/8th Bn. ARGYLL = SUTHERLAND HIGHLANDERS.

From 1st June 1916.

to

30th June 1916 .

152nd Inf. Bde. SECRET No. 154.

Headquarters,

152nd Infantry Brigade.

I send herewith War Diary for June, 1916, for Battalion under my Command.

R. K. Gardner

Lieut. Colonel,

Comdg. 1/ 8th Battn. A. & S. Highr

1st July, 1916.

1/8th Bn Arg. & Suth'd Highrs

Instructions regarding War Diaries and Intelligence Summaries are contained in F. S. Regs., Part II. and the Staff Manual respectively. Title pages will be prepared in manuscript.

WAR DIARY

~~or~~

~~INTELLIGENCE SUMMARY.~~

(Erase heading not required.)

Volume II

Sheet No 23

Army Form C. 2118.

Place	Date	Hour	Summary of Events and Information	Remarks and references to Appendices
	1916 June			
NEUVILLE ST VAAST	1	9-30pm	Bn moved from Bray to NEUVILLE ST VAAST, relieving 8th So. Lancashire Regt. Bn distributed Headqrs and B Coy	
do			in NEUVILLE ST VAAST, 'A' Coy in support to 5th Seaforths (Right Battn of Brigade in line) 'D' Coy at QUARRIES	
do			in support to 6th Seaforths (Left Battn of Brigade in line) 'C' Coy in Shelters in PYLONNES. 6th Bn Gordon	
do			Highlanders in Divisional Reserve at BRAY. Relief completed at 1-25 am 2nd June. 2 OR wounded.	
do	2		Bn in Bde Reserve 1 OR wounded	
do	3		do 1 OR wounded	
do	4		do	
do	5		do	
VIMY	6	5-35pm	Battn relieved 6th Seaforths in P. (Left 2 subsector) Firingline, 6th Gordons on right. 1 OR wounded	
(P. sector)	7		Battn in firing line 1 OR wounded	
do	8		do 1 OR wounded	
do	9		do 1 OR wounded	
do	10		do	
do	11		do 1 OR wounded	
do	12		Battn relieved by 6th Seaforths at 8pm, and at 1130 pm moved to Divisional Reserve Billets at MONT ST ELOY arriving at 3 am 13th	

1577 Wt. W10791/1773 500,000 1/15 D. D. & L. A.D.S.S./Forms/C. 2118.

1/8th Bn. Arg & Suthd Highrs

WAR DIARY

~~or~~

~~INTELLIGENCE SUMMARY.~~

(Erase heading not required.)

Volume II

Sheet No 24.

Army Form C. 2118.

Instructions regarding War Diaries and Intelligence Summaries are contained in F. S. Regs., Part II. and the Staff Manual respectively. Title pages will be prepared in manuscript.

Place	Date	Hour	Summary of Events and Information	Remarks and references to Appendices
	1916 June			
BRAY	13	11.30am	Battn moved from MONT ST ELOI to huts at BRAY	
do	14		Battn in Divisional Reserve	
do	15		do	
do	16		do. G.O.C 51st (H) Divn presented Medal Ribbons to Capt A C McIntyre (Military Cross)	
do			and Cpl Baker (D.C.M.) on Battn ceremonial parade and afterwards marched past.	
do	17		Battn in Divisional Reserve	
VIMY (P Sector)	18	10 am	Church Parade. At 10 pm moved to Left 2 subsector and relieved 6th Seaforths. 6th Gordons in Left 1 subsector, 5th Seaforths Bde Reserve NEUVILLE ST VAAST. Relief complete 1-55 am 19th	
do	19		Battn in firing line. 2 OR wounded. LIEUT W M BENNETT, killed.	
do	20		at 9.35 pm hostile mine exploded on front occupied by 'B' Company. Work of consolidation commenced but attempts of Germans to prevent our occupation of near lip resulted in a	
do			severe fight with Bombs and Lewis Guns for six hours when enemy retired. 2nd Lieuts R C M SMITH	
do			and 2nd Lieut J. INCH (9th Bn attached) killed. 2nd Lieut. J.C.F. PENDER wounded. 2 NCOs & 2 men killed.	
do			9 other ranks wounded. 2nd Lt J.C.F. Pender awarded Military Cross, Sgt A. McCallum awarded D.C.M.	
do			Sgt H. McGregor, Stretcher Bearers A. Thomson and P McCreank awarded Military Medals.	
do	21		Battn in firing line. LIEUT. R. FINLAY wounded.	
do	22		do. Lt Col. H.B.D. Baird, DSO. relinquished command on Staff appointment.	

1577 Wt. W10791/1773 500,000 1/15 D. D. & L. A.D.S.S./Forms/C. 2118.

1/8th Bn. Arg. & Suth^d High^rs.

Instructions regarding War Diaries and Intelligence Summaries are contained in F. S. Regs., Part II. and the Staff Manual respectively. Title pages will be prepared in manuscript.

WAR DIARY

~~or~~

~~INTELLIGENCE SUMMARY.~~

(Erase heading not required.)

Volume II

Sheet No 25.

Army Form C. 2118.

Place	Date	Hour	Summary of Events and Information	Remarks and references to Appendices
	1916 June			
VIMY	23		Batt^n in firing line. Severe Thunderstorm	
do	24		Batt^n relieved by 1/6th Seaforths and moved to NEUVILLE ST VAAST. Hdqrs and B Coy in NEUVILLE ST VAAST A Coy in support to 5th Seaforths (~~Right~~ Left 1) C and D in supports to 6th Seaforths (Left 1) 6th Gordons at BRAY Relief completed 2.45 am 25th 1 O.R. wounded.	
NEUVILLE ST VAAST	25		Batt^n in Brigade Reserve	
do	26		do	
do	27		do	
do	28		do	
do	29		do	
VIMY (P sector)	30	5.30pm	Batt^n relieved 1/6 Seaforths in left 2 sector. 6th Gordons in left 1 sector. 5 Seaforths to MONT ST ELOI 6th Seaforths to ACQ. 2nd Division First Army on left of Batt^n	

In the Field
30th June 1916.

J. R. Gardner
Lieut Colonel
Comdg 1/8 Bn A & S Highrs

152nd Brigade.

51st Division.

1/8th BATTALION

ARGYLL & SUTHERLAND HIGHLANDERS.

JULY 1 9 1 6

X 24

Vol 15

152nd Inf. Brigade / 51
SECRET No. 134.

WAR DIARY

of

1/8th Bn. Argyll & Sutherland Highlanders.

July, 1916.

1/8th Bn. Arg. Suth. Highrs.

WAR DIARY
~~or~~
~~INTELLIGENCE SUMMARY~~
(Erase heading not required.)

Volume II
Sheet No 24

Army Form C. 2118

Instructions regarding War Diaries and Intelligence Summaries are contained in F. S. Regs., Part II. and the Staff Manual respectively. Title Pages will be prepared in manuscript.

Place	Date 1916	Hour	Summary of Events and Information		Remarks and references to Appendices: Killed Off	Killed O.R.	Wounded Off	Wounded O.R.	Missing Off	Missing O.R.
VIMY RIDGE P (Left 2) Sector	July 1		Battn in fire trenches. 8 Platoons 2/18th Bn London Regt. (60th Division) attached for instruction	AM				1		
do	2		do 2 Coys 2/18th Bn London Regt (60th Divn) attached for instruction. 2 am Heavy bombardment and hostile mine exploded on Battn front. 10-15 pm Hostile mine exploded on battn front.	AM		5		12		
do	3		Battn in fire trenches.	AM				1		
do	4		do. 11pm Relief by 1/6th Bn Seaforth Highrs commenced	AM				1		
ON LINE OF MARCH.	5	2.15am	Relief by 1/6th Seaforth Highrs complete. Battn rendezvous at ACQ. 10 am Battn marched to rear Area arriving at 4-15 pm Hdqrs & A & B Coys at BAILLEUL AUX CORNAILLEUX, C & D Coys at MARQUAY	AM						
OSTERVILLE.	6	11 30am	Battn marched to OSTERVILLE arriving 1pm Remainder of Brigade in trenches & forward area Battn rearmed with Short L. E. Rifle Mk III & Bayonets.	AM						
do	7		Battn resting in rear Area. Battn bathed in ST POL.	AM						
do	8		do. Training & interior economy.	AM						
do	9		do. 6 pm Divine Service.	AM						
do	10		do. Training and interior economy.	AM						
ECOIVRES	11	9am	Battn marched to forward area, arrived ECOIVRES 4.15 pm	AM						
MAROEUIL	12		Battn took over mining fatigues in centre sector of Divisional line. B Coy to AU REITZ, C Coy to ANZIN D Coy to ABRIS CENTRAL, BN HQ & details of A not attached to other companies being at MAROEUIL Major R Campbell, Cameron Highlanders, assumed command of Battn. (Tempy Lt Col from this date.)	AM						
	13		Battn on mining fatigues.	AM				1		

1875 Wt. W593/826 1,000,000 4/15 J.B.C. & A. A.D.S.S./Forms/C. 2118.

1/8th Bn Arg & Suthd Highrs

WAR DIARY ~~or~~ ~~INTELLIGENCE SUMMARY~~

(Erase heading not required.)

Volume II

Sheet No. 25

Army Form C. 2118

Instructions regarding War Diaries and Intelligence Summaries are contained in F. S. Regs., Part II. and the Staff Manual respectively. Title Pages will be prepared in manuscript.

Place	Date 1916	Hour	Summary of Events and Information	Remarks and references to Appendices	Killed Offs	Killed O.R.	Wounded Offs	Wounded O.R.	Missing Offs	Missing O.R.
MAROEUIL	July 14		Battn on mining fatigues. 8 pm orders received to cease fatigues and concentrate at MAROEUIL.	AMy						
ECOIVRES & SUS ST LEGER	15	10am	Battn marched to ECOIVRES and travelled by Motor Lorries to SUS ST LEGER. Left ECOIVRES 1-30pm arrived SUS ST LEGER 4pm. Remainder of Brigade billetted in SUS ST LEGER.	AMy						
GEZAINCOURT	16	9.30am	Marched with Brigade to GEZAINCOURT arriving 4pm	AMy						
do	17		Battn (with Brigade) resting Short Route march	AMy						
do	18		do. Battn bathed at DOULLENS.	AMy						
do	19		do 9pm Transport left by road for FLESSELLES.	AMy						
	20	4pm	Battn marched to CANDAS and left by train at 8-45 pm for MERICOURT. Transport went by road to BUIRE.	AMy						
	21	1.15am	Arrived MERICOURT and marched to BUIRE 7.50 pm Battn marched with Brigade to Bivouac F4b (Sheet 62D NE) (1/20000)	AMy						
FRICOURT	22		Battn in bivouac. 4pm owing to being twice bombarded moved at 6pm to F4a. 8pm moved to Bivouac at F2d.	AMy						
do	23		Battn in Bivouac F2d.	AMy				4		
BECORDEL-BECOURT	24	9am	Battn moved to bivouac at E12b. Training	AMy						
do	25		Battn remained in bivouac Training	AMy						
MAMETZ WOOD	26		Battn moved to bivouac S20a (Sheet 57c SW 1/20000) arrived 10pm. at 10-25pm Battn suffered rapid bombardment of gas shells and shrapnel lasting 6 hours (4-30am 27th) 700 men on work parties.	AMy						
FRICOURT WOOD	27	2pm	Battn shifted Bivouac to MAMETZ WOOD. 7.40 pm Battn shifted bivouac to F4a (Sheet 62D NE 1/20000) 400 men on work parties.	AMy		3	1	14		3
					Gas	1	1	26		

1875 Wt. W593/826 1,000,000 4/15 J.B.C. & A. A.D.S.S./Forms/C. 2118.

1/8th Bn Arg Suth^d High^rs

WAR DIARY
~~or~~
~~INTELLIGENCE SUMMARY~~
(Erase heading not required.)

Volume II

Sheet No. 26

Army Form C. 2118

Instructions regarding War Diaries and Intelligence Summaries are contained in F. S. Regs., Part II. and the Staff Manual respectively. Title Pages will be prepared in manuscript.

Place	Date 1916	Hour	Summary of Events and Information		Remarks and references to Appendices: Killed Off.	Killed OR	Wounded Off.	Wounded OR	Missing Off.	Missing OR
FRICOURT WOOD	July 28		Batt^n in Bivouac	AW			Gas 1	6 / 44		
do	29		Batt^n in Bivouac	AW		1	Gas	3 / 13		
do	30		Batt^n in Bivouac	AW			Gas	1 / 1		
do	31		Batt^n in Bivouac	AW			Gas	2		

In the Field
31/7/16

R Campbell Lieut Colonel
Comdg 1/8th Bn A & S H^rs

1875 Wt. W593/826 1,000,000 4/15 J.B.C. & A. A.D.S.S./Forms/C. 2118.

152nd Brigade.

51st Division.

<u>1/8th BATTALION</u>

<u>ARGYLE & SUTHERLAND HIGHLANDERS</u>

<u>AUGUST 1 9 1 6</u>

Headquarters
152nd Inf Bde

SECRET.
No 16

Herewith WAR DIARY for August 1916.
(Vol. III Sheets 1, 2, & 3.)

R Campbell
Lieut Colonel
Comdg 1/8th Bn. A & S H.

1/9/16

1/8th Bn. Arg. & Suth^d Highr^s

Volume III

Sheet 1.

Army Form C. 2118.

CONFIDENTIAL. No 31 (A) HIGHLAND DIVISION

Instructions regarding War Diaries and Intelligence Summaries are contained in F. S. Regs., Part II. and the Staff Manual respectively. Title pages will be prepared in manuscript.

WAR DIARY

~~or~~

~~INTELLIGENCE SUMMARY.~~

(Erase heading not required.)

Place	Date 1916	Hour	Summary of Events and Information		Casualties Officers K	W	M	Other ranks K	W	M	Remarks and references to Appendices
	August										
FRICOURT	1		Battalion in Brigade Reserve at F 4 a (Sheet 62^D NE 1-20000)	am							
WOOD	2		——— do ———	am					48		
"	3		——— do ——— 2nd Lt J. Thomson, 11th Gordon Highrs (attached)	am		1			21		
"	4		——— do ———	am							
HIGH WOOD	5	12.45pm	Battalion moved ~~do~~ am to firing line in HIGH WOOD S.4 (Sheet 57^C S.W. 1/10000)	am				2	12		
"	6		Battalion in firing line	am				2	28		
	7	7.50am	Battalion relieved in firing line by 9th H.L.I. and marched to bivouacs at 7.2.d. (Sheet 62^D NE.)	am							
			11.45 am marched to Brigade Bivouacs at D18 (Sheet 62^D NE)	am							
BUIRE	8		Battalion resting 4pm Transports moved by road to CARDONETTE.	am							
	9	12.30pm	Battalion marched to EDGEHILL SIDING and entrained. Train left at 4.15pm arriving LONGPRE-LES CORPS SAINTS at 9.5 pm. To Billets. Transport arrived by road.	am							
LONGPRE LES-CORPS-SAINTS	10		Battalion resting	am							
	11		do.	am							
	12	7.21am	Battalion with Transport entrained and moved to THIENNES arriving 5.30pm. Marched to BLARINGHEM arriving 7.30pm. To Billets with Brigade.	am							
BLARINGHEM	13		Battalion resting. Divine Service and Communion at 10 am	am							

1577 Wt. W10791/1773 500,000 1/15 D. D. & L. A.D.S.S./Forms/C. 2118.

1/8th Bn. Arg v Suthd Highlanders

WAR DIARY
~~or~~
~~INTELLIGENCE SUMMARY.~~
(Erase heading not required.)

Volume III

Sheet 2

Army Form C. 2118.

Instructions regarding War Diaries and Intelligence Summaries are contained in F. S. Regs., Part II. and the Staff Manual respectively. Title pages will be prepared in manuscript.

Place	Date	Hour	Summary of Events and Information	Casualties Officers K. W. M.	Casualties O.R. K. W. M.	Remarks and references to Appendices
	1916 August					
BLARINGHEM	14		Battalion resting. Training Re inoculation of officers am			
"	15		do. do. am			
"	16		do. Route march. Companies instructed in Breastworks under R.E. am			
"	17		do. 2.30 pm Inspection of Battn by Brigade Commander. am			
	18	4.15am	Transports left by road for new area. 7.45 am Battalion marched to EBBLINGHEM entrained at 10.25 am for STEENWERCK. Detrained 11.30am marched to ARMENTIÈRES arrived 4 pm. Transports rejoined. am			
ARMENTIÈRES	19		Battalion with Brigade in Divisional Reserve. Resting am			
"	20		do. Divine Service in Battn Billet. am			
"	21		do. Training am			
"	22		do. 'B' Coy inspected in Gas Drill by Brigade Commander. Reinforcements arrived, 30 OR. from No 19 Base 72 OR. from No 2 Entrenching Battn. am			
"	23		Battn with Brigade in Divisional Reserve. 35 OR reinoculated. Wiring instruction under R.E. 4 officers 308 OR carrying party at night am			
"	24		Battn with Brigade in Divisional Reserve. Reinforcements inspected by Brigade Commander. 4 officers 268 other ranks carrying party at night am			
"	25		Battn with Bde in Divisional Reserve. 2 officers 150 OR on carrying party at night am			

1577 Wt. W10791/1773 500,000 1/15 D. D. & L. A.D.S.S./Forms/C. 2118.

1/8th Bn Arg. & Suth'd Highlanders.

Volume III

WAR DIARY
or
~~INTELLIGENCE SUMMARY.~~
(Erase heading not required.)

Sheet 3

Army Form C. 2118.

Instructions regarding War Diaries and Intelligence Summaries are contained in F. S. Regs., Part II. and the Staff Manual respectively. Title pages will be prepared in manuscript.

Place	Date	Hour	Summary of Events and Information	Casualties Officers K	Officers W	Officers M	O.R. K	O.R. W	O.R. M	Remarks and references to Appendices
	1916 Augt.									
ARMENTIÈRES	26	6.25 pm	Battn relieved 1/7th A&SH (154th Bde) in firing line (I.5 Sheet 36 N.W.4, 1-10000) 1/6th Seaforth Highrs on right, 153rd Bde on left. 30 OR Reinforcements from Base arrived. am							
"	27		Battalion in firing line. am				1			
"	28		do. am					7		
"	29		do Thunderstorm am							
"	30		do Sub-sector visited by Corps Commander. 25 O.R. reinforcements from Base am							
"	31		do. am							

In the Field
31st August 1916.

R. Campbell Lieut Colonel
Commanding 1/8th Bn A&S Highrs

SECRET
No. 134
152nd INF. BDE.

X. 26

Vol 17

W A R D I A R Y

of

1/8th Bn. ARG. & SUTH'D. HIGHLANDERS.

From

1st September, 1916.

To

30th September, 1916.

Headquarters
152nd Inf Bde

Herewith War Diary for September 1916, Vol III Sheets 4, 5, & 6.

R Campbell Lieut Colonel

1/10/16. Cmdg 1/8 Bn A&SH

1/8th Batt. Argyll & Sutherland Highrs.

WAR DIARY ~~or~~ ~~INTELLIGENCE SUMMARY.~~

Volume III

Sheet 4

Army Form C. 2118.

Instructions regarding War Diaries and Intelligence Summaries are contained in F. S. Regs., Part II. and the Staff Manual respectively. Title pages will be prepared in manuscript.

(Erase heading not required.)

Place	Date	Hour	Summary of Events and Information	Casualties: Officers K	W	M	Other ranks K	W	M	Remarks and references to Appendices
	1916 Sept									
ARMENTIERES	1		Battalion in firing line (I 5, Sheet 36 NW 4 1:10000) am							
"	2		do am					3		
"	3		do am					1		
"	4		do am							
"	5	6.25pm	Battalion relieved by 1/5th Seaforth Highlanders. Moved to Brigade Reserve Billets in Armentieres am							
"	6		Battn in Brigade Reserve. Furnishing working & carrying parties am							
"	7		do do am					3		
"	8		do do am							
"	9		do do am							
"	10		do Divine Service do am							
"	11		do do am							
"	12		do do am							
"	13		do do am							
"	14		do do am							
"	15		do. do. am				1			

1/8th Batt. Argyll & Sutherland Highrs.

Instructions regarding War Diaries and Intelligence Summaries are contained in F. S. Regs., Part II. and the Staff Manual respectively. Title pages will be prepared in manuscript.

WAR DIARY
~~or~~
~~INTELLIGENCE SUMMARY.~~
(Erase heading not required.)

Volume III
Sheet 5

Army Form C. 2118.

Place	Date	Hour	Summary of Events and Information	Remarks and references to Appendices
	1916 Sept			
ARMENTIERIES	16		Battn in Brigade Reserve. Furnishing working and carrying parties	am
"	17		do do	am
"	18		do do	am
BAILLEUL	19	9am	Marched to Training Camp near BAILLEUL arriving 12-15 pm Brigade relieved in line. 5 offrs 221 other ranks left in Armentieres as working party. 26 O.R. reinforcements arrived	am
"	20		With Brigade in training Camp. Training	am
"	21		do do	am
"	22		do do	am
"	23		do Route march, passed Army Commander. Armentieres detachment rejoined.	am
"	24		do Church Parade with 6 Gordon Highlanders Presentation of Certificates of	
"			Gallant Conduct	am
"	25		With Brigade in Training Camp. Training	am
"	26		do do	am
"	27		do do	am
"	28		do. Brigade Ceremonial Parade Presentation of Ribbons and inspection by	
"			Army Commander.	am

1577 Wt. W10791/1773 500,000 1/15 D. D. & L. A.D.S.S./Forms/C. 2118.

1/8th Batt. Argyll & Sutherland Highrs.

Volume III

Sheet 6.

Army Form C. 2118.

Instructions regarding War Diaries and Intelligence Summaries are contained in F. S. Regs., Part II. and the Staff Manual respectively. Title pages will be prepared in manuscript.

WAR DIARY

~~or~~

~~INTELLIGENCE SUMMARY.~~

(Erase heading not required.)

Place	Date	Hour	Summary of Events and Information	Remarks and references to Appendices
	1916 Sept			
BAILLEUL	29		With Brigade in Training Camp Training am	
"	30	11.28 pm	Entrained at Bailleul Main Station for Doullens on Divisional move am	

In the Field 30/9/16

R. Campbell Lieut. Colonel
Comdg 1/8th Bn. A & S. Highrs.

SECRET
No. 134
152nd INF. BDE.

X.27

CONFIDENTIAL
No 21(A)
HIGHLAND
DIVISION.

W A R   D I A R Y

of

1/8th Bn. ARGYLL and SUTHERLAND HIGHLANDERS.

Vol 18

From

1st October, 1916.

To

31st October, 1916.

****

1/8th Bn Args Suth^d High^rs

WAR DIARY

~~or~~

~~INTELLIGENCE~~ ~~SUMMARY~~.

(Erase heading not required.)

Instructions regarding War Diaries and Intelligence Summaries are contained in F. S. Regs., Part II. and the Staff Manual respectively. Title pages will be prepared in manuscript.

Volume III

Sheet 7.

Army Form C. 2118.

CONFIDENTIAL. NO 21(A) HIGHLAND DIVISION.

Place	Date	Hour	Summary of Events and Information	Casualties Officers K	Officers W	Officers M	O.R. K	O.R. W	O.R. M	Remarks and references to Appendices
	1916 Oct.									
GEZAINCOURT	1	5am	Detrained at DOULLENS and marched to GEZAINCOURT arriving 7-10 am aw							
BOIS du WARNIMONT	2	9.30am	Marched with Brigade to Bivouacs at BOIS du WARNIMONT aw							
do	3		In Bivouac aw							
CAILLY AU BOIS	4	11.45am	Marched to Bivouacs, in Brigade support. Hdqrs & A & B Coys to J.17.b. (57D N.E. 1/20000) relieving 10th Cornwalls. C & D Coys to FORT GROSVENOR (K.21.a. 57D N.E. 1/20000) relieving 2/So. Staffords. 1/6th Gordon Hrs & 1/5th Seaf Hrs to line, 1/6th Seaf. Hrs in reserve. aw							
	5		H.Q. & A & B Coys to Bivouacs K 25 a (57D N.E. 1/20000) Whole Battn on night working party. aw					2		
HEBUTERNE	6	6.20pm	Battn relieved 6/Gordon Highrs in line (Right sub sector) 6th Seaf. Hrs on left. Ox. & Bucks L.I on right aw							
	7	4.20pm	C & D Coys relieved by 7th So. Lancs. and moved to FORT GROSVENOR aw				1	5		
	8	6.20pm	H.Q. & A & B Coys relieved in line & C & D in FORT GROSVENOR by 4th Gordon Hrs (154th Bde) and							
BUS			marched to Bivouacs in BUS. Remainder of Brigade in LOUVENCOURT. 2nd Lt J.D. Kemp, wounded. aw		1					
"	9		Training aw							
"	10		Training, 9 officers from Base aw							
"	11		Training 20 O.R. from Base aw							
"	12		Training Work parties aw							
"	13		Training Work parties aw							

T.134. Wt. W708–776. 500000. 4/15. Sir J. C. & S.

1/8th Batt. Argyll & Suthe[rland] Highrs.

Instructions regarding War Diaries and Intelligence Summaries are contained in F. S. Regs., Part II. and the Staff Manual respectively. Title pages will be prepared in manuscript.

WAR DIARY
~~or~~
~~INTELLIGENCE~~ ~~SUMMARY.~~

(*Erase heading not required.*)

Volume III

Sheet 8

Army Form C. 2118.

Place	Date	Hour	Summary of Events and Information	Casualties Officers K	W	M	O.R. K	W	M	Remarks and references to Appendices
	1916 Oct									
BUS	14		Training Work parties am							
"	15		Church service am							
"	16		Training am							
[A]UCHONVILLERS	17	8.30am	Marched from Bus to BEAUMONT HAMEL Sector and relieved NELSON Battⁿ 189th Bde Naval Division am at 1.45pm in left sub sector of Brigade line 6th Gordon Highrs on right. 23rd Royal Fusiliers on left 5+6th Seaforths in Support and Reserve. B.D.C. Coys in line, A Coy in support							
"	18		In line am							
	19	12.40pm	Relieved in line by 6th Seaforth Highrs & moved to Bivouacs at P18b. Sheet 57D SE 1/10000. am							
[M]AILLY MAILLET	20		Battⁿ in Bivouacs 23 OR. reinforcements joined am					1		
"	21		do am							
[L]EALVILLERS	22	9am	Marched to Billets in LEALVILLERS arriving 11.30am. 3 officers from Base am							
	23	2.45pm	Marched to Bivouacs at P17d. Echelon B formed at P17a (Sheet 57D SE 1/20000) am							
[L]EALVILLERS.	24	2pm	Battⁿ returned to LEALVILLERS, Echelon B remaining at P17a am ~~1 officers joined~~ am am							
"	25		Battⁿ resting Work Parties. am							
"	26		Training Work parties am							
"	27		do. do. am							

T.2134. Wt. W708–776. 500000. 4/15. Sir J. C. & S.

1/8th Batt. Argyll & Sutherland Highrs.

Instructions regarding War Diaries and Intelligence Summaries are contained in F. S. Regs., Part II. and the Staff Manual respectively. Title pages will be prepared in manuscript.

WAR DIARY

~~or~~

~~INTELLIGENCE SUMMARY.~~

(*Erase heading not required.*)

Volume III

Sheet 9

Army Form C. 2118.

Place	Date	Hour	Summary of Events and Information		Casualties Officers K	W	M	O.R. K	W	M	Remarks and references to Appendices
	1916 Oct										
LEALVILLERS	28		Training. Work parties	AW							
"	29		Training Work parties	AW							
	30	10 40am	Battalion moved from LEALVILLERS "A" Coy + 3 platoons B Coy to AUCHONVILLERS, HQ + remainder of Battn to Bivouacs at P 17 d. 2 officers joined - reinforcements	AW							
	31		Work parties	AW					1		

In the Field 31/10/16

R. Campbell Lieut Colonel
Comdg 1/8th Bn. A & S Highrs

T.2134. Wt. W708–776. 500000. 4/15. Sir J. C. & S.

SECRET
No. 134
152nd INF. BDE.

X.28

Vol 19

W A R D I A R Y

of

1/8th Bn. ARGYLL and SUTHERLAND HIGHRS.

NOVEMBER.1916.

1/8th Bn Arg & Suth^d Highlanders

WAR DIARY ~~or INTELLIGENCE SUMMARY.~~

Volume III

Sheet 10.

Army Form C. 2118.

Instructions regarding War Diaries and Intelligence Summaries are contained in F. S. Regs., Part II. and the Staff Manual respectively. Title pages will be prepared in manuscript.

(Erase heading not required.)

Place	Date	Hour	Summary of Events and Information	Casualties Officers K	W	M	Other ranks K	W	M	Remarks and references to Appendices
	1916 Nov.									
MAILLY WOOD	1		Batt^n in Bivouacs. A & B Coys at AUCHONVILLERS Work parties am							
do	2		do do am							
do	3		do do am							
do	4		A & B Coys rejoined. Bn marched to FORCEVILLE for Church service 3 pm am							
do.	5		Batt^n in Bivouacs am							
FORCEVILLE	6	11.30am	Batt^n less Echelon B marched to Billets in FORCEVILLE. 6 OR reinforcements am							
do	7		Batt^n in Billets. Training. Work parties. am							
do	8		do do am							
do	9		do do am							
do	10		do do am							
do	11		do do. am							
do.	12	11am	Church Service. 9 pm Batt^n 21 officers 674 other ranks marched to assembly trenches preparatory to attack of german position BEAUMONT HAMEL. am							
	13	3.20am	Battalion in position for attack. 5.45 am Batt^n attacked BEAUMONT HAMEL gaining all objectives am	5	6	.	6 / 73	170	10	"A"
	14	9.10pm	Batt^n relieved in BEAUMONT HAMEL by one Company 6th Gordon Highlanders & moved into bivouac							

1577 Wt. W10791/1773 500,000 1/15 D. D. & L. A.D.S.S./Forms/C. 2118.

1/8th Bn. A & S Highlanders

WAR DIARY
or
~~INTELLIGENCE SUMMARY~~.
(Erase heading not required.)

Volume III

Sheet 11.

Army Form C. 2118.

Instructions regarding War Diaries and Intelligence Summaries are contained in F. S. Regs., Part II. and the Staff Manual respectively. Title pages will be prepared in manuscript.

Place	Date	Hour	Summary of Events and Information	Casualties: Officers K	W	M	Other ranks K	W	M	Remarks and references to Appendices
	1916 Nov.									
MAILLY WOOD	14		in Mailly Wood East Am							
do	15		Battn resting Am							
do	16		do Am							
do	17		do Am							
do	18		do Slight fall of snow Am							
TRENCHES	19	12.30pm	Battn moved to Reserve Trenches opposite BEAUMONT HAMEL providing work and carrying parties and clearing Battlefield Am							
do	20		Battn in reserve trenches 70 OR reinforcements Am							
do	21		do 84 OR reinforcements Am							
do	22		do Am					2		
do	23		do 3pm Echelon B officers and men moved to FORCEVILLE 7 OR reinforcements Am							
FORCEVILLE	24	6am	Battn relieved by 22nd Bn Manchester Regiments and moved to Billets in FORCEVILLE Am							
do	25		7 officers 38 OR reinforcements Am							
do	26		Church Service. Am							
SENLIS	27	1.30pm	Battn marched to billets in SENLIS, remainder of Brigade to BOUZINCOURT Am							
do	28		Battn resting. Training Am							

1577 Wt. W10791/1773 500,000 1/15 D. D. & L. A.D.S.S./Forms/C. 2118.

1/8th Bn Arg. & Suth. Highrs

Volume III

Sheets 12.

Army Form C. 2118.

WAR DIARY

~~or~~

~~INTELLIGENCE SUMMARY.~~

(*Erase heading not required.*)

Instructions regarding War Diaries and Intelligence Summaries are contained in F. S. Regs., Part II. and the Staff Manual respectively. Title pages will be prepared in manuscript.

Place	Date	Hour	Summary of Events and Information	Remarks and references to Appendices
	1916 Nov.			
SENLIS	29		Battn resting. Training. Drafts inspected by Brigade Commander. am	
do.	30		Battn resting. Training am	

[signature] Major,
Commanding 1/8th Bn A & S Hrs

1577 Wt. W10791/1773 500,000 1/15 D. D. & L. A.D.S.S./Forms/C. 2118.

REPORT ON THE OPERATIONS AT BEAUMONT HAMEL ON THE 13th.NOVEMBER, 1916.

On the night of the 12/13th.November, 1916, the Battalion moved up to its position in HUNTERS TRENCH. A halt of one hour was made just before the entrance to FOURTH AVENUE and ~~hit~~ hot soup issued to the men. Considerable difficulty was found in getting into HUNTERS TRENCH as it was very narrow in places, but the Battalion was ready in position at 3.20 a.m. on 13th.November.

Platoon Commanders at once set to work and cut away our own wire in places where necessary. Two minutes before Zero the left of the leading wave ("A" Company) movedout and lay down in front of our wire in touch with the 2nd.H.L.I.

Up to Zero the Battalion had suffered no casualties. The mist was of great assistance in helping us to get into the assembly trenches unseen.

At Zero the first wave went over followed immediately by the second, third and fourth waves. Each wave was composed of a full Company, and the Companies were placed in the order of "A", "B", "C" and "D". The Lewis Guns of each company went over immediately ~~after~~ in rear of their respective Companies. I had arranged ~~with~~ that each wave should move out as closely as possible on the heels of the wave preceding it, as I thought that the 6th.Seaforth Highlanders would probably be down into HUNTERS TRENCH almost before my battalion was clear of it. As it turned out the first wave of the 6th.Seaforth Highlanders came down into HUNTERS TRENCH just as the last wave of my battalion was leaving it. Theleading wave halted at about 15 yards from our own barrage, and as it lifted they rushed the front line, giving the Germans no time to get out of their dug-outs. The bombing parties were busily engaged until Zero plus 20 in clearing dug-outs, and they had considerable difficulty with German parties in the communication trenches.

In the meantime the second wave had carried the second line and commenced to clear it; this wave captured a Minenwerfer. They also sent down about 50 prisoners.

At 7 a.m. Lieutenant McCallum, commanding "B" Company re-organized the remains of his Company and started to lead them forward to reinforce the fourth wave, but as soon as they started away from the second German line they were fired on by some Germans concealed in shell holes near the German first line. They therefore retired and dealt with this party before going on. Having done so they advanced again and eventually reinforced the leading line of the battalion.

The third wave advanced on the third German line andwere entering it when the barrage lifted off it. This wave was considerably troubled by snipers on their right flank. There appears to have been a gap between the right flank of the Argylls and the left flank of the 5th.Seaforths, which was afterwards dealt with by a company of the 6th.Gordons. The third wave had orders to deal with two dug-outs located at Q.5.c.3.5.3.5., which lay between the objectives of the second and third waves; they left a guard on these as they passed.

From information derived from a captured German map a Battalion Headquarters was suspected at Q.5.c.5.0.5.5, which was just in front of the objective of the third wave. On obtaining the objective, therefore, the of the third wave, Lieutenant Munro, accompanied by 2nd.Lieutenant Miller, went forward to search for this dug-out, and there captured a Battalion Commander, four other officers and a staff of 45 men (believed to belong to the 2nd. Battalion of the 62nd.Regiment).

At 9.20 a.m. I received information from the officer commanding the fourth wave that they had entered the fourth German line. They were afterwards shelled out of it, and retired to the third German line. It appears a little doubtful whether this wave did actually reach the fourth German line; owing to the destructive effect of our artillery fire it was almost impossible to recognise the ground. It is, however, certain that they consolidated eventually with the third wave in the third German line, and remained there until the whole battalion moved forward later in the day to try and occupy the line of the WAGON ROAD.

The battalion was at this time (9.20 a.m.) in touch with the 2nd.H.L.I. on the left and the 5th.Seaforths on the right.

At 4.25 p.m. orders were received from the Brigade to seize and consolidate the line of the WAGON ROAD from its junction with the green line to Q.5.b.6.3. This movement was commenced at dusk, but the advance was stopped on the green line by our artillery barrage, which was turned on 150 yards east of the green line. The battalion therefore consolidated on the green line from Q.5.d.1.5. to Q.5.c.8.8., and continued to hold this line until finally relieved. Contact was obtained with the 2nd.H.L.I. on the left and the 6th.Gordon Highlanders on the right.

Two 'Tanks' proceeded up towards BEAUMONT HAMEL during the afternoon, but one stuck between the first and second German lines about Q.4.d.9½.1½.; the other proceeded to the northern part of BEAUMONT HAMEL and stuck the other side of the village.

The casualties for the battalion during the fight were estimated at 250; at the present time (November 18th) they have turned out to be 265.

Remarks on Operations are attached on a separate sheet.

(Sgd) R.Campbell

Lieut-Colonel,
Comdg: 1/8th.Bn. Argyll & Suth'd Highrs.

18th.November, 1916.

Casualties during action of
13/14 Nov. 1916.

Officers KILLED
Captain A. Macarthur
Lieut. J. T. McKellar
2nd Lt A. E. Brander 5
" D. Macgregor
" H Fraser

WOUNDED
Captain D. Macgregor
Lieut. G. McCallum
" A. Crawford 6
2nd Lt R. R. Spence
" H. P. F. McIntosh
" H. C. N. Baly

Other ranks
Killed 76
Died of wounds 6
Wounded 171
Missing 8
261

30/11/16.

List of Officers joining on 25/11/16

2nd Lt. (Temp. Lt.) A.R. Macfarlane-Grieve
2nd Lt. A.K. Wilkinson
" J.J. Crawford
" W. Jaffrey
" D.N. Morris
" J.P. Trotter
" J.S. Young.

SECRET
No. 134
152nd INF. B. X.29

CONFIDENTIAL.
No 21 (A)
HIGHLAND
DIVISION.

Vol 20

W A R D I A R Y

of

1/8th Bn. ARGYLL and SUTHERLAND HIGHRS.

From

1st December, 1916.

To

31st December, 1916.

Instructions regarding War Diaries and Intelligence Summaries are contained in F. S. Regs., Part II. and the Staff Manual respectively. Title pages will be prepared in manuscript.

1/8th Bn Arg. & Suth^d Highlanders. **WAR DIARY** ~~or~~ **INTELLIGENCE SUMMARY.** (Erase heading not required.)

Volume III Sheet 13.

Army Form C. 2118.

Place	Date	Hour	Summary of Events and Information	Casualties Officers K	Officers W	Officers M	Other ranks K	Other ranks W	Other ranks M	Remarks and references to Appendices
	1916 Dec^r									
SENLIS	1		Battalion resting. Training. A & B Coys Baths. am							
	2		do. do. C & D Coys Baths. am					1		
	3		do. Church Service. Inspection of Billets. am							
OVILLERS HUTS	4	9.30am	Battalion moved to OVILLERS HUTS. Q.M. Stores to AVELUY. Transport at CROMWELL HUTS. 63 other ranks reinforcements from No 19 Inf Base Dept. 250 men on Work parties. am							
	5		Batt^n with Brigade in reserve. 370 men on Work parties. 2nd Lt Duncan & 2nd Lt Norris with 56 other ranks to Detachment under 92nd Coy R.E. am							
	6		Batt^n in Brigade Reserve. 11 Military Medals awarded for 13 Nov 1916. 350 men on work parties. am							
	7		do. 350 men on work parties. am							
	8		do. 200 men on work parties. Lewis Gun Det. relieved guns of 9th Royal Scots in COURCELETTE sub-sector. Trousers issued for trench duty. am							
COURCELETTE	9	10.50pm	Batt^n relieved 9th Royal Scots in front line near COURCELETTE. A B & C in line, D in support. 6th Seaforths on right, 61st Division on left. 6th Gordons & 5th Seaforths in support. am				1	1		
	10		Batt^n in trenches. am				3	7		
	11		Batt^n in trenches. Snow am							
	12		Batt^n in trenches. am				5	12		

1/8th Bn Arg & Suth'd Highlanders

Instructions regarding War Diaries and Intelligence Summaries are contained in F. S. Regs., Part II. and the Staff Manual respectively. Title pages will be prepared in manuscript.

WAR DIARY
or
INTELLIGENCE SUMMARY.
(Erase heading not required.)

Volume III

Sheet 14

Army Form C. 2118.

Place	Date	Hour	Summary of Events and Information	Casualties: Officers K.	W	M	O.R. K	W	M	Remarks and references to Appendices
	1916 Oct.									
COURCELETTE	13	2 am	Battn relieved by 5th Seaforth Highrs and moved to Shelters in R 29. am				am X			
do	14		Battn in supports am							
do	15	10 pm	Battn relieved by 7th Black Watch and moved to BRUCE HUTS near AVELUY am							
SENLIS	16		Battn moved to Billets in SENLIS (conveyed by motor Bus.) 30 other ranks reinforcements from Base am							
do	17		Battn in Reserve with Brigade. am							
do	18		do. am							
do	19		do. am					1		
do	20		do am							
do	21		do. am							
OVILLERS HUTS	22		Battn moved to OVILLERS HUTS am							
do	23		Battn with Brigade in Support supplying work parties am							
do	24		do am							
do	25		do am							
do	26		do am							
	27	9.15 pm	Bn relieved 9th Royal Scots in left subsector COURCELETTE. A & D Coys in line, B & C to WOLFE HUTS am							

1/8th Bn. Argyll & Sutherland Highlanders.

WAR DIARY
or
~~INTELLIGENCE~~ SUMMARY

(Erase heading not required.)

Volume III

Sheet 15.

Army Form C. 2118.

Instructions regarding War Diaries and Intelligence Summaries are contained in F. S. Regs., Part II. and the Staff Manual respectively. Title Pages will be prepared in manuscript.

Place	Date	Hour	Summary of Events and Information		Casualties Officers K	W	M	Other ranks K	W	M	Remarks and references to Appendices
	1916 Dec										
COURCELETTE	28		A & D Coys in trenches. Captain J.L. Lauder killed.	am	1						
"	29		B & C Coys relieved A & D Coys in line. A & D Coys to WOLFE HUTS.	am					1		
"	30		B & C Coys in trenches. Lewis Gun teams relieved by 5th Seaforths. Major A Lockie to command 5th Seaforths. 72 Reinforcements arrived	am							
"	31		B & C Coys relieved in line by 5th Seaforth Highlanders & moved to OVILLERS HUTS. Detachments from 92nd R.E. returned to Battn	am							

In the Field 31·12·16

R Campbell
Lieut. Colonel
Comdg 1/8th Bn A & S Hrs

2449 Wt. W14957/M90 750,000 1/16 J.B.C. & A. Forms/C.2118/12.

152nd Inf. Bde. SECRET No. 134.

X-30

CONFIDENTIAL.
NO 21 (A)
HIGHLAND
DIVISION.

Vol 21

WAR DIARY

of

1/8th Battn. ARGYLL and SUTHERLAND HIGHRS.

FROM

1st JANUARY, 1917

TO

31st JANUARY, 1917.

CONFIDENTIAL.
No 21 (A)
HIGHLAND
DIVISION.

Secret.

H.Q.
152nd Inf. Bde.

Herewith War Diary for January 1917.

R. Campbell
Lieut Colonel
Cmdg 1/8 Bn A&SH

31/1/17

1/8th Bn Arg. & Suth'd High'rs

Instructions regarding War Diaries and Intelligence Summaries are contained in F. S. Regs., Part II. and the Staff Manual respectively. Title pages will be prepared in manuscript.

WAR DIARY

~~or~~

~~INTELLIGENCE SUMMARY.~~

(Erase heading not required.)

Volume III

Sheet 16

Army Form C. 2118.

CONFIDENTIAL. No HIGHLAND DIVISION.

Place	Date	Hour	Summary of Events and Information		Casualties K W M	Casualties K W M	Remarks and references to Appendices
	1917 JAN.						
OVILLERS	1		Battn in Brigade Reserve. HQ & B & C Coys in OVILLERS HUTS, A & D Coys & Lewis Gun Detachments in WOLFE HUTS.				
			Work parties provided by Battn. 18 OR. reinforcements from Base.	am			
AVELUY	2	10 am	H.Q. & B & C Coys moved to BRUCE HUTS, A & D Coys to BOUZINCOURT	am			
SENLIS	3	11.15 am	Battn moved to Billets in SENLIS	am			
SENLIS	4		Battn in SENLIS. Inspections of kit and interior economy	am			
"	5		do. Baths.	am			
"	6		do. Route march 18 OR. reinforcements from Base	am			
"	7		do. Church service Army Commander, Fifth Army, attended Battn. service	am			
"	8		do. Route march	am			
OVILLERS	9	11.15 am	Battn marched to OVILLERS HUTS Brigade in support	am			
"	10		OVILLERS HUTS Work parties	am			
"	11		do. do. Snow.	am			
SENLIS	12	9.30 am	Battn marched to Billets in SENLIS. 1st march to Rest area. 2nd Lt W.R. Lyon joined	am			
BEAUQUESNE	13	11 am	Battn marched from SENLIS to BEAUQUESNE (12 miles) arriving 12.30 pm Snow	am			
LE MEILLARD	14	9.5 am	BEAUQUESNE to LE MEILLARD (15 miles) arrived 3.40 pm	am			
YVRENCHEUX	15	8.15 am	LE MEILLARD to YVRENCHEUX (12 miles) arrived 12.30 pm	am			

T2134. Wt. W708—776. 500000. 4/15. Sir J. C. & S.

1/8th Bn Arg. & Suth'd Highlanders

Instructions regarding War Diaries and Intelligence Summaries are contained in F. S. Regs., Part II. and the Staff Manual respectively. Title pages will be prepared in manuscript.

WAR DIARY
~~or~~
~~INTELLIGENCE SUMMARY.~~
(Erase heading not required.)

Volume III

Sheet 17

Army Form C. 2118.

Place	Date	Hour	Summary of Events and Information	Casualties Officers K	W	M	OR K	W	M	Remarks and references to Appendices
	1917 Jan									
NOUVION en Ponthieu	16	10.5 am	YVRENCHEUX to NOUVION en Ponthieu (11 miles) arrived 2 pm. Rest area am							
en Ponthieu	17		Batt'n in Rest area Billeting. Snow am							
	18		do. Refitting Reinforcements from Base 71 OR. from 11th Ent. Bn 56 OR am							
	19		do. Refitting Reinforcements from 9th Ent. Batt'n 103 OR. am							
	20		do. Baths. Inspection of Billets am							
NOUVION EN PONTHIEU	21		do. Church service. Reinforcements 120 OR from 19 Inf Base. 2nd Lt W. Newall joined am							
	22		do. Training commenced am Severe frosty weather							
	23		do. Training do am							
	24		do Training Inspection of drafts by Brigade Commander do am							
	25		do Training do am							
	26		do. Training Leave stopped do am							
	27		do Training Corps commander visited training. do am							
	28		do. Church Service at LE TITRE do am							
	29		do. Training do am							
LE PLESSIEL	30	9.30 am	Batt'n moved to Billets in LE PLESSIEL vacated by 8th Royal Scots arriving 11.30 am do am							
do	31		LE PLESSIEL, Training do am							

In the Field
31/1/17

R Campbell
Lieut Colonel
Comdg 1/8th A & S Highrs

T.2134. Wt. W708—776. 500000. 4/15. Sir J. C. & S.

SECRET
No. 134
152nd INF. BDE.

X-31

Vol 22

WAR DIARY
of
1/8th Bn. ARGYLL & SUTHERLAND HIGHLANDERS.

from

1st FEBRUARY 1917.

to

28th FEBRUARY 1917.

1/8th Battn Arg. & Suth'd Highrs

WAR DIARY

~~or~~

~~INTELLIGENCE SUMMARY.~~

(Erase heading not required.)

Volume III

Sheet No 18

Army Form C. 2118.

Instructions regarding War Diaries and Intelligence Summaries are contained in F. S. Regs., Part II. and the Staff Manual respectively. Title pages will be prepared in manuscript.

Place	Date	Hour	Summary of Events and Information		Casualties Officers	Casualties Other ranks	Remarks and references to Appendices
	1917						
LE PLESSIEL	Feby 1		Battn in rest area. Training.	am			
do	2		do do	am			
do	3		do do	am			
do	4		do	am			
MAISON PONTHIEU	5	9.15am	Battn marched from LE PLESSIEL to MAISON PONTHIEU arriving 2.30pm (11 miles)	am			
NŒUX	6	9.10am	MAISON PONTHIEU to NOEUX 8 miles arriving 12.30pm.	am			
OEUF	7	8.45am	NŒUX to OEUF 11½ miles arriving 1.30pm	am			
CHELERS	8	9.40am	OEUF to CHELERS 15 miles arriving 4.45pm	am			
VILLERS BRULIN	9	10am	CHELERS to VILLERS BRULIN (Hd Qrs & B+C Coys) BERTHONSART (A & D) Coys	am			
MAROEUIL	10	9.30am	Battn less a detachment of 303 officers & men under Major Lockie marched to MAROEUIL. Classes of Instruction formed at VILLERS BRULIN	am			
ROCLINCOURT	11	2.30pm	Marched to trenches and relieved 8th Royal Highlanders in left subsector of Brigade. A22d - A23b. (ROCLINCOURT SHEET 51B N.W.1 1-10000) A & B Coys Front line, C & D Coys support line. 6th Seaforths on right, Canadian Divn on left. Q.M. Stores and Transport at MAROEUIL.	am			
do	12		Trenches	am			
do	13		Trenches A & B. Coys relieved C & D Coys.	am			

2353 Wt. W2544/1454 700,000 5/15 D. D. & L. A.D.S.S. Forms/C 2118.

1/8th Bn Arg. & Suth'd Highlanders

Instructions regarding War Diaries and Intelligence Summaries are contained in F. S. Regs., Part II. and the Staff Manual respectively. Title pages will be prepared in manuscript.

WAR DIARY

~~or~~

~~INTELLIGENCE SUMMARY.~~

(Erase heading not required.)

Volume III

Sheets 19.

Army Form C. 2118.

Place	Date	Hour	Summary of Events and Information	Casualties Officers	Casualties Other ranks	Remarks and references to Appendices
	1917 Feby					
ROCLINCOURT	14		Trenches am			
"	15		do am			
"	16		do am			
ECURIE	17	9.30pm	Batt'n relieved by 5th Seaforth High'rs & moved to ECURIE (B & D Coys) ANZIN (A Coy) ST. CATHERINES "C" Coy am			
"	18		Batt'n in Brigade supports providing working parties am			
"	19		do do am			
"	20		do do am			
"	21		do do. Detachment VILLERS BRULIN to MAROEUIL am	Nil		
"	22		do do am			
"	23		do do am			
"	24		do do am			
"	25		do do am			
"	26		do do am			
ECOIVRES	27	5.10pm	Batt'n relieved by 7th A&SH'rs and moved to huts at ECOIVRES. am			
"	28		Cleaning and Bathing. Detachments rejoined. am			

In the Field 28/3/17

[signature] Lieut. Colonel
Cmdg 1/8th Bn A&S Highrs

2353 Wt. W2544/1454 700,000 5/15 D. D. & L. A.D.S.S. Forms/C. 2118.

X . 32

SECRET
No. 134
152nd INF. BDE.

Vol 23

W A R   D I A R Y

of

1/8th Bn. A R G Y L L   A N D   S U T H E R L A N D   H I G H L A N D E R S.

From

1st M A R C H, 1 9 1 7.

to

31st M A R C H, 1 9 1 7.

Army Form C. 2118.

18th Bn Arg. & Suthd. Highlanders

Instructions regarding War Diaries and Intelligence Summaries are contained in F. S. Regs., Part II. and the Staff Manual respectively. Title pages will be prepared in manuscript.

WAR DIARY

~~or INTELLIGENCE SUMMARY.~~

(Erase heading not required.)

Volume III

Sheet No 20

Place	Date 1917	Hour	Summary of Events and Information	Casualties: Officers K	Officers W	Officers M	Other Ranks K	Other Ranks W	Other Ranks M	Remarks and references to Appendices
	March									
ECOIVRES	1		Battalion resting. Company training and work parties. AM							
do	2		do. do. do. AM							
ROCLINCOURT	3	2.10pm	Relieved 6th Battn Seaforth Highlanders in Right sub-sector. (Under 154th Brigade) AM							
do	4		In trenches AM							
do	5		do AM				3	2	-	
do	6		do AM							
do	7		do AM							
do	8		do. AM							
do	9	5pm	Relieved by 5th Battn Seaforth Highlanders and marched to ECOIVRES HUTS. AM							
ECOIVRES	10		Battalion resting. Bathing. AM							
do	11		Battalion training with Brigade. Presentation of ribbons by Corps Commander. 13 received ribbons AM							
do	12		Battalion training AM							
do	13		do AM							
do	14		do. 2 officers 75 other ranks to ARRAS for work. AM							
do	15		do AM					1		
do	16	9pm	B & D Coys moved to trenches preparatory to raid. AM							

2353 Wt. W2544/1454 700,000 5/15 D. D. & L. A.D.S.S. Forms/C 2118.

1/8th Battn Arg. & Suth'd Highlanders.

Volume III.

Sheet No 21.

Army Form C. 2118.

WAR DIARY
~~or~~ ~~INTELLIGENCE SUMMARY.~~

(Erase heading not required.)

Instructions regarding War Diaries and Intelligence Summaries are contained in F. S. Regs., Part II. and the Staff Manual respectively. Title pages will be prepared in manuscript.

Place	Date 1917	Hour	Summary of Events and Information		Casualties Officers K	W	M	Other Ranks K	W	M	Remarks and references to Appendices
	March										
ROCLINCOURT.	17	6.15 am	Raiding party, 13 officers 382 other ranks, raided German trenches from A 30 a 25. 3¾ to A 23 d. 8. 1. (Reference ROCLINCOURT 51B N.W.1) capturing 10 Prisoners and inflicting heavy loss and damage on germans. Bt Lt A.R.Macfarlane-Grieve and 2nd Lt R.Lyon, killed, 2nd Lt C.T.Brown, wounded and missing. 2nd Lts H.P.T. Macintosh, J.A.S. Henderson, J.D. Caskey, D. Duncan and D.N. Morris wounded	Am	2	5	1	19	82	25	"A"
ECOIVRES	18		Battalion resting.	Am							
do	19		Battalion training - work parties	Am							
do	20		do do	Am							
do	21		do do	Am							
AGNIERES &	22		H.Q. & A & D Coys to AGNIERES, B & C Coys under Major Lockie to CAUCOURT	Am							
CAUCOURT	23		Battalion training	Am							
do	24		do ARRAS detachment rejoined.	Am							
do	25		do Church services - Bathing	Am							
do	26		Battalion training	Am							
do	27		do	Am							
do	28		do	Am							
do	29		do.	Am							

1/8th Bn Arg & Suth'd Highlanders

Instructions regarding War Diaries and Intelligence Summaries are contained in F. S. Regs., Part II. and the Staff Manual respectively. Title pages will be prepared in manuscript.

WAR DIARY

~~or~~

~~INTELLIGENCE SUMMARY.~~

(Erase heading not required.)

Volume III

Sheet No 22

Army Form C. 2118.

Place	Date	Hour	Summary of Events and Information	Remarks and references to Appendices
	1917 March			
[..]GNIERES &	30		Battalion training	[illegible]
CAUCOURT	31		Battalion training	[illegible]
			In the Field 31/3/17 R Campbell Lieut. Colonel Cmdg 1/8 Bn A & S Highrs	

T2134. Wt. W708–776. 500000. 4/15. Sir J. C. & S.

REPORT ON RAID carried out by 1/8th Bn. Argyll & Suth'd Highrs. on 17th March, 1917 :-

1. The Raiding Party (12 Officers and 382 N.C.Os and men) left ECOIVRES HUTS at 9 p.m. on 16th March, and moved via MAROEUIL and ANZIN.

From ANZIN TO ROCLINCOURT owing to the state of the trenches the party moved over the open. I had arranged with a party of the 8th Royal Scots who were working in GENIE TRENCH the previous day, to make temporary bridges over the cross trenches to enable the raiding party to get over them. This had been done and the march up was simple.

The LILLE ROAD was reached at 12 midnight, and a long halt made near the junction of GENIE and FILATIERS. Hot soup and cake was issued to the men from the Divisional Soup Kitchen, and the necessary bombs, mobile charges, etc. were issued. Men's greatcoats, mess-tins and bayonet scabbards were sent back in limbers from this point.

The party proceeded on to the line at 1.45 a.m. and were up ready to move in at 3.40 a.m.

The 6th Gordon Highlanders vacated the old French line at 4 a.m. and the raiding party moved into position.

All was ready at 4.45 a.m.

The men worked extraordinarily well and quietly, and up to Zero there was nothing to arouse the enemy's suspicions.

2. Zero Hour had been fixed at 6.15 a.m., which meant the party waiting under cover for an hour of daylight, but it was hoped that the enemy would by then have "stood down".

Shortly before Zero two aeroplanes came over the area. I think this should certainly have been avoided.

At Zero - 3 the artillery away to our left fired a few rounds, and at Zero - 2 fired a heavy salvo. It would have been better if they had waited till Zero - 1 when the barrage was due. At Zero - 1 our barrage opened, and the opening salvo was not good, some of the rounds being short in 'no man's land'. The barrage was at once taken up, and at Zero - 30 when the raiders left their trench it was perfect. Both the 18-pdrs and the Stokes were perfectly accurate on the enemy's front line. It was so good that our party was up at the enemy's wire before the barrage lifted, and I did not see a single casualty.

3. As the barrage lifted the various parties attempted to enter the line. Unfortunately the enemy had repaired his wire on the left and right flanks, and both parties were held up.

The centre parties got in without much trouble, and caught the enemy as he was attempting to come out of his dugouts.

A sentry was found dead in left of centre group. Two prisoners were taken and sent over to our lines.

As it was obvious that there was going to be a stiff fight all through, the dugouts were at once dealt with with ammonal and a large number of the enemy were killed.

4. Meanwhile the parties on the left had been badly held up by the wire, and part of them were driven back towards our line by bombs and rifle fire, but the remainder engaged the enemy with close range rifle fire, and he suffered heavy casualties.

The O.C. Raid sent Coy Sergt-Major McKinnon to re-organize the left, as all three officers were casualties. He got the parties in at the gaps opposite ALLGAUER TRENCH and the gap to the left of it, and they worked down to the left and captured the whole of the First Line objective.

Large numbers of German dead were found in the area covered by these three left groups. The estimates average over 100. The dugouts were all bombed and all are known to have still contained Germans.

5/

5. On the right the parties were also held up by wire, but got in by a small gap partially closed by concertina wire. This gap had evidently been used by the 6th Gordons in their raid, as the bodies of two of their men were lying by it.

The delay owing to the wire did not matter much on this flank, as the party had to wait for the lift of the barrage and had begun to hunt for a gap before it lifted.

The enemy had not time to get out of his dugouts. 6 prisoners were taken. The remainder of the enemy did not come u and the dugouts were blown up at once with ammonal.

6. With regard to the Second Line,

21 enemy dead were found in KOMMANDEUR Trench and the Second Line just to the left of it. A large number of the garrison of the right half of the Second Line attempted to retire to the Third Line. They suffered some casualties from rifle fire from our right parties but more from the artillery, as they were badly caught by the barrage.

The dugouts were all blown up with ammonal, except one in Number VIII area which was only bombed. Some dugouts in this line had been previously destroyed and not repaired. Two prisoners were taken here.

7. The centre party only got half way up to their objective, but they held their ground there until the time was up.

8. The left parties (IV, V, VI) had very severe fighting. No.VI got through by the gap at the end of ALLGAUER Trench, and straight into their objective as the barrage lifted.

There was a very sharp fight in this area, as the two left hand parties had not got up owing to the front line wire.

The enemy, however, were eventually dealt with, and the dugouts bombed. Those of the enemy left above ground retreated to the Third Line, but very few got away.

9. Meanwhile the two left parties had come round by the gaps at ALLGAUER and the gap opposite 6 and 7 saps, and worked on to their objective from right to left. There was again sharp fighting, as the enemy had had time to man his trenches. In the fighting that ensued the majority of the enemy were killed; a few escaped to the Third Line. Heavy casualties to the enemy are reported in this Sector.

10. The fighting was extremely severe, especially on the left. It was too intense throughout to allow of prisoners being taken, and only 10 passed through Battalion Head Quarters. 12 more were claimed, but cannot be traced. They were supposed to have gone back on our right, but it seems probable that they were the ones we got through our lines.

11. The leading of the officers in the Raid was splendid throughout. 2nd.Lieut.J.E.Robertson, 2nd.Lieut.J.T.Young and 2nd.Lieut.R.Lyon were especially noticeable. The latter was unfortunately killed when following up the enemy almost to the Third German line.

Many of the men had never been under a barrage before, but the fighting was carried to a successful issue in spite of many difficulties.

The front line were absolutely up to the barrage at the First German line before it lifted.

12. Our casualties were heavy, but not in proportion to the damage inflicted on the enemy.

12/. The party went over :
12 Officers and 382 Other Ranks.

<u>Casualties;</u>

Officers Killed....... 2
" Wounded and Missing... 1
" Wounded........ 5
8.

Other Ranks Killed... 14
" " Wounded.. 76
" " Missing.. 12
102.

The raiders all agree that the enemy's casualties were very much heavier than ours.

His line was held in abnormal strength, and the garrison was exterminated.

13. Information has since been received that 5 prisoners who were sent back on the right were shot down by the enemy between the First and Second German lines.

[signature]
Lieut-Colonel,
Commanding 1/8th Bn. Argyll & Suth'd Highrs.

15 - 5 - 17.

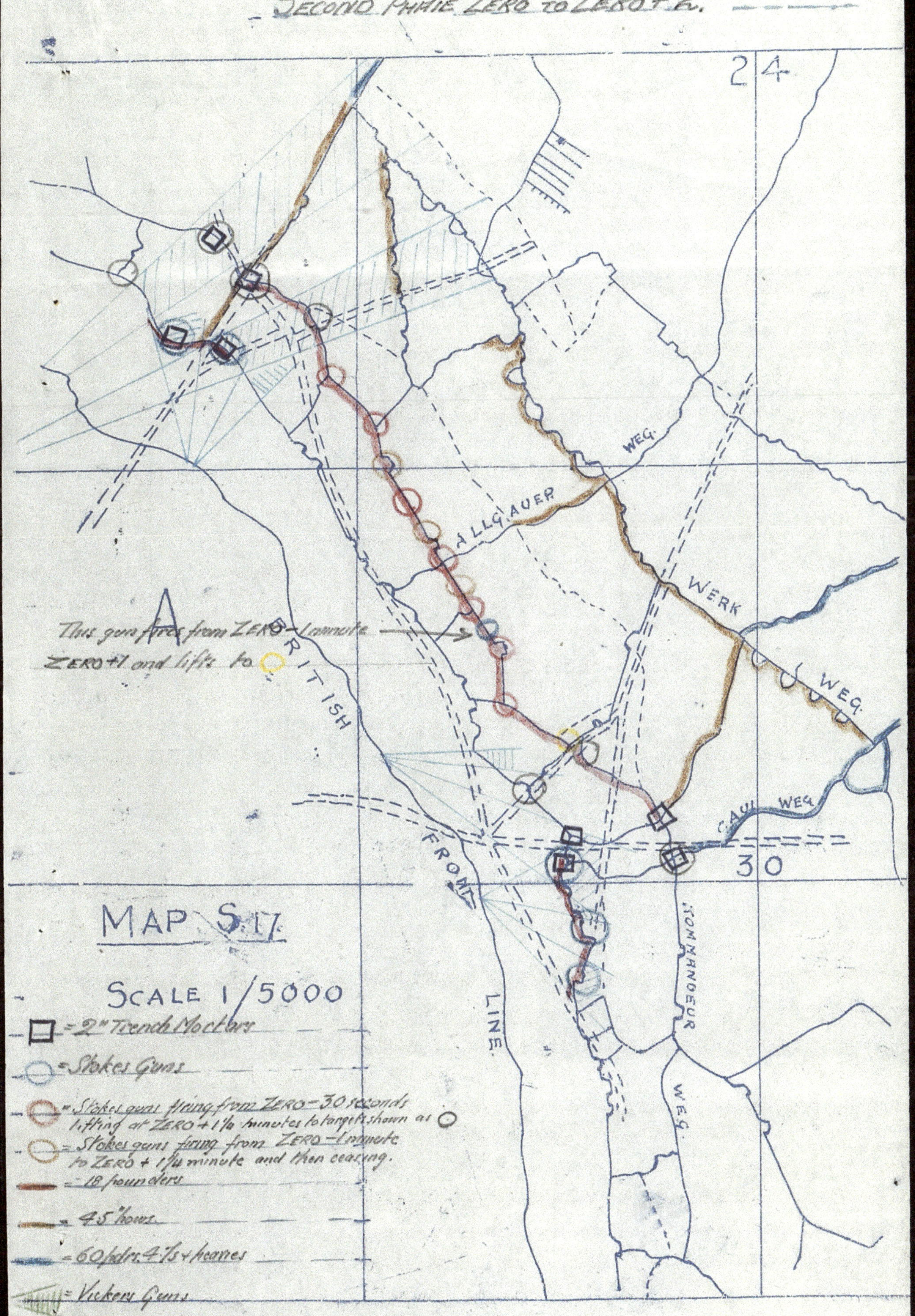
SECOND PHASE ZERO TO ZERO + 2.
24
WEG.
ALLGAUER
WERK
WEG.
This gun fires from ZERO – 1 minute
ZERO +1 and lifts to
A
BRITISH
FRONT
LINE
CAU WEG
30
KOMMANDEUR
WEG
MAP S.17
SCALE 1/5000
= 2" Trench Mortars
= Stokes Guns
= Stokes guns firing from ZERO – 30 seconds lifting at ZERO + 1½ minutes to targets shown at
= Stokes guns firing from ZERO – 1 minute to ZERO + 1¼ minute and then ceasing.
= 18 pounders
= 4.5" hows
= 60 pdrs 4.7's + heavies
= Vickers Guns

THIRD PHASE ZERO+12 TO ZERO+40.

24

WEG.

ALLGAUER

WERK

WEG.

A

BRITISH FRONT LINE.

CAUL WEG

30

KOMMANDEUR WEG.

MAP S.17.

SCALE 1/5000

= 2" Trench Mortars

= Stokes Guns

= 18 pounders

= 4·5 hows.

= 60 pdrs 4·7s + heavies.

= Vickers Guns.

FIRST PHASE ZERO-1 TO ZERO.

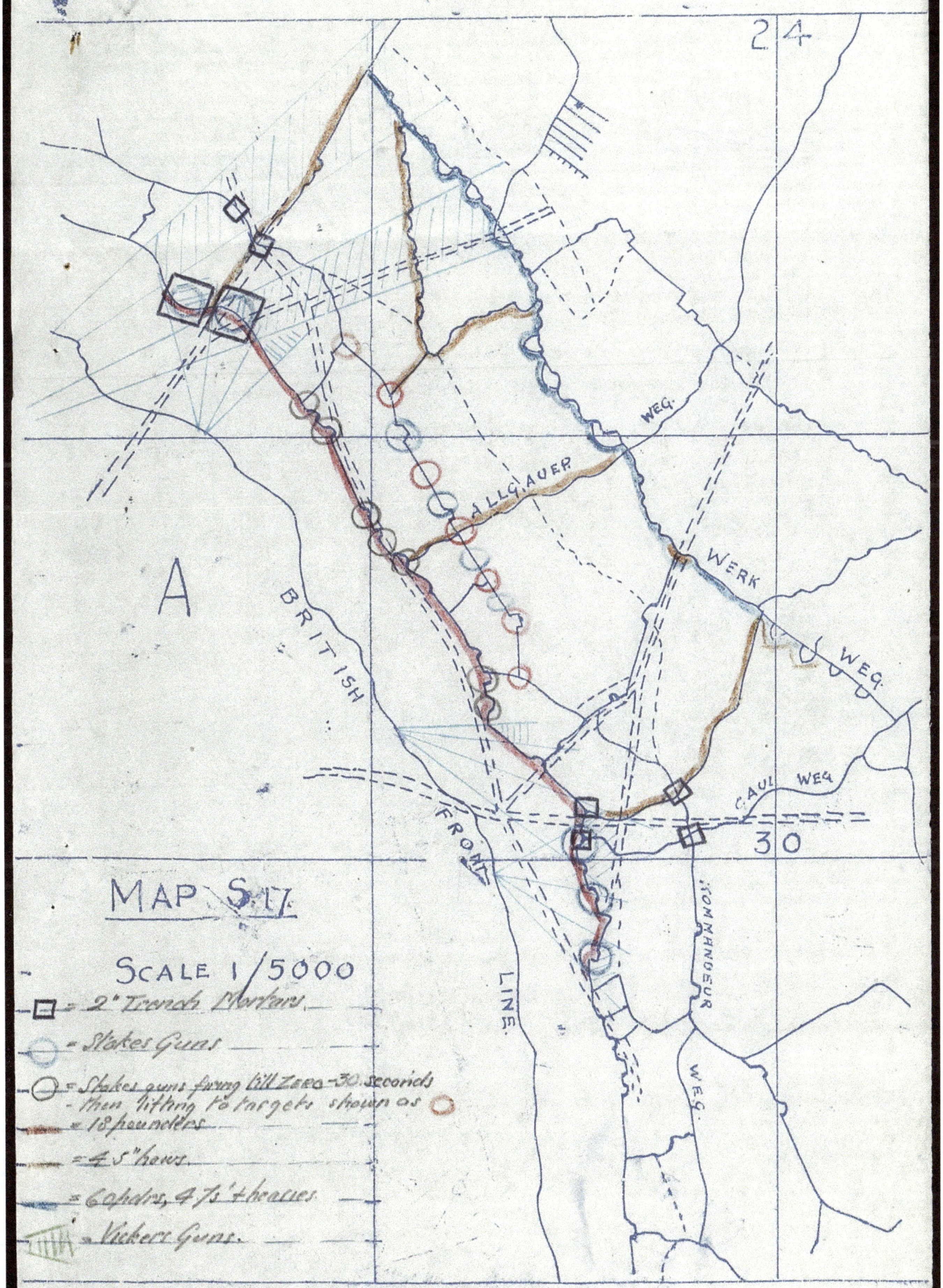

24

WEG.

ALLGAUER

WERK

WEG.

A

BRITISH

FRONT

LINE

CAUL WEG

30

KOMMANDEUR

WEG.

MAP S.17

SCALE 1/5000

= 2" Trench Mortars

= Stokes Guns

= Stokes guns firing till Zero-30 seconds - then lifting to targets shown as

= 18 pounders

= 4.5" hows.

= 60pdrs, 4.7s & heavies

= Vickers Guns.

APPENDIX III.

Action of Vickers Guns.

EMPLOYMENT. Eight guns of the 152nd Machine Gun Company will co-operate in keeping down the heads of the enemy and in preventing any enemy machine guns from coming into action from the flanks of the trenches raided, during the period Raiding Party are moving across "No Man's Land", and from enemy Front Line to Support Line, and during the period Party are returning.

The eight guns will be at following positions :-

Two guns at A.30.c.3.9., two guns at A.30.a.1.3., two guns at A.23.d.6.0. and two guns at A.29.a.6.8., and will deal with trenches as follows :-

1 gun with	A.30.c.5½.7¼	to	A.30.c.5½.9¼.
1 " "	A.30.c.5½.8¼	to	A.30.a.5.1½.
1. " "	A.30.a.5.0.	to	A.30.a.4.2½.
1 " "	A.30.a.4¾.1¾	to	A.30.a.2¾.3½.
1 " "	A.23.d.8.1¾	to	A.23.d.5¾.3.
1 " "	A.23.d.7.2½	to	A.23.d.5.3¾.
1 " "	A.24.c.1½.4	to	A.24.c.1.7½.
1 " "	A.24.c.1.5½	to	A.24.c.½.9½.

The Raid will be divided into four phases :-

(1) ZERO - 1 to ZERO (Time Artillery and Trench Mortars open fire) (Time Infantry advance.

(2) ZERO to ZERO plus 3 minutes (Time Infantry reach enemy Support Line.

(3) ZERO plus 3 minutes to ZERO plus 25 minutes (Time Infantry commence returning)

(4) ZERO plus 25 minutes to ZERO plus 40 minutes (Time Infantry have reached our Front Line)

The barrage will be carried out as follows :-

Phase 1. ZERO - 1 minute to ZERO. All guns will fire short bursts of fire and engage any enemy machine gun which opens.

Phase 2. ZERO to ZERO plus 3 minutes. All guns will open intense barrage on their allotted trenches.

Phase 3. ZERO plus 3 minutes to ZERO plus 25 minutes. All guns will remain laid on allotted trenches, ready to counter any enemy machine guns that may open.

Phase 4. ZERO plus 25 minutes to ZERO plus 40 minutes. All guns will open intense barrage on allotted trenches.

COMPOSITION /

"A"

S E C R E T.　　　　　　　　　　　　　　　　　　　　Copy No. 16

152nd Infantry Brigade Order No. 129.

Reference Trench Map
Sheet ROCLINCOURT
and attached
sketch maps.

14th March, 1917.

1. The 1/8th Bn. ARGYLL & SUTHERLAND HIGHRS. will repeat the Raid on the enemy's trenches carried out on 5th March by the 1/6th Bn. Gordon Hrs., on 17th March, 1917. ZERO hour will be 6.15 a.m.

2. The Sector of trenches to be raided are :-

German front line from A.30.A.$2\frac{1}{2}$.$3\frac{3}{4}$ to A.23.D.8.1.

German support line from A.30.A.$3\frac{1}{2}$.$4\frac{1}{2}$. to A.23.D.9.$2\frac{1}{2}$.

Length of frontage 480 yards.

Strength of raiders about 13 Officers and 378 O. R.

3. The Raid will be carried out on the "Leap Frog" principle and will be accompanied by a demonstration by the Artillery, 2" mortars, and Stokes Guns of flank Divisions and Brigades.

4. The action of Heavy Howitzers, 4.7 Guns, Field Artillery, 2" Mortars, Stokes Guns and Vickers Guns will be as shown in the attached sketch maps, each of the three maps representing one phase as follows :-

1st Phase. ZERO - 1 minute to ZERO, preliminary bombardment.

2nd Phase. ZERO to ZERO plus 2. Assault of German First Line.

3rd Phase. ZERO plus 2 to ZERO plus 40. Assault of German Second Line, destruction of enemy's defences and return of raiders.

5. The Artillery barrage will be shrapnel, will conform to the trace of the hostile trenches, and will not lift in parallel lines. When lifting off the Second German Line 50% of the 18 pdrs. will move on to the German Third Line by successive stages so as to knock out enemy machine guns or Riflemen if posted in the open,

The /

The remaining 50% 18 pdrs. will lift direct on to the German Third Line.

~~At ZERO plus 25 some part of the 18 pdrs. will drop to a line 100 yards East of the German Second Line, quickening their rate of fire for the first minute after doing so to cover the withdrawal, firing H. E. This drop in the barrage will serve as a warning to all raiders that they must evacuate the German Second Line.~~

Groups detailed to form blocks in Communication Trenches in advance of the Second Line should be supplied with as many carefully synchronized watches as possible.

A smoke barrage will be placed by 2" Mortars on the Right flank of the Raiders throughout.

6. The following appendices are attached :-

Appendix I. Programme of Raid.

Appendix II. Allotment of ammunition and rate of fire.

Appendix III. Action of Vickers Guns.

7. The Raiders and all trench weapons will take the time for ZERO - 1 minute from the opening of the Artillery. The Artillery in its turn will take its time from a salvo fired by a selected battery under arrangements made by the C.R.A. 51st Division.

8. To ensure that all are fully prepared by ZERO - 1 minute watches will be synchronized on the evening of Y day with a watch which will be taken round to the H.Q. of Units by a representative of the Brigade Staff.

9. 2" Trench Mortars, Vickers and Stokes Guns will fire at their best rate from ZERO - 1 minute to ZERO plus 3, and from ZERO plus 25 to ZERO plus 40, these being the periods when the assaulting Infantry will be above ground in their advance to

and /

APPENDIX II.

Rate of fire and ammunition.

Rate of Fire - 18 pdrs. 1080

Zero minus 1 minute to Zero plus 5 minutes.	4 rounds per gun per minute.	216
Zero plus 5 minutes to Zero plus 25 minutes.	2 rounds per gun per minute.	108 = 2160
Zero plus 25 minutes to Zero plus 35 minutes.	4 rounds per gun per minute.	1080.
Zero plus 35 minutes to Zero plus 40 minutes.	3 rounds per gun per minute.	324
Zero plus 40 minutes to Zero plus 43 minutes.	1 round per gun per minute.	164
Zero plus 43.	Stop firing.	4808

Rate of Fire 4.5" Howitzers.

Zero minus 1 minute to Zero plus 5 minutes.	2 rounds per How. per minute.
Zero plus 5 minutes to Zero plus 25 minutes.	1 " " " " "
Zero plus 25 minutes to Zero plus 40 minutes.	2 " " " " "
Zero plus 40 minutes to Zero plus 43 minutes.	½ " " " " "
Zero plus 43 minutes.	Stop firing.

4.5" Howitzers will not fire nearer than 200 yards to our Infantry.

Ammunition Allotment. The following allotment of ammunition has been asked for and approved.

4.7"	-	200.
6" How.	-	150.
8" How.	-	100.
9.2" How.	-	30.

PROGRAMME FOR TRENCH MORTARS.

TIME	NATURE	REMARKS.
Zero minus 1 min. to Zero plus 4 min.	8 Mortars 2" Medium.	2 rounds per mortar per minute.
Zero plus 4 min.to Zero plus 25 min.	do.	1 round per mortar per minute
Zero plus 25 min.to Zero plus 40 min.	do.	1½ rounds per mortar per minute.
Zero plus 40 min. to Zero plus 43 min.	do.	½ round per mortar per minute.

The mortars firing on the flanks will fire smoke bombs throughout, as available.

APPENDIX No. 1.

Programme of Raid.

ZERO - 1 minute - Preliminary bombardment opens.

ZERO - First wave assaults First German Line.

ZERO plus 2 - Second wave assaults Second German Line.

ZERO plus 25 - Second wave withdraws from Second German Line.

ZERO plus 35 - First wave withdraws from First German Line.

COMPOSITION OF GUN TEAMS. Each Team will consist of 1 N.C.O. and 3 Other Ranks.

POSITION READY FOR RAID. Guns, equipment and personnel will be in positions, ready for Raid, 1 hour previous to ZERO hour.

TIME. Watches will be synchronized on the night previous to the Raid.

At ZERO a battery will fire a salvo, and all times of barrage will be taken from this salvo.

and retirement from the German Lines.

10. In addition to targets shown on attached sketch maps, the 4.7" Guns and Heavy Hows. will fire on the following :-

<u>1st Phase.</u>

4.7's and Heavy Hows. from A.30.a.95.55 to A.24.c.00.80.

<u>2nd Phase.</u>

4.7's	(A.30.a.70.05 to A.30.b.35.30 to A.30.b.75.70. (A.30.a.95.60 to A.30.b.75.70 (A.24.a.10.00 to A.24.a.15.85
Heavy Hows. on selected points & trench junctions.	(A.30.b.33.33 to A.30.b.70.65 (A.24.c.75.34 to A.24.a.45.55 (A.24.a.63.74 to A.24.a.15.90 (A.17.d.36.23 to A.18.c.24.83 (A.24.b.24.94 to A.24.b.60.55 (B.19.a.0.04 to B.19.c.34.38 (B.19.c.50.13 to B.25.b.38.28

<u>3rd Phase.</u>

As Second Phase.

11. ~~In order to distract the enemy's attention 2 red rockets, similar to those used by the enemy as his S.O.S. on the occasion of the Raid of the 1/6th Bn. Gordon Highrs. will be sent up by the Battalion holding the Right Sub-sector from the extreme Left of the Front Line in the Right Sub-sector at ZERO plus 30 seconds.~~

12. No badges, shoulder straps or identity discs will be worn by the Raiding Party, nor will any documents or other marks of identification be carried.

All Raiders will be warned that in the event of capture they are not to disclose their unit or Division.

13. The Raiding Party will enter the old French Trench on their return and gradually make their way along it to FISH TUNNEL (A.29.b.90.45) as a hostile barrage is most unlikely to be put down on the French Trench. The route from the French Trench to FISH TUNNEL will be marked out by blue and white signalling flags under arrangements to be made by O.C. 1/8th Bn. Argyll and Sutherland Highrs.

14. Prisoners will be sent down to Brigade Headquarters, MADAGASCAR, under escort as soon as the hostile barrage permits.

All papers etc. should be taken from them at the earliest possible moment, the effects of each prisoner being tied up in a separate bundle. The bundles should be brought to Brigade Headquarters in sandbags by the escort, and handed over to the Brigade Major. Documents captured in the Raid will also be forwarded to Brigade Headquarters, MADAGASCAR as early as possible.

15. ACKNOWLEDGE.

F. W. Bewsher
Captain.
Brigade Major.
152nd Inf. Brigade.

Issued at ___________

Copy No. 1. 51st (H) Divn. "G"
2. " " " "G"
3. " " " "A"
4. C.R.A. 51st (H) Divn.
5. 154th Inf. Brigade.
6. 153rd Inf. Brigade.
7. 103rd Inf. Brigade.
8. 2nd Canadian Inf. Brigade.
9. 256th Brigade R.F.A.
10. 255th " "
11. 64th " "
12. D. S. T. M.
13 to 18. 152nd Inf. Brigade Units.
19. 1/8th Bn. Arg. & Suth. Hrs. (2nd copy)
20. B. S. C.
21. Staff Captain.
22. W. D.
23. File.

Amendment No. 1 to 152nd Infantry Brigade Order No. 129.

Para 5 delete from "At ZERO plus 25 some part" down to "evacuate German Second Line"

and substitute

"At ZERO plus 25 the 18 pdrs. will quicken their rate of fire and change from shrapnel barrage to an H.E. barrage to serve as a warning to all Raiders that they must evacuate the German Second Line".

(Sgd) F. W. BEWSHER, Capt.
Brigade Major,
152nd Infantry Brigade.

Addenda to 152nd Inf. Bde. Order No. 129.

The Divisional Soup Kitchen near the junction of GENIE and FIL[illegible]TIERS AVENUES will be reserved for the Raiding Party on Y-Z night from 11.P.M. to 12 mid-night.

On arrival at the Soup Kitchen soup will be issued to the Raiders, but as there are insufficient cups each man must take his canteen with him and these will be dumped at the SOUP KITCHEN and returned to Battalion H.Q., in the limbers which are carrying up additional charges, bombs etc.,.

On Y day each man will also be issued with a portion of cake for consumption with the soup mentioned above.

Addition to 152nd Infantry Brigade Order No. 129.

1. At ZERO plus 25 one green rocket will be fired from our Front Line as a signal to the Raiders to withdraw. This will be repeated if necessary, single green rockets being fired at intervals.

S E C R E T. Copy No.______

OPERATION ORDER No. 21

by

Lieut. Colonel R. CAMPBELL, D.S.O., Commanding 1/8th (The Argyllshire) Battalion Princess Louise's (Argyll & Sutherland) Highlanders.

Monday, 13th March 1917.

1. OBJECT. To gain information regarding the enemy and his trenches; to obtain prisoners and to damage trenches and dug-outs.

2. OBJECTIVE. The German Front Line from A.23.d.80.10 to A.30.a.2½.5½, and the Second Line from A.23.d.90.20 to A.30.a.33.40.

3. ZERO HOUR AND DATE. Raid will take place on 17th March.
Zero hour will be notified later.

4. TIME TABLE.

Zero minus 1 minute.	Artillery barrage on German Front Line.
Zero.................	Barrage lifts to German Second Line: troops assault German First Line.
Zero plus 2 minutes.....	Barrage lifts to German Third Line: troops assault German Second Line.
Zero plus 25 minutes...	Part of 18 pdrs. drop to a line 100 yards East of German Second Line, quickening the rate of fire (Signal of withdrawal from Second German Line).
Zero plus 35 minutes...	All Raiders withdraw from German Lines.
Zero plus 40 minutes...	Barrage ceases.

5. BARRAGE. Barrage will be shrapnel: will conform to trace of enemy's trenches and not lift in parallel lines. When lifting off the Second German Line 50% of the 18 pdrs. will move on to the German Third Line by successive stages so as to knock out enemy machine guns or Riflemen if posted in the open, the remaining 50% 18 pdrs. will lift direct on the German Third Line.
At Zero plus 25 some part of the 18 pdrs. will drop to a line 100 yards East of the German Second Line, quickening their rate of fire for the first minute after doing so to cover the withdrawal. This drop in the barrage will serve as a warning to all Raiders that they must evacuate the German Second Line.
Smoke barrage will be placed by 2" Mortars on the Right Flank of the Raiders throughout.

6. STRENGTH. 12 Officers and 378 men. ("B" and "D" Coys.).

7. O.C. RAID. Captain R. A. MACTAGGART will command the Raiding Party from old French Trench at head of No. 5 Sap.

8. FORMING UP. The Raiding Party will move from ECOIVRES HUTS at 9 P.M. on 16th March in order "D" Company (Parties 10,7,9,11,8).
"B" Company (Parties 1,4,2,5,3,6.).
and march via MARCEUIL, ANZIN, alongside GENIE TRENCH to junction of FILATIERS with LILLE ROAD. There a halt of 1½ hours will be made to issue soup and mobile charges and bombs. Companies will proceed to old French Trench as follows :-
"D" Company by FILATIERS, THURSDAY, FISH and SEAFORTH.
"B" Company by FILATIERS, THURSDAY, FISH and FISH TUNNEL.
Parties will use the saps as per Appendix "A".
Absolute silence will be observed during the movement to the assembly position and while in the old French Trench.
Smoking is forbidden.

9. ACTION. All men engaged are arranged in groups (1 N.C.O. and 8 men) with definite objectives - each area being an Officer's command as shewn in ~~Appendix "B"~~ attached map "A"

First Line Groups and Communication Trench Groups move first, followed by those who are to occupy German Second Line. The Second Line Groups re-organise in German First Line, with the exception of Groups IV.A, V.A, X.A, X.B, VIII.C, and XI.C. All Groups will attack across the open. The Groups named will attack up the Communication Trenches and form Blocks at their respective objectives.

10. MOPPING UP. When Parties reach their objective, all Germans found in trench will be at once shot. Mills bombs should not be thrown when rushing the trenches. All entrances to dug-outs will be secured, two sentries being left at each. Occupants are invited to come out; if they hesitate a Mills bomb is thrown down one entrance and a further opportunity of coming up given. If no response the entrances are guarded, and just before time of withdrawal, petrol and "P" bombs are used at one entrance, the other being left open for occupants being driven up.

Mobile charges will be used for tunnels and dug-outs. If occupants come up readily the dug-outs will be searched for identifications and documents before being destroyed.

11. EQUIPMENT. Men will not wear any equipment. Rifle with bayonet fixed will have 9 rounds in magazine and one in breech. Safety catches down. 10 rounds will be carried in left tunic pocket. 2 Mills bombs will be carried by each man in the right tunic pocket. "P.H." Helmets will be worn in "Gas Alert" position.

Groups will carry bombs, petrol and explosives according to attached list ~~already issued~~.

Blocking Groups I.A, IV.A, V.A, IX.B, X.A, and XI.C. will carry one pick and one shovel. Throwers attached to these Groups will wear waistbelt and side-arms.

Each Second Line man will have the number of his Group on cardboard disc sewn on back of tunic.

12. DOCUMENTS, PRISONERS etc. All available documents, maps, etc. are to be brought back; prisoners are to be searched and all weapons and papers removed; prisoners will be headed towards FISH TUNNEL - escort 1 per 20; where a party will be detailed to receive them. Every endeavour must be made to get as many prisoners as possible. Machine Guns and Trench Mortars must be carried back to the British Lines immediately on capture.

13. MEDICAL ARRANGEMENTS. Every effort will be made to bring back Casualties.

Two stretchers will accompany last wave ~~in~~ to First German Line near ALLGAUER TRENCH. First Aid Post will be established in FISH TUNNEL.

14. IDENTIFICATION. All papers, letters and shoulder titles will be left behind. If a man is captured, he is only obliged to state his Number, Rank, Name and Regiment, NOT the Battalion. Nothing whatsoever about trenches, dispositions, or any other information must be disclosed.

15. SYNCHRONIZATION OF WATCHES. All watches will be synchronized before moving up. Zero - 1 minute will be taken from first salvo of Artillery.

Groups detailed to form Blocks in Communication Trenches in advance of the Second Line should be supplied with as many carefully synchronized watches as possible.

16. RETURN OF PARTY. Raiding Parties will withdraw in accordance with Time Table (Order No. 4).

A green rocket will be fired from head of Sap 5 at Zero plus 25, but this signal will not be waited for, and withdrawal from Second German Line will commence at Zero plus 25.

Raiding /

Raiding Parties will return to old French Trench, thence by Saps to Front Line.

Parties on the Right will move out by SEAFORTH.

" : " Left " " " " FISH TUNNEL.

No parties will stop in FISH TUNNEL, but will move straight through as quickly as possible.

All parties will move independently to ANZIN CHURCH.

17. <u>BATTALION HEADQUARTERS.</u> Battalion Headquarters will be established in FISH TUNNEL.

18. <u>ACKNOWLEDGE.</u>

(Signed) A. MACDONALD, Lieutenant,
Adjutant, 1/8th Bn. A. & S. Hrs.

APPENDIX "A".

	Parties.
Sap 1.	IX a.b.c.d.e. XI a.b.c.
Sap 3.	VIII a.b.c.d.e.
Sap 4.	VII a.b.c.d.
Sap 5.	III b and c. X a.b.c.d.
Sap 6.	III a. VI a.b.c.d.
Sap 7.	II a.b.c.d. V c and d.
Sap 8.	I b and c. VI b and c. V a and b.
Sap 9.	IV a. I a.

ADDENDA to REPORT on RAID BY 1/8th Bn. A. & S. Highrs.

14. BARRAGE.

(i) With regard to the Barrage (para.2), when the Raid was first decided on it was suggested that we should have a H.E. Barrage;

The Shrapnel Barrage assisted by the Stokes Guns was perfect, and I do not think it would have been possible to have got as close up to a H.E. Barrage as we did to the Shrapnel Barrage.

(ii) The Smoke Barrage on the flanks appears not to have been noticed by anyone.

15. The men had been instructed that they were to deal with the enemy by close-range rifle fire and not by bombs, and there is no doubt that this proved most extraordinarily effective and should be strongly impressed on all ranks taking part in Attacks and Raids.

R. Campbell

Lieut-Colonel,

Commanding 1/8th Bn. Argyll & Suth'd Highrs

18 - 3 - 17.

Stores carried by Groups

GROUP.		No. 5 Bombs.	No. 23 Bombs.	Ammonal.	"P" Bombs.	$\frac{1}{2}$ Tins Petrol.	Remarks
1.	A.	42	12	2	4	1	
	B.	38	-	2	4	1	
	C.	38	-	2	4	1	
2.	A.	38	-	2	4	1	
	B.	38	-	2	4	1	
	C.	38	-	2	4	1	
3.	A.	38	-	2	4	1	
	B.	38	-	2	4	1	
	C.	38	-	2	4	1	
4.	A.	42	12	3	4	1	
	B.	38	-	2	4	1	
	C.	38	-	2	4	1	
5.	A.	42	12	-	4	1	No dugouts ?
	B.	38	-	2	4	1	
	C.	38	-	2	4	1	
	D.	38	-	2	4	1	
6.	A.	38	-	2	4	1	
	B.	38	-	2	4	1	Officers dug-
	C.	38	-	2	4	1	out in B or C.
	D.	38	-	2	4	1	
7.	A.	38	-	2	4	1	(Shelter & Store
	B.	38	-	2	4	1	(require alteratio
	C.	38	-	2	4	1	
	D.	38	-	2	4	1	
8.	A.	38	-	2	4	1	
	B.	38	-	2	4	1	
	C.	38	-	2	4	1	
	D.	38	-	3	4	1	
	E.	38	-	2	4	1	
9.	A.	38	-	2	4	1	
	B.	38	-	3	4	1	(M.G. Empmt. and)
	C.	38	-	2	4	1	(Bomb Store)
	D.	38	-	3	4	1	Tunnel.
	E.	42	12	1	4	1	Bomb Store.
10.	A.	42	-	3	-	-	White Star
	B.	38	12	2	4	1	(B should form
	C.	38	-	3	4	1	(block.
	D.	38	-	2	4	1	
11.	A.	38	-	3	4	1	
	B.	38	-	2	4	1	
	C.	42	12	1	4	1	
		1618	72	87	164	41	

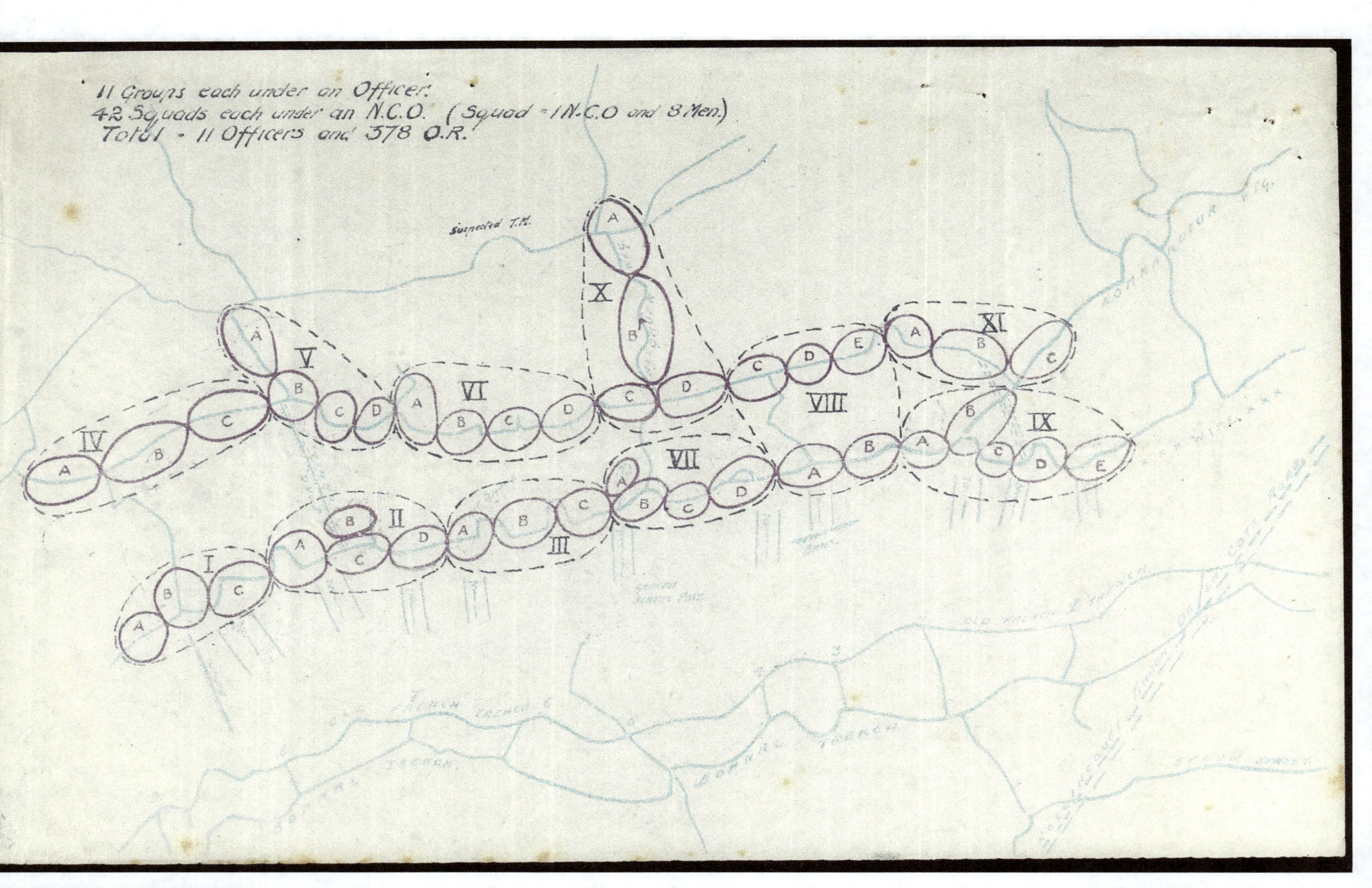

11 Groups each under an Officer.
42 Squads each under an N.C.O. (Squad = 1 N.C.O and 8 Men.)
Total - 11 Officers and 378 O.R.
Suspected T.M.
I
II
III
IV
V
VI
VII
VIII
IX
X
XI
OLD FRENCH TRENCH 6
OLD FRENCH 1 TRENCH
SOMMAL TRENCH
SPOON STREET

Any Answer to this Letter must be Prepaid.

On His Majesty's Service.

~~The Secretary~~,

~~Historical Sction, Military Bran~~ch,

~~Committee of Imperial Defence~~,

~~2, Cavendish Square, W.1.~~

WAR OFFICE.

If undelivered, to be returned to the Officer Commanding at the place shown in the post mark of origin.

R.

X.33 152/51

Vol 24

W A R D I A R Y

of

1 / 8 th Bn. ARGYLL & SUTHERLAND HIGHLANDERS

for

A P R I L , 1 9 1 7.

****

1/8th Bn Arg + Suth Highrs

Instructions regarding War Diaries and Intelligence Summaries are contained in F. S. Regs., Part II. and the Staff Manual respectively. Title pages will be prepared in manuscript.

WAR DIARY
~~or~~
~~INTELLIGENCE SUMMARY.~~
(Erase heading not required.)

Army Form C. 2118.

Volume III
Sheet No 23

Place	Date 1917	Hour	Summary of Events and Information	Officers K	Officers W	Officers M	Other Ranks K	Other Ranks W	Other Ranks M	Remarks and references to Appendices
AGNIERES + CAUCOURT.	April 1		Presentation of ribbons by Corps Commander. GmG							
do	2		Battalion Training. GmG							
do	3		do GmG							
do	4		do GmG							
do	5		Battalion marched to tents in BOIS DE MAROEUIL. GmG							
BOIS DE MAROEUIL	6		Preparing for Operations. GmG							
do	7		do GmG							
do	8		Church Services GmG							
		7.30pm	Battalion moved to proceed to the Assembly Trenches E. of Roclincourt, for the Attack. GmG							
ROCLINCOURT	9	5.30am	Battalion attacked E. of ROCLINCOURT. ~~Brigade~~ Battalion Frontage: A30a 4.2 to A29b 90.95. (Ref. map ROCLINCOURT 51B N.W.1). Order of Battle from S. to N:- 6th Bn. The Gordon Highlanders and 6th Bn. Seaforth Highlanders, attacked the 1st German System of trenches. The 1/8th Arg. Suth. Highrs and the 5th Bn Seaforth Highrs attacked the 2nd + 3rd ~~line~~ Systems of German trenches. The 103rd Infy Brigade Advanced on the right of the Battalion, and the 5th Seaforth Highrs on the left. The Battalion reached the line B19 d. 15.03 to B19 d. 2.7. (Ref. ROCLINCOURT 51B N.W.1). GmG							"B"

1/8th Bn Arg + Suthd Highrs

WAR DIARY
or
~~INTELLIGENCE SUMMARY.~~
(Erase heading not required.)

Volume III

Sheet No 24

Army Form C. 2118.

Instructions regarding War Diaries and Intelligence Summaries are contained in F. S. Regs., Part II. and the Staff Manual respectively. Title pages will be prepared in manuscript.

Place	Date 1917	Hour	Summary of Events and Information	Officers K	Officers W	Officers M	Other Ranks K	Other Ranks W	Other Ranks M	Remarks and references to Appendices
ROCLINCOURT	April 9	8.0pm	5th Bn The Gordon Highlanders relieved the Battalion which was withdrawn to the line B19c5.1. to B19c1.9. The Battalion went into action with 22 Officers, and 622 Other Ranks. 2nd Lieut. P.S. Watson, and 2nd Lieut. W.L. Wilkinson, killed. 2nd Lieut J.F. Campbell, and 2/Lieut. A.K. Williamson, died of wounds. Capt. A.C. McLaren, Lieut. + Adjt. A. Macdonald, 2nd Lieuts. M. Gillies, J.J. Young, M.C., J.P. Trotter and A.R. Muir, wounded. 2nd Lieut. R.M. MacRae, wounded remaining on duty. Three machine guns were captured by the Battalion, two of which were brought in.	2	9	-	38	168	6	
do	10		In trenches, holding support position.							
		10pm	Relieved by 7th Bn The Gordon Highlanders, and withdrawn to reserve in Old British Line.							
do	11	3pm	Relieved by 22nd Bn The Essex Regt. and marched to X Hutments, ECOIVRES.							
ECOIVRES	12		Resting.							
do	13	11.45am	Marched to Huts on ACQ – HAUT AVESNES road at E7b1.4 (Ref map 51C) – Bathing.							
ACQ.	14		Resting.							
do	15		Battalion Training. – Church Services.							

2353 Wt. W2544/1454 700,000 5/15 D. D. & L. A.D.S.S./Forms/C. 2118.

1/8th Bn. Arg. & Suthd. Highrs.

Instructions regarding War Diaries and Intelligence Summaries are contained in F. S. Regs., Part II. and the Staff Manual respectively. Title pages will be prepared in manuscript.

WAR DIARY
or
~~INTELLIGENCE SUMMARY.~~
(Erase heading not required.)

Volume III
Sheet 25.

Army Form C. 2118.

Place	Date 1917	Hour	Summary of Events and Information	Officers K	Officers W	Officers M	Other ranks K	Other ranks W	Other ranks M	Remarks and references to Appendices
	April									
ACQ.	16	10 a.m.	Battalion moved to ARRAS in motor 'Busses. Billeted in ARRAS in Divisional Reserve.							
ARRAS.	17		Training. Officers reconnoitred support positions near ATHIES.							
do	18	6.15 pm	Battalion moved to trenches N. of FAMPOUX. In support in GAVRELLE - OPPY line.							
FAMPOUX.	19		In trenches in Support.							
		8.30 pm	Relieved 6th Bn. Black Watch in front line from H 18 b.2.6 to HYDERABAD WORK (H12a 0.0) (Ref. map. 51B N.W.)					2		
do	20		In trenches. Heavily shelled by 5.9" howitzers. - Draft of 249 Other Ranks reported at ARRAS.		1		6	7		
do	21		do do					7		
do	22	12 m.n.	Relieved by 7th Bn. The Gordon Highrs, who were moving into position for the Assault. Marched to billets in ARRAS.				2	4	1	
ARRAS	23		In Divisional Reserve.							
do	24	7.30 a.m.	Battalion warned to be ready to move to the line at ½ hours notice.							
		2.30 pm	Moved under orders to go into line. Reached ST. LAURENT BLANGY. Orders cancelled, and Battalion moved to old British trenches near ST. NICHOLAS. Bivouaced.							
ST. NICHOLAS	25		In Bivouacs.							
do	26	9.30.	Battalion moved in motor 'Busses to Huts on ACQ.-HAUT AVESNES road (E 17 b 1.4)							

2353 Wt. W2544/1454 700,000 5/15 D. D. & L. A.D.S.S. Forms/C. 2118.

1/8th Arg. & Suthd. Highlanders.

Instructions regarding War Diaries and Intelligence Summaries are contained in F. S. Regs., Part II. and the Staff Manual respectively. Title pages will be prepared in manuscript.

WAR DIARY
or
~~INTELLIGENCE SUMMARY.~~
(Erase heading not required.)

Volume III

Sheet 26

Army Form C. 2118.

Place	Date 1917	Hour	Summary of Events and Information	Remarks and references to Appendices
	April			
ACQ	27		Resting. GMcG	
do	28	11 a.m.	Battalion marched to TERNAS (Sheet 51c). 12 Officers reported for duty. GMcG	
TERNAS.	29		Church Services – 4 Officers and 85 Other ranks joined for duty. GMcG	
do	30		Battalion training. GMcG	

In the Field
30/4/17

R. Campbell Lieut. Colonel
Commdg 1/8th Arg. & Suth. Highrs.

2353 Wt. W2544/1454 700,000 5/15 D. D. & L. A.D.S.S. Forms/C 2118.

X-34

W A R D I A R Y

of

1/8th Bn. Argyll and Sutherland Highlanders,

MAY,1917.

1/8th Bn Arg & Suth Highlanders.

WAR DIARY
or
~~INTELLIGENCE SUMMARY.~~
(Erase heading not required.)

Volume III Sheet No 27

Army Form C. 2118.

Instructions regarding War Diaries and Intelligence Summaries are contained in F. S. Regs., Part II. and the Staff Manual respectively. Title pages will be prepared in manuscript.

Place	Date 1917	Hour	Summary of Events and Information		Officers K	W	M	Other Ranks K	W	M	Remarks and references to Appendices
	May										
TERNAS	1		Battalion Training	GmJ							
do	2		do	GmJ							
do	3		do	GmJ							
do	4	2pm	do Battalion Sports	GmJ							
do	5	10-30am	do G.O.C. Division present while Battalion carries out attack practice	GmJ							
		5.30pm	Brigade Tug of War Competition. Battalion team beat 5th Seaforth Highlanders in the final pull								
do	6		Church Services	GmJ							
do	7		Battalion Training 14 Other Ranks joined.	GmJ							
do	8		do	GmJ							
do	9		do	GmJ							
do	10		Battalion entrains at LIGNY-ST. FLOCHEL, and proceeded to ARRAS. Billets in the SCHRAMM BARRACKS	GmJ							
ARRAS	11	7.30pm	Battalion marched to bivouacs W. of railway embankment at H 13 b 9.2 (Ref. map 51B NW)	GmJ							
do	12	9.0pm	Battalion marched to trenches E of CHEMICAL WORKS (I.13 and 14), via ATHIES and FAMPOUX. Battalion HQ. in quarry at I 13 a 2.1. Frontage held by Battalion: CORONA trench from I 19 b 5.8. to I 14 a. 2.3. The Battalion relieved elements of the 11th Infantry Brigade								

2353 Wt. W2544/1454 700,000 5/15 D. D. & L. A.D.S.S. Forms/C 2118.

1/8th Bn Arg & Suth Highlanders

WAR DIARY
or
~~INTELLIGENCE SUMMARY.~~
(Erase heading not required.)

Volume III Sheet No 28

Army Form C. 2118.

Instructions regarding War Diaries and Intelligence Summaries are contained in F. S. Regs., Part II. and the Staff Manual respectively. Title pages will be prepared in manuscript.

Place	Date 1917	Hour	Summary of Events and Information	Officers K	Officers W	Officers M	Other Ranks K	Other Ranks W	Other Ranks M	Remarks and references to Appendices
	May									
FAMPOUX	12		The 2nd Bn. Seaforth Highlanders took over the line on our right, and that on the left was held by the 17th Division. Trenches hastily dug, very shallow in places. Were dug into. GmF							
do	13	10pm	In trenches. Battalion ordered to advance one company and occupy the sunken road from about I.20.a.30.35 to I.14.c.5.2½ (See 152 Inf Bde Order No 143). The advance was carried out at 10pm. No opposition was encountered and a trench (COLOMBO) was dug just W. of the road, and joined up with the 5th Seaforths on the right. D Company under CAPT J.V.F. MACDONALD carried out the advance. Two platoons of C Company (CAPT. W.D. MUNRO, [illegible]) were swung forward and dug in to link up new trench with CORONA. GmF				6	27	-	Appendix "A"
do	14		In trenches. Junction of COLOMBO and CORONA trenches completed. Enemy bombardment with 4.2" and 5.9" howitzers fairly heavy. 2/Lieut F.L. Sinclair wounded.	-	1	-	5	51	-	
do	15		In trenches. A day of heavy bombardment by the enemy, the CHEMICAL WORKS and Battalion HQ receiving most attention. CAPT. J.V.F. MACDONALD, LIEUT. G. BOYD, and 2nd LIEUT. H.R.H. GORRIE, wounded. GmF	-	3	-	12	27	-	
do	16	3.0am	After an intense bombardment, the enemy launched a heavy attack against our front. The line was held and the enemy beaten off with heavy losses, except for a short stretch on the left, at the junction with the 17th Division, where							Appendix "B"

2353 Wt. W2544/1454 700,000 5/15 D. D. & L. A.D.S.S. Forms/C. 2118.

1/8th Arg + Suth Highlanders

Instructions regarding War Diaries and Intelligence Summaries are contained in F. S. Regs., Part II. and the Staff Manual respectively. Title Pages will be prepared in manuscript.

WAR DIARY
or
~~INTELLIGENCE SUMMARY~~
(Erase heading not required.)

Volume III Sheet No 29.

Army Form C. 2118

Place	Date	Hour	Summary of Events and Information	Officers K	Officers W	Officers M	Other Ranks K	Other Ranks W	Other Ranks M	Remarks and references to Appendices
	1917 May									
FAMPOUX.	16		he succeeded in penetrating our line, and pushed parties along the railway as far as I 13 C 3.5. These parties were at once engaged and destroyed, and the CHEMICAL WORKS cleared of the enemy. Fifty one prisoners were captured.							Appendix "C"
		9.30a.m.	The 153rd Infy Bde. counter attacked and drove the enemy out of the remaining trenches occupied by him. During these operations, CAPT. M.A. MACTAGGART, and 2nd LIEUT. A.G. POLLARD, were killed, the former having continued to lead his men after having been twice wounded. 2nd LIEUTS R.D. McILROY, R.A. WATSON, and E.D. HENDRY, were wounded, and CAPT. W.D. MONRO, M.C., and 2nd LIEUTS. W. McN. SNADDEN, T.P. JOHNSTON, and A.D. HUMBLE missing.	2	3	4	25	97	60	
		10p.m.	The Battalion was relieved and marched to bivouacs at H.13.a. (near ST. LAURENT-BLANGY)							
ST. LAURENT BLANGY.	17	4p.m.	Marched to Billets in ARRAS. In Divisional Reserve.							
ARRAS.	18		Battalion resting, and bathing. do							
do	19		Battalion refitting. Capt. W. H. C. Kidston, 2nd Lieut A. D. Cameron, and 25 other ranks joined.							
do	20		Church Services. In Divisional Reserve							
do	21		Battalion training do							
do	22		do do							
do	23		do do							
do	24		do do							
do	25		do do 14 Other Ranks joined.							

1875 Wt. W593/826 1,000,000 4/15 J.B.C. & A. A.D.S.S./Forms/C. 2118.

1/8th Batt. Arg. and Suth. Highlanders

Volume III,
Sheet No 30.

Army Form C. 2118

WAR DIARY
or
~~INTELLIGENCE SUMMARY~~
(Erase heading not required.)

Instructions regarding War Diaries and Intelligence Summaries are contained in F. S. Regs., Part II. and the Staff Manual respectively. Title Pages will be prepared in manuscript.

Place	Date 1917	Hour	Summary of Events and Information		Officers K	Officers W	Officers M	O. Ranks K	O. Ranks W	O. Ranks M	Remarks and references to Appendices
	May										
ARRAS.	26		Battalion Training, In Divisional Reserve	G.M.J.							
do	27		Church Services. do	G.M.J.							
do	28		Battalion Training do	G.M.J.							
do	29		do do	G.M.J.							
do	30	1.30p.m.	Battalion moved to TERNAS (Ref map 51B) by motor busses.	G.M.J.							
TERNAS	31		Battalion Route march. 184 other ranks joined.	G.M.J.							
			Total Strength of Battalion 31/5/17 35 officers 886 other Ranks. Numbers actually with unit. 26 officers 813 other Ranks.	G.M.J.							

A. W. Lockie
Major.
Commanding, 1/8th Arg. & Suth. Highrs.

1875 Wt. W593/826 1,000,000 4/15 J.B.C. & A. A.D.S.S./Forms/C. 2118.

Copy No. 1

Copy.

OPERATION ORDER,
by
Lieut.-Colonel R. Campbell, D.S.O., Commanding 1/8th (The Argyllshire) Battalion Princess Louise's (Argyll & Sutherland) Highlanders.

13th May, 1917.

1. The Battalion will carry out an advance to-night with one company as follows:-

(a) At 10 p.m. "D" Coy will advance from a portion in CORONA trench I.19.b.5.7. to I.14.C.Q.4. and occupy the sunken road from about I.20.A.30.35 to I.14.C.5.2½. and join up with 2 platoons of 5th Sea: Highrs. at I.20.A.30.35.
Having occupied sunken road, if they are too thick, "D" Coy will thin out and consolidate posts.

(b) As soon as "D" Coy are firmly established in the new posts "C" Coy will link up a line of posts from the left of "D" Coy to I.14.A.25.1. in CORONA trench.

2. The advance will be carried out without a barrage.
At 10.15 p.m. a slight barrage will be played on HAUSA and DELBAR wood.

3. The advance will be at 5 paces' extension in a double wave. Each man will be told his objective, and the distance to it. The advance will not be checked until the objective is reached except that everyone will lie down if a Very Light is thrown up. As soon as it is out the advance will continue. The advance will be made in absolute silence.

4. "A" Coy will at 10 p.m. move into position at present held by "D" Coy. Absolute silence is essential.

5. "B" Coy will as soon as the situation permits of it begin work on a support line running from I.19.b.4.9. in a north-easterly direction to I.13.D.97. where it will join existing line. It will be dug in parts and joined up afterwards.

6. 3 platoons of 8th Royal Scots will be at disposal of battalion to dig communication trench forward to new line.
O.C. "A" Coy will detail 3 reliable guides to report at Battn. Headquarters at 8.35 p.m. They will be sent on to meet these platoons and will guide them to CORONA trench, "D" Coy's present position. They will dig a communication trench forward to the sunken road.

7. "D" will carry picks and shovels in their equipment.

8. Zero will be at 10 p.m.

9. ACKNOWLEDGE.

(Sgd) R. CAMPBELL, Lt-Col.,

Commanding 1/8th Bn. A. & S. Highrs.

Copy No. 1....Filed.
2 - 5....Companies.

OPERATIONS, 16TH MAY, 1917.

1. On the morning of the 16th at 3 a.m. the enemy launched a powerful counter-attack on the whole of the sector of the front held by my Battalion.
The barrage was very heavy.

2. The following appears to be the history of the fight.

Disposition of Battalion.
1½ Companies in COLOMBO TRENCH, ½ Coy in CORONA TRENCH between COLOMBO and the railway; 1 Coy in CORONA from its junction with COLOMBO to junction with 5th Seaforth Highrs; 1 Coy in CORONA Support with one platoon on the north of the railway; Battalion Headquarters in the QUARRY at I.13.a.15.05.

Two Companies 6th Seaforth Highrs. were in process of relieving Dorset Regiment in CUPID TRENCH and were to have come under my orders on completion of relief.

The two Companies on the right of my line were to have been relieved by two Companies of the 6th Gordon Highrs., but relief had hardly started.

3. When the attack commenced the 1½ Companies in COLOMBO Trench held their ground and inflicted extremely heavy losses on the enemy. They remained in possession of the COLOMBO line throughout the entire operations.

The two platoons in the front line in CORONA trench north of COLOMBO were, however, driven out and several captured. The enemy attack broke through here and also on the north of the railway where the Seaforths and Dorsets were occupied in relieving.
The result of this was that the whole of my line on the north of the railway and the CORONA line immediately south of it to the junction of COLOMBO was in the hands of the enemy.
In the fighting that ensued the platoon of CORONA support line north of the railway was driven back through the Chemical Works to the south of the railway, and the whole of CORONA support line to the south of the railway was then turned and attacked from the rear, the garrison being driven back towards the rear.
The Companies holding CORONA and CORONA support continued fighting, and ultimately about 8 a.m. CORONA support was recaptured.
A certain proportion of the garrison of CORONA support appear to have been driven back westwards when the line was first turned, but these came into action again in the fighting that ensued later for the Chemical Works.
While this fighting was in progress the enemy had swept through the Chemical Works and had reached CARDIGAN Trench on the north of the railway and CEYLON on the south by 4 a.m.
I at once attacked the party north of the railway from the QUARRY with every man from Battalion Headquarters. Rifle grenades were employed with great success for driving the enemy from the shell holes.

The whole/

The whole of this party was either killed or captured by 6.45 a.m.
At this time heavy rifle fire was taking place on the south side of the railway, and I therefore advanced the party and took up a position on the top of the railway bank.
I found that the position on the south side of the railway was that the enemy were in parts of CEYLON trench and COLON, and were held up by the party of the 6th ~~Sandem~~ Highrs. who were firing on them from CORDITE Seaforth trench. Another party of the 6th Seaforths were firing on them from CLIP trench at the same t ime.
I at once sent my Adjutant to order the party of 6th Seaforths from CORDITE trench to advance as soon as I opened fire from the railway. They did so, and the whole of t his party of the enemy were either killed or captured.

4. The line was reformed, 6th Seaforths on the right, 8th Argylls on the left (north of the railway) and the Chemical Works were swept clear of the enemy, the line being established on the eastern edge of the Works.
It was now 8 a.m. and I received orders from the Brigade that the 153rd Brigade were to make a counter-attack, the creeping barrage for which was to start from the western end of the Chemical Works at 8.30 a.m.
CAWDOR I therefore withdrew my men from the esatern edge back to CARDIGAN and ~~CC CORDITE~~ trenches, and ordered the 6th Seaforth Highrs. to do the same on the south side of the embankment to CEYLON and CORDITE trenches.
The barrage opened at 9.30, and the 153rd Brigade passed through us to the attack.

5. On receiving the orders at 8 a.m. for the counter-attack, I at once sent back 2/Lieut.FAIRLIE, R.F.A., my Liaison Officer, to Brigade Headquarters to explain the position. The barrage was therefore cancelled for the southern side of the railway.

6. Barrage. The enemy barrage was the most severe that I have seen.
His bombardment of the previous day was also ~~extremely~~ extraordinarily heavy.
Our own barrage apparently failed to see the "S.O.S." signal, as there was no response. The "S.O.S." signal was sent up by the front line companies and from Battalion Headquarters.

7. Communication. Communication both to the front and rear was extremely difficult. All wires were cut both forward to Brigade Headquarters and to the artillery. Pigeon service was used, and the remainder of the messages were sent through by runner.

8. Casualties. The casualties for the 4 days in the line were heavy -
15 Officers,
290 Other Ranks.

R Campbell

Lieut-Colonel,
18-5-17. Commanding 1/8th Bn. A. & S. Highrs.

1/8th Bn. Argyll & Sutherland Highlanders.
****

CASUALTIES FOR MONTH OF MAY, 1917.

~~OFFICERS~~
~~KILLED~~:-

13th May, 1917.

OTHER RANKS KILLED. (6)
S/5113, Pte. W.J.Graham, "A" Coy.
S/5206, L/C. J.Hamilton, "A" "
10150, " H.Johnstone, "A" "
S/11669, Pte. G.M.Livingstone, "A"
303152, L/C. J.McHardy, "D" "
276709, Pte. W.Mackie, "A" "

OTHER RANKS WOUNDED. (27)
301319, Cpl. J.Boyd, "A" Coy.
301844, Pte. T.M.Borthwick, "A" Coy.
S/7216, " E.E.Browning, "A" "
303352, " D.Connell, "B" "
302827, " J.Divers, "B" "
303166, " T.Ferguson, "A" "
40034, " J.Fleming, "B" "
303190, " J.Gaitens, "C" "
300765, " A.Gillies, "B" "
303162, L/C. J.Hitchin, "A" "
'234, Pte. T.Hill, "C" "
S/8445, " J.Kelly, "C" "
301770, " J.G.McAllister, "C" "
301380, " R.McGill, "A" "
300138, Cpl. A.McIntyre, "A" "
300510, Pte. A.McKinnon, "A" "
301397, " H.McMillan, "D" "
301773, " R.S.McMorrow, "C" "
S/3727, " G.McGraw, "C" "
302875, L/C. D.Melvin, "C" "
303177, Pte. J.Mewha, "A" "
303143, " H.Moffat, "D" "
303417, " W.Murphy, "B" "
303339, Sgt. J.Seymour, "C" "
252, Pte. T.Wight, "C" "
301123, " G.Balmer, "B" "
301063, " P.Laverty, "A" "

14th May, 1917.

OFFICERS WOUNDED. (1)
2nd.Lieut. G. I. SINCLAIR.

OTHER RANKS KILLED. (5)
303261, Pte. G. Brodie, "C" Coy.
300878, " J. Bailey, "D" "
303002, " W. Carroll, "C" "
S/40183, " T. Elliott, "C" "
275684, L/C. W. McAulay, "A" "

OTHER RANKS WOUNDED. (51)
303094, Pte. A. Bamford, "A" Coy.
302993, " R. Barr, " "
302994, " J. Bauld, "C" "
302899, L/C. R.N.Boyd, "D" "
301723, Pte. J.W.Brown, "B" "
302907, Cpl. J.Burnett, "D" "
S/15473, Pte. J.Bryson, "C" "
303082, " C.Cook, "C" "
S/10658, L/C. J.Crockhart, "B" "
301651, Pte. T.Dean, "C" "
325579/

(2) 16th May, 1917.

OTHER RANKS WOUNDED (contd.)

S/16893,	Pte.	J. Aird,	"C"	Coy.	
301360,	"	J. Anderson,	"A"	"	
300535,	L/C.	C. Bradley,	"C"	"	
303226,	Pte.	D. Brodie,	"A"	"	
300467,	L/C.	B. Burchell,	"A"	"	
301806,	Pte.	J. Barclay,	"B"	"	
325433,	"	R. Ballantyne,	"B"	"	
S/4838,	"	A.E. Bluckett,	"B"	"	
S/1731,	"	R. Brown,	"C"	"	
301729,	"	A. Cardle,	"C"	"	
303246,	"	J. Cochrane,	"A"	"	
303107,	"	T. Connolly,	"A"	"	
300572,	"	H. Conner,	"C"	"	
301719,	"	D. Cowell,	"D"	"	Remd. on duty.
303230,	"	W. Cowie,	"A"	"	
301234,	"	G. Craig,	"C"	"	
302404,	"	R. Craig,	"A"	"	Remd. on duty.
301573,	"	J. Crilley,	"B"	"	
S/6398,	"	H. Callogly,	"B"	"	
302977,	"	E. Docherty,	"C"	"	
302841,	"	R. Docherty,	"A"	"	
300864,	L/C.	M. Dolan,	"B"	"	
~~3668~~					
301081,	Pte.	J. Davidson,	"A"	"	
300188,	"	A. Ferguson,	"C"	"	
300359,	"	A. Ferguson,	"C"	"	
301057,	"	W. Fitzsimmons,	"A"	"	
303336,	"	D. Fleming,	"A"	"	
265351,	"	W. Fraser,	"B"	"	
1253,	L/C.	J. Fleeting,	"C"	"	
8 94,	Pte.	J. A. Fleming,	"B"	"	
303075,	"	J. Goodwin,	"A"	"	
S/7002,	"	J.W. Gaffney,	"A"	"	
300310,	"	J. Gillies,	"A"	"	
301405,	"	J. Harvey,	"A"	"	
301045,	"	G. Hornby,	"B"	"	
325217,	"	D. Hopkins,	"A"	"	
S/15841,	"	J. Hume,	"A"	"	
S/2379,	"	M. Holloran,	"B"	"	
S/7243,	"	W. Henshaw,	"C"	"	
303057,	"	W. Jack,	"D"	"	
303129,	"	J. Johnson,	"C"	"	
301235,	"	W. Johnson,	"C"	"	
301308,	"	A. Curr,	"A"	"	
202202,	Cpl.	T. Kendal,	"B"	"	
301596,	Pte.	F. Lyon,	"D"	"	Remd. onduty.
303258,	"	R. McAllister,	"B"	"	
300562,	"	D. McColl,	"B"	"	
301339,	L/C.	M. McAskill,	"B"	"	
302918,	Pte.	E. McCracken,	"B"	"	
303341,	"	D. McCudden,	"D"	"	
303260,	"	P. McCue,	"B"	"	
300382,	"	J. McGregor,	"A"	"	
300250,	"	D. McIntyre,	"A"	"	
300014,	CSM.	D. McKinnon,	"B"	"	
303292,	Pte.	J. McLean,	"B"	"	
303026,	"	J. McLellan,	"D"	"	
300031,	Cpl.	D. McNair,	"C"	"	
325689,	Pte.	W. McWilliams,	"B"	"	
9519,	L/C.	J. McDonald,	"A"	"	
S/7191,	Pte.	A. McPhee,	"A"	"	
S/9216,	"	T. K. McLean,	"A"	"	
4/8657,	"	W. McCulloch,	"B"	"	
S/7000,	"	J. McLeod,	"C"	"	
S/6812,	"	M. McPherson,	"C"	"	
303331,	"	J. Martin,	"C"	"	
302926,	"	W. May,	"D"	"	
303036,	"	A. Miller,	"D"	"	
301805,	"	W. Morham,	"C"	"	

301487/

14th May, 1917.

325579, Pte. A. Esbie, "C" Coy.
302814, L/C. L. Forrest, "B" "
300613, Sgt. A. Fraser, "A" "
302190, Pte. H. Gibson, "C" "
303312, L/C. W. Gillies, "D" "
S/4007, Pte. W. J. Gribben, "A" Coy.
S/7665, " A. Gowans, "A" Coy.
300441, " J. Gilmour, "C" "
S/13276, " E. Hoyle, "A" "
S/3434, " A. Hamilton, "B" "
325273, " J. Kay, "A" "
4/9258, " W. Kerr, "B" "
S/6623, " J. Kelly, "D" "
303149, " W. McDade, "D" "
300428, " D. McFarlane, "B" "
303159, " M. McLellan, "D" "
S/5920, " L. McKendrick, "A" "
S/15275, " C. McMorran, "C" "
8688, " S. McChayne, "C" "
S/12142, " J. McGarrity, "C" "
40375, " J. McDougall, "B" "
303032, " G. Maxwell, "D" "
300576, " M. Mitchell, "D" "
S/6389, " J. Murdoch, "C" "
/2349, " J. Murphy, "D" "
S/7713, " H. Neil, "D" "
18714, " W. Paterson, "A" " remd. on duty.
300981, " H. Rawding, "A" "
302405, " D. Robins, "D" "
300968, " W. Roberts, "D" "
S/7325, " G. Reid, "B" "
300837, " E. Sewell, "C" " remd. on duty.
303241, " P. Sorley, "C" "
S/17051, " C. Simmons, "A" "
S/6161, " R. Shaw, "D" "
S/8615, " R. Turner, "D" "
303438, " P. Wason, "D" "
303239, " T. Weir, "C" "
303353, " J. Wilson, "D" "
S/3730, " R.P. White, "C" "
302207, " W. McEwan, "A" "

15th May, 1917.

OFFICERS WOUNDED. (3)
Captain J.V.F. MACDONALD.
Lieut. G. BOID.
2/Lieut. H. GORRIE.

OTHER RANKS KILLED. (12)
300672, Pte. A. Beveridge, "D" Coy.
S/5444, " R. Brooks, "C" "
8860, L/C. R. Cunningham, "A" "
276605, Pte. A. Fairweather, "A" "
S/14694, L/C. J. Harkes, "C" "
303153, Pte. D. McKellar, "D" "
276579, " W. McNaughton, "B" "
S/5004, " J. McKay, "C" "
303269, " D. Nicolson, "C" "
300806, " D. Quinton, "D" "
302931, " J. Scott, "D" "
302919, " A. Thomson, "C" "

OTHER RANKS WOUNDED. (27)
301686, Pte. J. Brown, "A" Coy.
S/7136, " W. Barber, "A" "
301977, L/C. R. Craig, "B" "
300700, " B. Crook, "D" " Remd. on duty.
301206, Pte. D. Ferguson, "C" "

301814/

15th May, 1917.

303814, Pte. R.T.Forsyth, "B" Coy.
S/40399, " P.Fleming, "A" "
300458, Sgt. J.M. Girvan, "D" "
300175, Pte. R.Graham, "B" "
S/17173, " J.Harris, "C" "
302004, " A.M.Lamont, "D" " Remd. on duty.
303158, " W.McLeish, "D" "
S/8718, " W.McIntosh, "D" "
S/6713, " T.V.McKimmie, "C" "
S/19022, " H.Morris, "B" "
S/8481, " W.Miller, "D" "
302346, " A.C.Neilson, "C" "
303412, " G.Paton, "B" "
303215, " E.Smith, "C" "
303070, " J.Stewart, "D" "
S/9938, " D.Sanderson, "C" "
9410, " J.Simpkin, "D" "
300405, " A.Thomson, "B" "
303428, " R.Thomson, "D" "
300823, " W.Todhunter, "D" "
325929, " J.J.Watson, "B" "
S/8642, " T.C.Waddell, "D" "

16th May, 1917.

OFFICERS KILLED. (2)
Captain M. A. MACTAGGART.
2/Lieut. A. G. POLLARD.

OFFICERS WOUNDED. (3)
2/Lieut. R. D. McILROY.
2/Lieut. R. WATSON.
2/Lieut. E. D. HENRY.

OFFICERS MISSING. (4)
Captain W. D. MUNRO, M.C.
Lieut. W. McN. SNADDEN.
2/Lieut. T.P. JOHNSTONE.
2/Lieut. A.D. HUMBLE.

OTHER RANKS KILLED. (25)
303169, L/C. J. Boyd. "A" Coy.
301227, " D. Brown, "B" "
300153, Pte. C. Campbell, "D" "
300169, " A. Campbell, "D" "
303328, " W. Dodds, "B" "
300119, " J.Ferguson, "D" "
S/15492, " J.Fraser, "C" "
302024, " J.Logan, "A" "
301358, L/C. P.McGilp, "C" "
325331, CSM. J.McCleary, "A" "
S/14725, Pte. S.McGregor, "A" "
300913, " A.Morrison, "A" "
303189, " J.Drysdale, "C" "
300462, " F.North, "B" "
303046, " W.Rankin, "D" "
301271, " J.Rodger, "B" "
S/15928, " T.Sloan, "A" "
9043, L/C. N.Shirlaw, "C" "
300209, Pte. J.Taylor, "B" "
300195, Cpl. W.Wyllie, "A" "
278886, Pte. E.Wilks, "A" "
300492, Cpl. J.A.Morris, "A" "
303358, Pte. P.Allan, "B" Coy.
S/15602, " Q.Aughey, "B" "
S/4111, " J.Smith, "A" "

OTHER RANKS WOUNDED. (91)
300723, Pte. H. Allan, "C" Coy. Remd. on duty.
303092, " R. Anderson, "A" "
303208, L/C.W. Anderson, "A" "

S/16893/

OTHER RANKS WOUNDED (Contd.).

301487, Cpl. D.Munro, "B" Coy.
S/1656, Pte. C. Martin, "C" "
S/5090, " J. Miller, "D" "
275243, " R. Peacock, "A" "
1816, " J.Preston, "A" "
S/1979, " R. Quinlan, "C" "
303332, " J. Reid, "B" "
S/15704, " R. Ross, "C" "
302853, Sgt. N. Sharkey, "A" "
301342, Pte. D. Stewart, "A" "
S/14902, " R. Steven, "C" "
S/12337, " E. Smith, "C" "
275354, " A. Somerville, "B" "
303319, Sgt. W. Thomson, "A" "
S/11627, Pte. A. Tevendale, "C" "
856, " G. Tanton, "C" "
326090, " A. Thomson, "A" "
361, L/C. P. Vesey, "B" "
303183, Pte. T. Walker, "B" "
301137, " J. Wallwark, "B" "
301883, " R. Wilson, "A" "
3053, " D. Wilkie, "A" "
S/14931, " J. Wyllie, "B" "
276546, " C. Wright, "B" "
4046, " W. Young, "B" "
S/14717, " A.G. Carruth, "A" "

OTHER RANKS. MISSING. (60)

301128, Pte. R. Alexander, "D" Coy.
~~303388, " .... "B"~~
~~S/15662~~ ....
S/16163, " A.Armstrong, "C" Coy.
S/10409, " W.Anderson, "A" "
303400, " J.P.Blair, "B" "
303097, " H. Bremner, "A" "
301200, " D.A.Brown, "B" "
300544, " S.C.Brown, "A" "
S/14239, " R.Brown, "A" "
40014, " A.Burns, "B" "
300293, " J.Cameron, "C" "
302976, " R.Campbell, "A" "
300469, " G.H.Cliff, "A" "
303055, " D.Cuthbertson, "C" "
301391, " D.Carlin, "B" "
302380, " J.Dowling, "B" "
302989, L/C. N.Duncan, "A" "
S/13007, Pte. F.Devine, "A" "
276641, " D.Duncan, "B" "
S/4398, " T.Downie, "C" "
S/6565, " T.Duncan, "C" "
301149, Cpl. T.Forster, "A" "
301202, Pte. J.Foster, "C" "
301180, " W.Glynn, "C" "
[illegible]5174, " G.Grant, "B" "
S/12859, " W.Goldie, "B" "
301192, " W.Harrison, "B" "
303015, " A.Hughes, "A" "
201203, " A.Harrow, "B" "
325586, " J.Hennings, "B" "
302887, " J.McBride, "C" "
301183, Cpl. A.McCall, "D" "
300565, Pte. A.McCallum, "B" "
300207, " D.McCallum, "A" "
303018, " J.McCallum, "C" "
301548, " P.McGill, "B" "
300944, " J.McGregor, "D" "
302818, " W.McGougan, "C" "
300123/300093, " J.McIvor, "B" "

 16th May, 1917.

OTHER RANKS MISSING (Contd.).

300053, Sgt. J. McLean, "B" Coy.
4/8982, Pte. W. McColl, "B" "
10376, " D. McColl, "B" "
7400, " F. McCormack, "B" "
303299, " J. Malley, "C" "
303202, L/C. W. Mason, "B" "
303240, Pte. A. Millar, "A" "
300575, " J. Muir, "C" "
275101, " J. Muir, "A" "
S/7624, L/C. B. Morgan, "B" "
S/3234, " J. Mather, "C" "
300200, Pte. D. O'May, "B" "
301666, " C. Perston, "B" "
303263, " J. Smith, "C" "
326192, " J. Sweeting, "A" "
S/2998, " R. Smith, "B" "
S/7704, " W. Taylor, "C" "
300986, " L. Walker, "B" "
301050, " T. Walker, "A" "
301101, Cpl. C. Wilson, "A" "
303079, Pte. H. Wilson, "B" "
300443, " D. Watson, "B" "

ROLL OF OFFICERS WHO TOOK PART IN OPERATIONS, 12/17th May, 1917.

Lieut-Colonel R. Campbell, D.S.O.

Major A. Lockie.

Capt. G. McCallum, M.C. A/Adjutant.

2/Lieut. J. Ross. Intelligence Officer.

" " A. G. Pollard. Bombing Officer.

" " G. M. Warnock. Lewis Gun Officer.

"A" Coy:-

2/Lieut. R. D. McIlroy.

" " N. Newall.

" " G. C. Haldane.

" " R. A. Watson.

"B" Coy:-

Captain M. A. Mactaggart.

Lieut. G. Boyd.

Lieut. W. McN. Snadden.

2/Lieut. T. P. Johnstone.

"C" Coy:-

Capt. W. D. Munro, M.C.

Lieut. J.A. McGregor.

2/Lieut. A.D. Humble.

" " E.D. Hendry.

"D" Coy:-

Capt. J. V. F. Macdonald.

2/Lieut. J. S. Aikman.

" " G. I. Sinclair.

" " H.R. H. Gorrie.

****

WO 95/2865 ⟨8⟩ + ⟨9⟩
END.

PUBLIC RECORD OFFICE

document(s), being

(8) Trench Map 1:20,000 Special Sheet
Part of 51B NW & NE. BIACHE, 1917

(9) Trench Map 1:10,000 Sheet 51B NW3.
ARRAS, 1917

has been removed to the Map Room, reference: MFQ 1251 (8) + (9)

Date: 27th August 1991   Signed: [illegible]

X.35

Vol 26

; W A R   D I A R Y

of

1/8th Bn. ARGYLL and SUTHERLAND HIGHLANDERS.

JUNE, 1917.

1/8th Bn. Argyll & Suth. Highrs.

WAR DIARY

~~or~~

~~INTELLIGENCE SUMMARY.~~

(Erase heading not required.)

Volume III, Sheet No. 31

Army Form C. 2118.

Instructions regarding War Diaries and Intelligence Summaries are contained in F. S. Regs., Part II and the Staff Manual respectively. Title pages will be prepared in manuscript.

Place	Date	Hour	Summary of Events and Information	Officers K	Officers W	Officers M	Other Ranks K	Other Ranks W	Other Ranks M	Remarks and references to Appendices
	1917 June									
TERNAS	1	~~6 am~~ GmJ	Battalion Resting. Company Route marches. GmJ							
do	2		do GmJ							
do	3.		do Church Services. GmJ							
do	4	6·15 a.m.	Battalion marched to HESTRUS – EPS area (ref. map France LENS 11). 34 Other ranks joined. GmJ							
HESTRUS										
do	5		Battalion marched to DENNEBRŒUCQ (ref. map France HAZEBROUCK 5.A) GmJ							
DENNEBRŒUCQ	6		Battalion Resting. GmJ							
do	7		do GmJ							
do	8		Battalion marched to WIZERNES (ref. map France HAZEBROUCK 5A) GmJ							
do	9		Battalion marched to RECQUES (ref. map France HAZEBROUCK 5A) GmJ							
RECQUES	10		Battalion Resting. Church Services. GmJ							
do	11		do Companies Training. GmJ							
do	12		do Battalion Firing on Rifle Range. GmJ							
do	13		do Companies Training GmJ							
do	14		do do GmJ							
do	15		do do GmJ							

2353 Wt. W2544/1454 700,000 5/15 D. D. & L. A.D.S.S. Forms/C 2118.

1/8th Bn. Arg. & Suth. Highrs.

Volume III. Sheet No 32.

Army Form C. 2118

WAR DIARY
or
~~INTELLIGENCE SUMMARY~~

(Erase heading not required.)

Instructions regarding War Diaries and Intelligence Summaries are contained in F. S. Regs., Part II. and the Staff Manual respectively. Title Pages will be prepared in manuscript.

Place	Date 1917	Hour	Summary of Events and Information		Remarks and references to Appendices
	June				
RECQUES	16		Battalion Resting. Company Training. Bathing	GMG	
do	17		do Church Services.	GMG	
do	18		do Company Training	GMG	
do	19		do do.	GMG	
do	20		do do.	GMG	
do	21		do Battalion Training. Vth Army Commander present.	GMG	
ST. MOMELIN	22	5.30am	Battalion marched to ST. MOMELIN (ref. map HAZEBROUCK 5A).	GMG	
do	23		Battalion Resting. Inspection of Kit.	GMG	
do	24		do Church Services.	GMG	
do	25		do Company Training. CAPT. H.A. LUCAS, R.A.M.C. transferred from the Battalion. CAPT. J.W. BENNETT, R.A.M.C., took over duties of Battalion M.O.	GMG	
do	26		do Company Training.	GMG	
do	27		do do	GMG	
do	28		do do	GMG	
do	29		do do	GMG	
do	30		do do Total Strength of Battalion at 30/6/17 35 Officers 1020 O.R. Total with unit 32 Officers 939 O.R.	GMG	

R. Campbell
Lieut Colonel
Commanding 1/8th Arg. & Suth. Highrs.

1875 Wt. W593/826 1,000,000 4/15 J.B.C. & A. A.D.S.S./Forms/C. 2118.

4th Bn. Arg. & Suth. Highrs.

WAR DIARY
or
~~INTELLIGENCE SUMMARY~~
(Erase heading not required.)

Volume III, Sheet No 33

Army Form C. 2118

Vol 27

Instructions regarding War Diaries and Intelligence Summaries are contained in F. S. Regs., Part II. and the Staff Manual respectively. Title Pages will be prepared in manuscript.

Place	Date 1917	Hour	Summary of Events and Information	Officers K	Officers W	Officers M	Other Ranks K	Other Ranks W	Other Ranks M	Remarks and references to Appendices
	July									
ST. MOMELIN	1		Battalion Resting. Church Services.							
do	2		do. Company Training.							
		2.15 p.m.	Transport moved by road to forward area (O.O. No 34).							
do	3	2.30 p.m.	Battalion marched to ST. OMER and entrained for POPERINGHE. On arrival Battalion marched to billets at A.30 Central (Sheet 28 N.W.) near VLAMERTINGHE.							
VLAMERTINGHE	4		In Bde. Reserve.							
do	5		do							
do	6		do							
do	7	7.40 p.m.	The Battalion marched to the trenches in C 14 & 15 (ref. map 28 N.W.), and relieved the 1/5th Bn. Seaforth Highlanders. Lieut. R. H. J. CLARK, 2/Lieuts. J. RUSSELL, G. C. M. GARDNER, and T. A. HAMILTON, wounded	-	4	-	-	1	-	
YSER CANAL	8		In trenches in C 14 & 15.	-	-	-	-	3	-	
	9		do do					9	-	
	10		do do. Battalion relieved by 1/9th Bn. The Royal Scots, and marched to camp at A.30 central (Ref. map 28 N.W.)					1	-	

1875 Wt. W593/826 1,000,000 4/15 J.B.C. & A. A.D.S.S./Forms/C. 2118.

1/8th Bn. Arg. & Suth. High^rs

Volume III, Sheet No 34

Army Form C. 2118

Instructions regarding War Diaries and Intelligence Summaries are contained in F. S. Regs., Part II. and the Staff Manual respectively. Title Pages will be prepared in manuscript.

WAR DIARY

~~or~~

~~INTELLIGENCE SUMMARY~~

(Erase heading not required.)

Place	Date 1917	Hour	Summary of Events and Information	Officers K	Officers W	Officers M	Other Ranks K	Other Ranks W	Other Ranks M	Remarks and references to Appendices
	July									
VLAMERTINGHE	11	9.30am	Battalion marched to POPERINGHE, and proceeded by Train to ST. OMER. On arrival, Battalion marched to Billets in the LEDERZEELE area. Gm.G							
LEDERZEELE	12		Battalion Resting Gm.G							
do	13		do Gm.G							
do	14		do Company Training. Gm.G							
do	15		do Church Services. Bathing Gm.G							
do	16		do Battalion Training on the attack course. Gm.G							
do	17		do do Gm.G							
do	18		do do 1 Officer + 30 OR. to forward area to form dumps etc. Gm.G							
do	19		do do Gm.G							
do	20		do Brigade attack Practice. Gm.G							
do	21		do Inspection of Fighting Kit. Gm.G							
do	22		do Church Services. Gm.G							
do	23		do Preparing for Operations. Completing kit etc. Gm.G	-	-	-	-	9	.	
do	24	3pm	Battalion moved to forward area by bus. Debussed at PROVEN							

1875 Wt. W593/826 1,000,000 4/15 J.B.C. & A. A.D.S.S./Forms/C. 2118.

1/8th Bn. Arg. & Suth. Highlanders

Volume III, Sheet No 35

WAR DIARY

~~or~~

~~INTELLIGENCE SUMMARY.~~

(Erase heading not required.)

Army Form C. 2118.

Instructions regarding War Diaries and Intelligence Summaries are contained in F. S. Regs., Part II. and the Staff Manual respectively. Title pages will be prepared in manuscript.

Place	Date 1917	Hour	Summary of Events and Information	Officers K	Officers W	Officers M	Other Ranks K	Other Ranks W	Other Ranks M	Remarks and references to Appendices
PROVEN	July 24		Battalion marched to Camp at A. 30 central, ref map sheet 28 N.W. GMJ							
A. 30. central	25		Battalion Resting GMJ							
do	26		do GMJ							
do	27		do 1 Officer & 10 O.R. rejoined from dump party GMJ							
do	28	8.15pm	Bn. H.Q., and A and B Coys. moved to assembly trenches & took over garrison of the line GMJ					1		
do	29		C & D. Coys at A 30. central. HQ. and A & B Coys in trenches GMJ					1		
do	30	6.30pm	C & D. Companies marched to the Assembly Trenches. GMJ							
N. of YSER CANAL	31	3.50am	The Battalion attacked the German front line system from C. 15. a. 65.13 to C.14.b. 80.23. The 1/5th Bn. Seaforth Highlanders attacked on the right of the Battalion and the 1/7th Bn. Gordon Highlanders on the left. Three platoons of B Coy attacked the German front line in the first wave. One platoon of A Company attacked the German Second line (CALEDONIAN SUPPORT). The Second wave, consisting of 2 platoons of A Coy and 3 of D Coy passed through and captured the third German line (Calendar Reserve) and FORT CALEDONIA. The Third wave, consisting of 1 platoon of A Coy and 1 platoon of D. Coy went							Ref. map: ST. JULIEN Sheet 28 N.W. 2 Edition 6A. Appendix "D"

D. D. & L., London, E.C. (A7883) Wt. W809/M1672 350,000 4/17 Sch. 52a Forms/C/2118/14

1/8th Bn. Arg. & Suth. Highlanders.

Volume III, Sheet No 36

Army Form C. 2118.

Instructions regarding War Diaries and Intelligence Summaries are contained in F. S. Regs., Part II, and the Staff Manual respectively. Title pages will be prepared in manuscript.

WAR DIARY

~~or~~

~~INTELLIGENCE SUMMARY.~~

(*Erase heading not required.*)

Place	Date 1917	Hour	Summary of Events and Information	Officers K	Officers W	Officers M	Other Ranks K	Other Ranks W	Other Ranks M	Remarks and references to Appendices
N. of YSER CANAL	July 31		through and captured and consolidated MULLER'S COT and BELOW FARM respectively. All objectives were reached and captured, and the 1/6th Bn. Seaforth Highlanders passed through the Battalion to attack the further objectives. C Company was held in reserve at HARDY'S TRENCH. At about 11.30 a.m. orders were received from the Brigade, to advance 2 platoons of the reserve Company to BRITTANIA FARM where the were to come under the orders of the O.C. 1/6th Seaforth Highlanders. This was done and these platoons (Nos 9 & 10) were sent to reinforce the firing line just S.W. of the STEENBECK River. Later, they crossed the river and occupied and consolidated the MAISON DU RASTA, but were ultimately withdrawn from there by order of O.C. 1/6th Seaforth Highlanders. Casualties. - 2/Lieut. J. CRERAR, Killed. Capt. W. H. L. KIDSTON, 2/Lieuts. A.M. SMITH, G.R. SWAN and A.D. CAIRNS, wounded.	1	4	-	14	94	9	

[initials]

R Campbell [signature]

Lieut. Colonel.

Commanding, 1/8th Arg. & Suth. Highlanders.

D. D. & L., London, E.C.
(A7883) Wt. W803/M1672 350,000 4/17 Sch. 52a Forms/C/2118/14

SECRET.   Copy No. 9.

OPERATION ORDER, No.43,
by
Lieut-Colonel A. Campbell, D.S.O., Commanding 1/8th (The Argyllshire) Battalion Princess Louise's (Argyll & Sutherland) Highlanders.

Ref: Map ST.JULIEN, 1/10,000.

Wednesday, 25th July, 1917.

1. The Fifth Army will attack the enemy's lines North and East of YPRES, on a date to be notified later.

2. The 51st Division will attack with the 152nd.Bde on the Right and the 153rd Bde. on the Left. The 117th Bde (39th Divn) will attack on the Right of the 152nd.Bde.

3. On "Z" day at Zero the Battalion will attack and capture the German Front Line system of trenches.
The 7th Gordon Highrs. will attack on the left of the 8th Argylls. The 5th Seaforth Highrs. will attack on the Right. The 6th Seaforth Highrs. will pass through the Battalion and capture further objectives.

4. BOUNDARIES OF ATTACK.
The various boundaries of the attack are shown on the ST.JULIEN map issued to Companies. The boundaries of the Battalion Attack are :-

On the Left - C.14.b.8023
C.14.b.9529.
C.15.a.4.8.
C.15.a.5697.

On the Right - C.15.a.6513.
C.15.a.9940.
C.15.b.4474.

5. The Battalion will assemble for the Attack in the British front line trench from C.14.d.5065 to C.15c.3074. ready to advance in waves as already detailed.

6. OBJECTIVES AND METHOD OF ATTACK.
The first objective, CALEDONIA Trench and CALEDONIA Support, will be captured by 5 platoons (3 platoons of "B" Coy for CALEDONIA Trench, and 1 platoon of "B" and 1 platoon of "A" Coy for CALEDONIA Support).
These two trenches will be captured in one rush.
The second objective, CALEDONIA RESERVE (BLUE line) - will be captured by 5 platoons (3 platoons of "D" Coy and 2 platoons "A" Coy). The platoon of "A" Coy on the right flank will detail 2 sections to clear MULLERS COT.

The third objective, BELOW FARM and FORT CALEDONIA, will be captured by 1 platoon of "D" Coy (BELOW FARM) and 1 platoon of "A" Coy (FORT CALEDONIA).

The first wave of 5 platoons (4 "B" and 1 "A") will advance at Zero hour.
The second wave of 5 platoons (3 "D" and 2 "A") will advance at 50 paces' distance from the preceding wave.
The third wave of 2 platoons (1 "D" and 1 "A") will advance 50 paces in rear of the second wave.
"C" Company will be in reserve in HARDY'S TRENCH.

7. As each of the objectives is captured and the succeeding wave passes through, the troops who have captured their objectives become available as a reserve to assist in the assault of further objectives. The Commander on the spot will call on them on his own initiative, informing Battalion H.Q. by runner.

8. As each objective is captured, every Commander will at once get touch with the troops on his flanks, and if necessary will energetically attack any parties of the enemy who are holding up his neighbours. Failure to

OPERATION ORDER No.43, Continued:-

8/. to do so would result in succeeding waves being held up.
A special party will be detailed by O.C."D" Coy to go out from BELOW FARM to the left as soon as the objective is captured, to get in touch with a party of 7th Gordon Highrs. who will be sent to meet them. This party will be under command of a senior N.C.O. of this platoon.

9. ACTION ON CAPTURE OF OBJECTIVES.
(a) The platoons who capture the first objective will consolidate on the line gained. 2 Officers and 100 men of these platoons will be held available for work on making an artillery track across no man's land' when called for by R.E.
(b) The 5 platoons who capture the BLUE line will, when the attacking waves of the 6th Seaforth Highrs. of the BLACK LINE have passed through them, be withdrawn behind the crest of the hill and consolidate a line 50 yards in rear of the crest, with observation posts on the crest of the hill.
(c) The 2 platoons who capture the third objective will consolidate an outpost line, BELOW FARM, N.E. end of FORT CALEDONIA towards Battalion Boundary on the line of WELSH FARM.
All consolidation will be done in groups.

10. DRESS, EQUIPMENT, RATIONS AND WATER.
As laid down in Section XI. Brigade Instructions (issued to Companies), except that the kilt apron will not be worn.

11. LEWIS GUNS.
30 filled magazines per gun will be taken into action.

12. PIGEONS.
One station of 2 birds will be sent with platoons detailed for the capture of the BLUE LINE.

13. AEROPLANE CONTACT PATROL.
Flares white or red will be lit by the foremost lines of troops only, whenever the aeroplane calls for them either by a succession of "A's" on the Klaxon Horn or by a succession of white lights.
On no account must flares be lit by troops in rear of the foremost line.

14. BARRAGE.
The Barrage will be shrapnel, and will lift in accordance with the Barrage Map issued to Companies.

15. "S.O.S".
From Zero onwards, S.O.S. is 4 lights,(2 red, 2 green) fired rapidly in that order, and repeated until artillery opens. They will be fired either -
(a) By S.O.S. rifle grenades, i.e 1 signal grenade bursting into 2 red and 2 green;
(b) By rockets ,2 red, 2 green; or
(c) By Very lights, 2 red, 2 green.

16. PRISONERS.
Prisoners will be taken to Brigade Headquarters at FOCH FARM; escorts will return to their Companies as soon as they hand them over.

17. LOCATION OF AID POST.
HEADINGLY LANE.

18. HEADQUARTERS.
Brigade H.Q. - FOCH FARM, C.20.d.1.9.
Battalion H.Q. - British Front Line, C.14.d.7075.

19. /

OPERATION ORDER No.43. Continued:-

19. In order to avoid information falling into the hands of the enemy, no documents, maps or papers, including private letters, will be taken into action except those enumerated in Section XX. of Brigade Instructions (issued to Companies). All papers and letters must either be placed in the packs, or collected under Company arrangements, and stored in the Pack Store.

20. Packs, blankets, greatcoats, and entrenching tools will be stored at 31, RUE DE L'HOPITAL, POPERINGHE.

21. DISTINGUISHING MARKS.
Distinguishing Marks will be worn by troops detailed for objectives as under :-

Front Line - - Nil.
CALEDONIA Support - - Yellow.
BLUE LINE - - - - Dark Blue.
BLUE Outpost Line - - Light Blue.
Carrying Parties - - Yellow band on the arm.

22. ACKNOWLEDGE. ackd

Gavin McGallen

Lieut.,
A/Adjt.,
1/8th Bn. Argyll & Suth'd Highrs.

Issued at 9.45 p.m.
Copy No.1....Filed.
2 - 5...Companies.
6....Hdqrs.
7....Q.M. & T.O.
8....Brigade.
9....O.C.7th Gordon Hrs.
10....O.C.5th Seaforth Hrs.
11....O.C.6th Seaforth Hrs.

1/8th Bn. Arg. & Suth'd Highlanders.

Volume III Sheet 37

152/51

Army Form C. 2118.

Instructions regarding War Diaries and Intelligence Summaries are contained in F. S. Regs., Part II, and the Staff Manual respectively. Title pages will be prepared in manuscript.

WAR DIARY

~~or~~

~~INTELLIGENCE SUMMARY.~~

(Erase heading not required.)

Vol 28

Place	Date 1917	Hour	Summary of Events and Information	Officers K	Officers W	Officers M	Other Ranks K	Other Ranks W	Other Ranks M	Remarks and references to Appendices
YSER CANAL	August 1		Holding captured trenches in front of YSER CANAL. 2 Platoons of C Coy attached to 6th Seaforth Highlanders in the Green Line, near FERDINAND FARM (Ref. map: ST JULIEN 1:10,000). A and D Companies dug in near GERMAN 2nd line. B Coy withdrawn to original British Front line. 2 Platoons of C. Coy in reserve in HARDY'S TRENCH.							
		3.30pm	Battalion withdrawn from the trenches and marched to Camp at A.30. Central (Ref. map: Sheet 28 N.W.)							
A.30 central	2		Battalion resting							
do	3		do , Refitting.							
do	4	3.50pm	Battalion marched to SIEGE CAMP (B.20d.6.7 Sheet 28 N.W.)							
SIEGE CAMP	5		Battalion resting. Church services							
		10.45pm	Enemy aeroplane dropped six bombs in camp.				1	6	-	
do	6		Battalion resting and refitting. Training of Rifle Grenadiers & Lewis Gunners							
do	7		do do Company training in anti-M.G. tactics.							
do	8	6.0am	Battalion marched to School Camp, ST. JANSTER BIEZEN (Ref. map Sheet 27, 1:40,000)							

D. D. & L., London, E.C. (A7883) Wt. W807/M1672 350,000 4/17 Sch. 52a Forms/C/2118/14

1/8th Bn. Arg. & Suth'd. Highlanders. Volume III, Sheet 38.

WAR DIARY

~~or~~

~~INTELLIGENCE SUMMARY.~~

(*Erase heading not required.*)

Army Form C. 2118.

Instructions regarding War Diaries and Intelligence Summaries are contained in F. S. Regs., Part II, and the Staff Manual respectively. Title pages will be prepared in manuscript.

Place	Date	Hour	Summary of Events and Information	Officers K	Officers W	Officers M	Other Ranks K	Other Ranks W	Other Ranks M	Remarks and references to Appendices
	1917 August									
ST. JANSTER BIEZEN	9		Battalion Resting. Company Training. GMcF							
do	10		do do { Stress laid on training in the use of GMcF							
do	11		do do { rifle grenades & method of dealing with GMcF							
do			{ machine Guns in the attack.							
do	12		do. Church Services GMcF							
do.	13		do Company Training GMcF							
do	14		do do 2nd Lieuts. V. McD. POOLE, W.B. WHYTE, and A.R. ALLAN joined. GMcF	-	.	-	-	1	-	
do	15		do do Brigade Rifle Grenade Competition, C. Coy, gained 1st prize. GMcF							
do	16		do do 2nd Lieut J.A. BEVERIDGE joined. GMcF							
do	17		do do GMcF							
do	18		do do GMcF							
do	19		do Church Services. GMcF							
do	20		do Companies Training GMcF							
do	21	3.0pm	do. The Corps Commander, XVIIIth Corps presented medal ribbons to Brigade. 18 ribbons received. The Brigade was afterwards inspected by the Field Marshal Commanding-in-Chief. GMcF							

D. D. & L., London, E.C. (A7683) Wt. W803/M1672 350,000 4/17 Sch. 52a Forms/C/2118/14

1/8th Bn. Arg. & Suth'd. Highlanders.

Volume III, Sheet 39

Army Form C. 2118.

WAR DIARY
or
~~INTELLIGENCE SUMMARY.~~
(Erase heading not required.)

Instructions regarding War Diaries and Intelligence Summaries are contained in F. S. Regs., Part II. and the Staff Manual respectively. Title pages will be prepared in manuscript.

Place	Date 1917	Hour	Summary of Events and Information	Remarks and references to Appendices
ST. JANSTER -	August			
BIEZEN	22		Battalion Resting. Companies Training	G.W.J.
do	23		do . do Brigade Drill Competition. No 3 Platoon and	
			No 12 Platoon ties for 3rd place.	G.W.J.
do	24		Battalion Resting. Companies Training. 2nd Lieuts. J. CLEMENT, C. MACTAGGART,	
do			H.H. DUFF, A. MUIR, A.S. MURRAY and J.S. HENDERSON joined for duty	G.W.J.
do	25		Battalion Resting, Companies Training 2nd Lieut D. McCHLEARY joins for duty	G.W.J.
do	26		do Church Services	G.W.J.
do	27		do Companies Training CAPT. D. McGEE joins for duty	G.W.J.
do	28		do do CAPT. S.J. MALCOLM joins for duty	G.W.J.
do	29	3.15p	Battalion moved by train from POPERINGHE to REIGERSBURG, and marches to bivouacs	
			near MORAT FARM	
		7.45p	Battalion relieved 6th Seaforth Highlanders in dug-outs on YSER CANAL BANK, near ESSEX FARM	G.W.J.
ESSEX FARM	30		In Brigade Reserve.	G.W.J.
do	31		do Total strength at 31/8/17 44 off. 1020 OR. Actually with unit 33 off. 887 OR.	G.W.J.

R. Campbell Lieut Colonel
Commanding, 1/8th Bn. Arg. & Suth'd Highlanders.

D. D. & L., London, E.C.
(A7883) Wt. W803/M1672 350,000 4/17 Sch. 52a Forms/C/2118/14

1/8th Bn. Arg & Suth'd Highlanders

Volume III Sheet No 40

WAR DIARY
~~or~~
~~INTELLIGENCE SUMMARY.~~
(*Erase heading not required.*)

Army Form C. 2118.

Instructions regarding War Diaries and Intelligence Summaries are contained in F. S. Regs., Part II. and the Staff Manual respectively. Title pages will be prepared in manuscript.

Vol 29

Place	Date 1917	Hour	Summary of Events and Information	Officers K	Officers W	Officers M	Other Ranks K	Other Ranks W	Other Ranks M	Remarks and references to Appendices
	September									
ESSEX FARM	1		In Brigade Reserve							
do	2		do							
		7.10pm	Battalion marches to front line and relieved the 6th Bn. Gordon Highlanders in the right battalion sector. Battalion H.Q. at MON BULGARE (C.5.C.8.8. Sheet: ST. JULIEN 1:10,000). Front consisted of small posts along the line VIEILLES MAISONS (C 6 b 40.35), BULOW FARM, to the LEKKERBOTERBEEK at U 30 C.6.7. (Sheet: POELCAPPELLE 1:10,000) "B" Coy holding the right of the front from VIEILLES MAISONS to BULOW FARM, "C" Coy from BULOW FARM to U 30 C 6.7. "D" Coy in support in dug-outs at MON DU RASTA (C.5.a.) "A" Coy in reserve W. of Canal Bank.							
LANGEMARCK LINE	3		In trenches. Enemy consistently barraged the area between the LANGEMARCK – ST JULIEN ROAD and the STEENBEEK.	-	-	-	-	3	-	+ 38
do	4	11.0pm	In trenches. Intercompany relief "A" Coy relieved "B" Coy, and "D" Coy relieved "C" Coy.	-	-	-	-	12	-	
do	5		In trenches.	-	-	-	3	-	-	
do	6	7.30am	do The 5th Bn Seaforth Highlanders on our left, raided the enemy in PHEASANT TRENCH, with 3 officers and 100 O.R. The barrage which the enemy put down in reply was not so heavy as it had been on the previous day.							

D. D. & L., London, E.C. (A7883) Wt. W803/M1672 350,000 4/17 Sch. 52a Forms/C/2118/14

1/8th Bn. Arg. + Suth'd Highlanders

Volume III. Sheet No 41

WAR DIARY
~~or~~
~~INTELLIGENCE SUMMARY.~~
(Erase heading not required.)

Army Form C. 2118.

Instructions regarding War Diaries and Intelligence Summaries are contained in F. S. Regs., Part II, and the Staff Manual respectively. Title pages will be prepared in manuscript.

Place	Date 1917	Hour	Summary of Events and Information		Officers K	Officers W	Officers M	Other Ranks K	Other Ranks W	Other Ranks M	Remarks and references to Appendices
	September										
LANGEMARCK LINE	6	8.30am	(?) At about 8.30 am a party of the enemy raided our right posts near VIEILLES MAISONS and succeeded in entering the block-house occupied by 2nd Lieut G.C. HALDANE and the platoon headquarters of No 3 Platoon. After the action 2nd Lieut G.C. HALDANE and 11 Other Ranks were found to be missing								
		10 pm	The Battalion was relieved by the 1/9th Bn. Royal Scots. On relief companies marched to ESSEX FARM, where hot food was provided, and thence marched to DIRTY BUCKET CAMP (A 30 central).	GMcG			1	2	8	11	
DIRTY BUCKET CAMP	7		Battalion Resting. Bathing.	GMcG							
do	8		do Companies Training	GMcG							
do	9		do Church Services	GMcG							
do	10		do Companies Training	GMcG							
do	11		do do	GMcG							
do	12		do do Range Practices. LIEUT. H.P.F. MACINTOSH joined	GMcG							
do	13		do do do	GMcG							
do	14	6.30pm	do 8 Off and 46 O.R. proceeded by Light Railway to forward area to work on Cable burying during the night	GMcG					1		

D. D. & L., London, E.C. (A7883) Wt. W803/M1672 350,000 4/17 Sch. 52a Forms/C/2118/14

1/8th Bn. Arg & Suth'd Highrs — WAR DIARY — Volume III. Sheet 42. — Army Form C. 2118.

WAR DIARY

~~or~~

~~INTELLIGENCE SUMMARY.~~

(Erase heading not required.)

Instructions regarding War Diaries and Intelligence Summaries are contained in F. S. Regs., Part II. and the Staff Manual respectively. Title pages will be prepared in manuscript.

Place	Date 1917	Hour	Summary of Events and Information	Officers K	Officers W	Officers M	Other Ranks K	Other Ranks W	Other Ranks M	Remarks and references to Appendices
DIRTY BUCKET CAMP.	Sept. 15		Battalion Resting.							
do	16		Working Parties in forward areas, and constructing rifle ranges at SIEGE and MURAT CAMPS. GMcF							
do	17		Battalion Resting Companies Training GMcF							
do	18		do do Preparing for operations GMcF							
do	19	9.50pm	Battalion marched to vicinity of VARNA FARM, COMEDY FARM, GOURNIER FARM, CANE TRENCH, and CANE AVENUE. In reserve to 154th Inf. Bde. Battalion HQ at VARNA FARM, "A" Coy H.Q. COMEDY FARM, 'B' and 'C' Coys in vicinity of CANE POST, 'D' Coy GOURNIER FARM. (Ref map: Sheet PILKEM 1:10,000) GMcF							
VARNA FARM	20	5.40am	The 154th Inf. Bde attacked on a frontage from C.6.b.35.05. to U.30.a.00.80 (ref. map. Sheet POELCAPPELLE 1:10,000). The 9th Bn Royal Scots attacked on right, and 4th Bn Seaforth Highlanders on the left. Inter-battalion boundary: the LEKKERBOTTERBEEK. These battalions were allotted the capture of the dotted Blue Line. The 7th Bn Arg & Suthd Highrs on the right, and the 4th Bn Gordon Highrs on the left, passed through the leading battalions and captured the Blue Line.							
		10.15am	Orders received from H.Q., 154 Bde. to move 1 Company to reinforce 4th Gordon Highrs							

D. D. & L., London, E.C. (A7883) Wt. W803/M1672 350,000 4/17 Sch. 52a Forms/C/2118/14

1/8th Bn. Arg & Suth's Highrs.

Volume III, Sheet No 43.

Instructions regarding War Diaries and Intelligence Summaries are contained in F. S. Regs., Part II. and the Staff Manual respectively. Title pages will be prepared in manuscript.

WAR DIARY

~~or~~

~~INTELLIGENCE~~ SUMMARY.

(Erase heading not required.)

Army Form C. 2118.

Place	Date 1917	Hour	Summary of Events and Information	Officers K	Officers W	Officers M	Other Ranks K	Other Ranks W	Other Ranks M	Remarks and references to Appendices
VARNA FARM	Sept. 20		on the left sector, near PHEASANT FARM CEMETARY. A Company moved at 11.15 am via MILITARY BRIDGE and SNIPE HOUSE, and reported to OC 4th Gordon Highrs. under whose orders they came. At the same time, C Company moved from CANE TRENCH to COMEDY FARM, and "B" Company was ordered to stand by ready to move at							
		1.30 pm	10 minutes notice. At 1.30 pm orders to move 1 Company to report to O.C. 7th Arg. Suth'd Highrs. at BULOW FARM, were received. "B" Company proceeded there at 3 pm via MON BULGARE.							
		6.0 pm	At 6.0 pm the enemy opened an extremely heavy bombardment on our lines from PHEASANT TRENCH to the STEENBEEK, and at the same time counter attacked with the Division. The two remaining companies ("C" and "D") were ordered forward to reinforce the 4th Gordon Highlanders on the left, and moved up through the hostile barrage, via MILITARY BRIDGE.							
		9.0 pm	Battalion HQ moved to SNIPE HOUSE. At this time the situation remained obscure in front, but the troops were reorganised, and "C" and "D" Companies with the remnants of "A" Company took up a position from V. 25. C. 05. 95. to U.30. a. 95. 95., with posts of 4th Seaforths and 4th Gordons in front. "B" Company							

D. D. & L., London, E.C.
(A7883) Wt. W809/M1672 350,000 4/17 Sch. 52a Forms/C/2118/14

1/8th Bn. Arg & Suth'd High'rs

Volume III, Sheet No 44

WAR DIARY

or

~~INTELLIGENCE SUMMARY.~~

(*Erase heading not required.*)

Army Form C. 2118.

Instructions regarding War Diaries and Intelligence Summaries are contained in F. S. Regs., Part II. and the Staff Manual respectively. Title pages will be prepared in manuscript.

Place	Date 1917	Hour	Summary of Events and Information	Officers K	Officers W	Officers M	Other Ranks K	Other Ranks W	Other Ranks M	Remarks and references to Appendices
SNIPE HOUSE	Sept 20		still remained under the control of O.C. 7th Arg & Suth'd High'rs	2	3	1	12	73	8	
do	21		Holding positions taken on the 20th Consolidating "Shell-holes". Enemy shelling very heavy in rear of Pheasant Trench. At 6.5pm the enemy was seen massing opposite our front. The S.O.S. signal was put up by the right Company and our artillery opened fire and dispersed the enemy. GmY							
		9.0pm	Two Companies 5th Seaforth High'rs relieved our Companies on the Cemetery line. Companies were withdrawn to a position slightly in front of Pheasant Trench. The 5th Seaforth High'rs also relieved the posts of 4th Seaforths and 4th Gordons in front. GmY	-	-	-	1	11	-	
do	22		In support to 5th Seaforth Highlanders.							
		11.0pm	Relieved by 2 Companies 6th Gordon Highlanders. On relief the Battalion proceeded to DIRTY BUCKET CAMP. "B" Company rejoined the Battalion.							
			During the operations described above, the following Officers sustained casualties. Capt S.J. MALCOLM, Killed. 2nd Lieut W.B. WHYTE, Killed.							

D. D. & L., London, E.C. (A7683) Wt. W803/M1672 350,000 4/17 Sch. 52a Forms/C/2118/14

1/8th Bn. Arg & Suth'd Highlanders. Volume III, Sheet No 45

WAR DIARY
or
~~INTELLIGENCE SUMMARY.~~
(Erase heading not required.)

Army Form C. 2118.

Instructions regarding War Diaries and Intelligence Summaries are contained in F. S. Regs., Part II. and the Staff Manual respectively. Title pages will be prepared in manuscript.

Place	Date 1917	Hour	Summary of Events and Information		Officers K	Officers W	Officers M	Other Ranks K	Other Ranks W	Other Ranks M	Remarks and references to Appendices
	Sept.										
SNIPE HOUSE	22		2nd Lieut A. MUIR, missing. Lieut H.P.F. MACINTOSH, wounded. 2nd Lieuts C MACTAGGART and H.H. DUFF, wounded and remained on duty. Major A.W. ROGERSON, wounded	Gnu?	-	1	-	1	9	-	
DIRTY BUCKET CAMP	23		Battalion Resting. Bathing	Gnu?							
do	24	1.0 pm	Battalion marched to SIEGE CAMP.	Gnu?							
SIEGE CAMP	25		Battalion resting. Range practices. Bathing	Gnu?							
do	26		do Range practices	Gnu?							
do	27		do	Gnu?							
do	28		do	Gnu?							
do	29	10.30 pm	do Enemy bombed camp. 2nd Lieut J.A. Beveridge, wounded	Gnu?	1	-	-	-	-	-	
do	30	2.30 am	Battalion marched to PROUEN and entrained for BAPAUME	Gnu?							

R Campbell Lieut. Colonel
Commanding 1/8th Arg & Suth'd Highlanders

D. D. & L., London, E.C.
(A7883) Wt. W803/M1672 350,000 4/17 Sch. 52a Forms/C/2118/14

X.39

CONFIDENTIAL
No 21 (A)
HIGHLAND
DIVISION.

War Diary

152/51

Vol 30

October 1919.

8th Arg & Suth Hrs.

1/8th Battn. Argyll & Sutherland Highlanders.

War Diary

October 1917.

Volume III

Sheets, 46, 47, 48.

1/8th Bn. Arg & Suth'd High'rs

Volume III, Sheet No 46.

WAR DIARY
~~or~~
~~INTELLIGENCE SUMMARY.~~
(Erase heading not required.)

Army Form C. 2118.

Instructions regarding War Diaries and Intelligence Summaries are contained in F. S. Regs., Part II. and the Staff Manual respectively. Title pages will be prepared in manuscript.

Place	Date 1917	Hour	Summary of Events and Information	Officers K	Officers W	Officers M	Other Ranks K	Other Ranks W	Other Ranks M	Remarks and references to Appendices
	October									
ACHIET-LE-PETIT	1	3·45am	Battalion detrained at BAPAUME and marched to Camp at ACHIET-LE-PETIT (Ref. map. LENS 11. 1:100,000.)							
do	2		Battalion Resting. Range Practices. 2nd Lieuts. G.A. RITCHIE and T.R. ALLISON and 21 Other ranks joined for duty.							
do	3		Battalion Resting. Range Practices.							
do	4		do do. 2nd Lieuts. W.M. McLEAN, J.W. CRAWFORD, J.C. BROWN, and A.J. GILCHRIST joined.							
do	5		do do							
BOISLEUX AU MONT	6	8·45am	Battalion marched to camp at S.17.a, near BOISLEUX AU MONT (Sheet 51B S.W.)							
do	7		Battalion resting							
do	8		do Companies training.							
do	9		do do							
do	10		do do							
do	11		do Range practices. Capt. & Adjt. A. MACDONALD and 2nd Lieut. J. STEEL joined for duty.							
do	12		Battn resting. Company training.							
do.	13		do do.							

D. D. & L., London, E.C.
(A7883) Wt. W803/M1672 350,000 4/17 Sch. 52a Forms/C/2118/14

1/8th Battn Arg & Suth Highrs

WAR DIARY
or
~~INTELLIGENCE SUMMARY.~~
(Erase heading not required.)

Volume III
Sheet No 41

Army Form C. 2118.

Instructions regarding War Diaries and Intelligence Summaries are contained in F. S. Regs., Part II. and the Staff Manual respectively. Title pages will be prepared in manuscript.

Place	Date	Hour	Summary of Events and Information		Casualties Officers K	W.	M	OR K	W.	M	Remarks and references to Appendices
BOISLEUX au MONT	1917 Oct 14		Battalion resting. Divine Service 2nd Lt H H Duff to England.	am							
do.	15		do Company training	am							
do	16	2pm	Battn relieved 4th Gordon Highrs in Support, (152nd Inf Bde relieved 153rd Inf Bde) from T.5.a.6.7								
HENINEL			to N 28 d. 3.0. (Map 51B S.W. 1/20000)	am							
do	17		Battn in support. Work parties	am							
do.	18		do do. Major R.G. Mori, MC joined	am					1		
do	19		do do. 2nd Lt A R Allan to England.	am							
do	20		do do	am							
do	21		do do.	am							
do	22	1.30pm	Relieved 6th Gordon Highrs in Right Front subsector from U 1 a 2.6 to O 31 b 2.0.								
HENINEL			(Sheet 51B S.W.) A & C Coys front, B & D Coys support.	am							
do.	23		Battalion in trenches.	am					1		
do	24		do	am							
do	25		do. B & D to front line A & C to support	am							

(A7092) Wt W12839/M1293. 750,000. 1/17. D. D. & L., Ltd. Forms/C.2118/14.

1/8 Bn A & S Highrs

WAR DIARY
~~or~~
~~INTELLIGENCE SUMMARY.~~
(Erase heading not required.)

Instructions regarding War Diaries and Intelligence Summaries are contained in F. S. Regs., Part II, and the Staff Manual respectively. Title pages will be prepared in manuscript.

Volume III
Sheet 48

Army Form C. 2118.

Place	Date	Hour	Summary of Events and Information	Casualties: Officers K	Officers W	Officers M	OR K	OR W	OR M	Remarks and references to Appendices
	1917 Oct									
HENINEL	26		Battn in trenches. am							
do	27		do am					1		
do	28		do am				2	5		
do	29		do Ech B marched to DAINVILLE. Lt W.H. McFarlane 2nd Lt E. Bannerman & 2nd Lt K.P. Craigie joined. 21 OR joined as reinforcements am							
do	30		Battn in trenches. 1 off 24 OR rejoined from 404 Coy R.E. am							
	31	1.30pm	Battn relieved by 26th Bn Northumberland Fus. (103rd Inf Bde) and entrained at HENIN SUR COUJEEL for DAINVILLE, thence march to WARLUS billets. Arrived 7 pm. Capt J.W. Bennett RAMC to England. Lt H.T. Wickert, M.O. R.C. U.S.A. joined am					1		

[illegible] Major
Comdg 1/8 Bn A & S Highrs

D. D. & L., London, E.C.
(A7683) Wt. W803/M1672 350,000 4/17 Sch. 52a Forms/C/2118/14

152nd Brigade.

51st Division.

<u>1/8th BATTALION</u>

<u>ARGYLE & SUTHERLAND HIGHLANDERS</u>

<u>NOVEMBER 1917</u>.

Appendices :-

Reports on Operations 20th - 23rd.

1/8th Battn Arg & Suth'd Highlanders.

Instructions regarding War Diaries and Intelligence Summaries are contained in F. S. Regs., Part II. and the Staff Manual respectively. Title pages will be prepared in manuscript.

WAR DIARY
or
~~INTELLIGENCE SUMMARY.~~
(Erase heading not required.)

Volume III
Sheet 49

Army Form C. 2118.

Place	Date	Hour	Summary of Events and Information	Casualties Officers K	W	M	O.R. K	W	M	Remarks and references to Appendices
WARLUS	1917 Nov. 1		Battalion in Rest Billets, K.36 (Sheet 51C 1-40,000) Resting AW							
do	2		do. Bathing. Interior economy AW							
do	3		do. Bathing do. AW							
do	4		do. Church Services AW							
do	5		do. Battalion Training. AW							
do	6		do. Brigade Training AW							
do	7		do. Company Training AW							
do	8		do. Battalion Training AW							
do	9		do. Brigade Training AW							
do	10		do. Company Training & Range practice AW							
do	11		do. Church Services AW							
do	12		do. Company Training & Range practice AW							
do	13		do Beaumont Hamel Anniversary (Holiday)							
do	14		do Coy Training - Attack practise							
do	15		do Attack practise.							
do	16		do Equipping etc preparatory to move to Area of Attack							

D. D. & L., London, E.C. (A7883) Wt. W803/M1672 350,000 4/17 Sch. 52a Forms/C/2118/14

1/8th Bn Argyll & Sutherland Highlanders.

VOLUME III.

Sheet No 50.

Army Form C. 2118.

WAR DIARY
or
~~INTELLIGENCE SUMMARY.~~

(*Erase heading not required.*)

Instructions regarding War Diaries and Intelligence Summaries are contained in F. S. Regs., Part II. and the Staff Manual respectively. Title pages will be prepared in manuscript.

CASUALTIES.

Place	Date	Hour	Summary of Events and Information	Officers K	Officers W	Officers M	O.R. K	O.R. W	O.R. M	Remarks and references to Appendices
	Novr									
WARLUS.	17.	5.50 a.m.	Battalion left WARLUS for ROCQUIGNY. Entraining BEAUMETZ-LES-LOGES. Detraining BAPAUME, thence by March Route.							
ROCQUIGNY.	18.	5.30 p.m.	Battalion moved by March Route to METZ-en-COUTRE.							
METZ-en-COUTRE.	19.		At 12 noon half Battalion moved to Assembly Positions – Remainder moved at 12 midnight [on 19th/20th.					1		
	20.		The Battalion attacked at 6.20 a.m. and took all its objectives, reaching the	1	2	-	9	39	-	
	20.		Railway 1000 yards South of FLESQUIRES.							
	21.		The Battalion attacked at 6.35 a.m. and took all its objectives, reaching the FLESQUIRES Ridge and Sunken Road running through L.20.c. & L.8.b. (The Red Dotted Line) and consolidation begun by 8.30 a.m.					4		
	22.		Battn rested in FLESQUIRES, having been relieved that morning at 2 a.m. by 5th [Seaforth Highrs.							
	23.		The objective of the Battalion was to form a Right Defensive flank from the FONTAINE-CAMBRAI Railway to a point about 1300 yds. due South, the line running just East of FONTAINE-NOTRE-DAME. The attack of 5th Seaforth Hrs and 6th Gordon Hrs being held up by Machine Gun fire, it was impossible to conform with this plan, and a position was consolidated about 1000 yds South of FONTAINE.	-	5	-	10	53	-	
	24.		At 2 a.m. the Battalion was relieved, partly by the 3rd Coldstream Guards and partly by the Irish Guards, and marched to FLESQUIRES.					1		

D. D. & L., London, E.C.
(A7883) Wt. W803/M1672 350,000 4/17 Sch. 52a Forms/C/2118/14

1/8th Bn A. & S. Highrs

Volume III
Sheet No 50

Army Form C. 2118.

WAR DIARY
or
~~INTELLIGENCE SUMMARY.~~
(*Erase heading not required.*)

Instructions regarding War Diaries and Intelligence Summaries are contained in F. S. Regs., Part II, and the Staff Manual respectively. Title pages will be prepared in manuscript.

Place	Date	Hour	Summary of Events and Information	Casualties: Officers	Casualties: O.R.	Remarks and references to Appendices
FLESQUIRES.	Novr 25		The Battn having rested all day, marched to YTRES, arriving there for entrainment at 8 p.m.			
YTRES.	26.		Having spent the night of 25th/26th in the open at YTRES Station, the Battalion			
AVELUY, BOUZINCOURT			entrained at 10.30 a.m., and arrived at AVELUY at 2.15 p.m. Thence by			
			march route to Billets in BOUZINCOURT. [illegible]			
BOUZINCOURT.	27.		Battalion rested. Re-fitting and cleaning up. [illegible]			
do	28		do. do do. [illegible]			
do	29		Company Training. Musketry, etc. Lt. G. Cumming, 5th Seaforths attached for duty as Battn Sig Officer [illegible]			
do	30.		Route March to MILLENCOURT and back to BOUZINCOURT by SENLIS. [illegible]			
do.		1 p.m.	Warned for move at one hour's notice. Ordered to march to ALBERT at 4.30 p.m. Entrained at ALBERT arriving BAPAUME 8.45 p.m. Marched to BARASTRE, arriving 1 a.m. 1st Dec. [illegible]			

[illegible] Major
for Lt Col Comdg 8th A. & S. Highrs.

D. D. & L., London, E.C.
(A7583) Wt. W809/M1672 350,000 4/17 Sch. 52a Forms/C/2118/14

1/8 A. & S. Hrs.

Headquarters,
152nd Inf. Brigade.

I forward herewith various Appendices dealing with the action of the 8th Argyll & Sutherland Highlanders during Operations on the 20th 21st and 23rd November, 1917. West of CAMBRAI.

Since the Infantry were being preceded by Tanks and not the usual Barrage, and it was not possible for the majority of the men to see the battle ground before the actual attack, the Training before the Battle was chiefly confined to teaching the men:-

(a) to keep far enough behind the Tanks;
(b) Map Reading and study of Model Course;
(c) rapidly extending after passing through the gaps in the wire made by Tanks;
(d) Sectional rushes.

Owing to the Tanks moving so slowly, the tendency was to get too close to them, and the actual practice with the Tanks did much to make the Officers and men realise the slowness of advance compared with the sudden lifts of an ordinary Barrage to which they had been accustomed.

The value of the training given to the men of rapidly extending after passing through gaps in the wire was revealed again and again, and did much to keep the casualties down to a minimum.

As it was only possible for Platoon Commanders to see the actual ground, all N.C.O's, Scouts and Runners were familiarised with the ground as much as possible by a close study of the Map and the Model Course. Since there was no bombardment, all landmarks were easily discernible in the actual ground.

R. G. [illegible] Major

[illegible]

A

On the afternoon of the 19th November, two platoons of each of the Companies detailed to attack the Front Line, Triangle Support, Supporting System and the Railway Embankment, took over the actual battle frontage from the 36th Division. This was a great advantage, as besides having six platoons in the line the men had an opportunity to see the lie of the country. The other two platoons of these three Companies, and the Reserve Company, started from METZ at 12 midnight and marched to positions of assembly. All Companies were in their assembly positions by 4.30 a.m. on the morning of 20th November, two Companies being assembled in the Front Line (DERBY Trench) and two Companies in Support Line (DERBY SUPPORT and STAFFORD SUPPORT) – roughly a frontage of 320 yards in each case.

Before Zero Hour all men had a hot meal.

Zero Hour was at 6.20 a.m., and this time proved to be practically ideal.

The objectives of the Battalion were as follows:-

(i) { The outpost line (2 Sections)
Hindenburg Front Line (3 platoons).

(ii) Triangle Support (3 platoons)

(iii) Mole Trench up to the Grand Ravine inclusive. (2 platoons).

(iv) The Railway Embankment (4 platoons).

At 6.20 a.m. (Zero hour) the Barrage opened. This was the sign for the infantry to start the attack At this time the Tanks were only 40 yards in front of the British Front Line except Tanks Nos 16, 17 and 18, which were just crossing our front line. The troops for the first objective, however, immediately advanced and lay down 50 yards from the British Front Line, and allowed the Tanks to advance 150 yds in front; the sections detailed for the outpost line, keeping close behind the Tanks. The only place in the outpost line which gave trouble was the crater in K. 36. c. 1. from which two machine-guns opened fire. Two Tanks, however, successfully dealt with them, and the 3 platoons for the Hindenburg Front Line continued the advance by short rushes. This objective, after a certain amount of resistance from hostile machine guns and bombers, was eventually captured at 7.30 a.m., and touch was obtained on both flanks.

By this time all the Tanks were inclining towards the right of our objective and the advance became slow, as the left of the objective was left uncovered. Heavy machine-gun fire was encountered. The Tanks eventually spread out and overcame the hostile machine gun fire, and objective (ii) was captured at 7.55 a.m, touch being obtained on both flanks.

~~Tank Crossings~~

After the capture of the second objective the two platoons detailed for the 3rd objective pushed forward and captured MOLE Trench without assistance; two machine guns complete with teams, however, were captured between MOLE trench and the RAVINE — the latter place being captured by 8.20 a.m.

By this time the Company detailed for the Railway Embankment were close up and passed through, following within 200 yards of the Tanks, which were well extended and covering the whole front. The only point which gave any resistance being RAVINE ALLEY, in which 2 officers and 35 other ranks were captured, besides 2 machine guns.

The Railway Embankment was finally reached at 9 a.m, when the position was consolidated.

At this juncture it may be pointed out that the value of the training was again exemplified as Tank crossings were made to enable not only the Tanks for the Second objective to cross the trenches without mishap, but they were afterwards used by both Cavalry and Artillery.

After the 6th Seaforth High^rs had passed through, the Battalion was reorganized and consolidated in depth as follows :-

2 Coys on Railway Embankment.
2 Coys consolidated between the GRAND RAVINE and MOLE Trench.

Operations on 21st Nov: 1917.

B 1. Assembly:-

At 6 a.m. on the 21st all Companies were assembled South of the Railway Embankment as follows:-

3 Companies under cover of the Embankment and just south of it.

1 Company in Sunken Road running through K. 30. a.

The objective of the Battalion was the Sunken Road running through L.1.D, L.2.c. and L.8.b. (the Red dotted line) within the original boundaries of the left Battalion of the 152nd Inf. Bde.

Two Companies were detailed to capture this objective. Each Company was on a frontage of two platoons, the two leading platoons of each Company being leapfrogged by the two rear platoons when they had reached a point 400 yards North of ORIVAL WOOD.

A third Company was detailed for support and to consolidate in depth in line with the Northern edge of ORIVAL WOOD.

The fourth Company was in Battalion Reserve and remained at the Railway Embankment.

This attack was not proceeded by Tanks and only a very slight barrage.

At 6.25 a.m, the leading waves of the 2 companies detailed for the final objective (Red Dotted Line) advanced to the Attack. After passing through the 6th Seaforth High^rs who had made good the ground as far as the/

as far as the BEETROOT FACTORY, only slight resistance was met with: (a) from some dug outs in Sunken Road running through L.8.C. and A. and (b) from House at Cross Roads in L.8.b. At (a) 5 or 6 enemy were killed and 12 prisoners taken, while at (b) 21 prisoners were taken, together with a machine gun. This machine gun and its section was taken complete after an advance had been made against it by sectional rushes.

The final objective was captured, and consolidation begun, by 8.30 a.m., touch being obtained on right and left. Patrols were at once pushed forward to see if CANTAING was occupied. These patrols were allowed to advance as far as the front belt of wire, in front of the village when heavy fire was opened on them, and it was found that the village and particularly a trench south west of the village were strongly held. Just after these patrols came back with information, the leading waves of the 154 Inf. Bde. passed through and began the attack on the village with assistance of Tanks which advanced from a S.E. direction.

About 2 a.m., on the 22nd Nov. the Battalion was relieved by the 5th Seaforth High.rs and withdrew from FLESQUIRES, where billets were found and the men rested during the 22nd.

Operations on 23rd November, 1917.

C/

By 6 a.m. on the 23rd inst. all Companies had assembled in ORIVAL WOOD, after which hour the men had breakfast and had as much rest as possible, before Zero hour, which was at 10.30 a.m.

The objective of the Battalion was to form a right defensive flank from the Railway running from CAMBRAI to FONTAINE to F. 22. central, a frontage of nearly 1350 yards. Two Companies were detailed to form this defensive flank, and 2 companies which were in Battalion Reserve were ordered to consolidate in depth as follows:-

One Coy in vicinity of Sunken Road in F. 21. c. facing Northwards.

One Coy in vicinity of Sunken Road in F. 21. b. and d. facing Eastwards.

At 10.30 a.m. the 2 leading companies detailed for the final objective debouched from ORIVAL WOOD and eventually came within 500 yards of the rear wave of the 6th Seaforth High^rs and 6th Gordon High^rs. The Companies in Bat^n Reserve followed 500 yards ~~from~~ behind the leading two Companies. This formation was kept in spite of a fairly heavy artillery barrage until the 6th Gordon H^rs were met with extremely heavy machine gun fire from the right flank (LA FOLIE WOOD) and frontal fire from the Village of FONTAINE-NOTRE-DAME. The fire was so intense that it was impossible to make any further advance; and one company was pushed forward to form a left defensive flank to the 6th Gordon High^rs who were consolidating about F. 21. c. 45. The other 3 Companies were/

were consolidated in depth in 26b. 27a. and 27c.

At 3.45 p.m. 2 Companies were formed up in 20.d. and 21.c. and one Company in support ready to cooperate with the attack made by the 5th Seaforth Highrs on west end of village, but as this attack did not develop it was impossible to push ~~for~~ home the frontal attack on account of heavy frontal and flank machine-gun fire, and all Companies re occupied their original positions.

F

Signal Communications.

All signal communication forward of Batt^n Hdqrs was done by visual, mainly lamp. The lamp proved itself to be most useful and reliable.

An attempt was made to run a line from first headquarters to German Front Line, but size of the wooden drums of wire were insufficient, and by the time the linesmen returned for more wire the headquarters had moved forward.

When Batt^n Hdqrs. had moved forward to the German second line and to the Gun Pits near FLESQUIRES, we were without telephone communication for some considerable time. In the second instance, we managed after some difficulty in joining up with 6th Seaforth High^rs in FLESQUIRES, but this wire to rear was unreliable. The line we ran direct to RIBECOURT answered requirements.

Regarding the third day's attack, much difficulty and labour would have been saved had we been able to run a line from LA JUSTICE up the Sunken Road as far as the cross roads near where Batt^n Hdqrs. were to be, during the quiet of the previous night or early morning.

Tanks.

D

The action of the Tanks was beyond all praise, and all my officers report that it is impossible to pick out any special Tanks which distinguished themselves – as all did so well.

E

Casualties :-

	OFFICERS.			OTHER RANKS.		
	Killed.	Wnded.	Missing.	Killed.	Wnded.	Missing
19th.	-	-	-	-	1	-
20th.	1	2	-	9	37	2
21st.	-	-	-	-	4	-
22nd.	-	-	-	-	-	-
23rd.	-	5	-	10	52	1
24th.	-	-	-	-	1	-
TOTALS.	1	7	-	19	95	3

Instructions regarding War Diaries and Intelligence Summaries are contained in F. S. Regs., Part II. and the Staff Manual respectively. Title pages will be prepared in manuscript.

WAR DIARY
or
~~INTELLIGENCE SUMMARY~~.
(*Erase heading not required.*)

Army Form C. 2118.

8th A & S Hrs

Vol 32

Place	Date	Hour	Summary of Events and Information	Casualties Officers K	W	M	ORs K	W	M	Remarks and references to Appendices
BARASTRE	DECR 1		The Battn stood at 1 hours notice ready to move into line during German Counterattack at GOUZEACOURT.							
BARASTRE / FREMICOURT	2		Left BARASTRE at 10.30 AM & Marched to MIDDLESEX Camp FREMICOURT							
FREMICOURT	3		The Battn rested							
FREMICOURT	4		The BATTn moved to the Line at LOUVERVAL into Front & Support lines.	-			[illegible]			
LOUVERVAL	5.		In the line as above.	-	-	-	1	-	-	
do	6		do do 2/Lt. J.A.S Henderson rejoined from Hospital	.	.	.	1	3	-	
do	7		do do							
do	8		do do	.	.	.	-	1	.	
do	9		do do.	.	.	.	-	1	.	
LOUVERVAL / FREMICOURT	10		Battn was relieved in the line by 7th Gordons & marched to Tents in FREMICOURT.							
FREMICOURT.	11		The Battn rested							
do	12		The Battn was engaged in camp improvements etc.							
do	13		do do. Lt.Col. Campbell left for England - Lt. J.S. Cameron, " J.R Ramsay, " E.B. McCall, " F.V. [illegible] } Joined for duty.							
do / BANCOURT	14		The Battn moved Camp to new Ground at BANCOURT.							
BANCOURT.	15		The Battn was engaged in Camp impr[illegible]							

D. D. & L., London, E.C.
(A7683) Wt. W803/M1672 350,000 4/17 Sch. 52a Forms/C/2118/14

Instructions regarding War Diaries and Intelligence Summaries are contained in F. S. Regs., Part II. and the Staff Manual respectively. Title pages will be prepared in manuscript.

WAR DIARY
or
INTELLIGENCE SUMMARY.
(Erase heading not required.)

Army Form C. 2118.

Place	Date	Hour	Summary of Events and Information		Officers K	Officers W	Officers M	O.R. K	O.R. W	O.R. M	Remarks and references to Appendices
	DEC.										
BANCOURT.	16.		Company Training - Musketry - Route Marching.	DWH							
"	17		Training	DWH							
"	18		do	DWH							
"	19		do	DWH							
"	20		do	DWH							
"	21		do	DWH	-	-	-	-	1	-	
"	22		do	DWH							
"	23		do Enemy Aeroplanes bombed vicinity at 6 30 pm.	DWH	-	-	-	1	1	-	
"	24		do	DWH							
"	25		~~do~~ Christmas day Holiday.	DWH							
" DEMICOURT }	26		Moved to line in front of DEMICOURT. (A + C Coys + Bn H.Q.) B + D left at BANCOURT.	DWH							
DEMICOURT	27		In the line. B + D Coys moved from BANCOURT to LEBUCQUIERE.	DWH	-	-	-	-	3	-	
"	28		do.	DWH	-	-	-	-	1	-	
"	29		do	DWH							
" FREMICOURT }	30		{ do. The Battn was relieved by 9 RS at 5.25 pm. + marched to FREMICOURT	DWH							
do	31		The Battn rested.	DWH							

(A7883) Wt. W809/M1672 350,000 4/17 Sch. 52a Forms/C/2118/14 D. D. & L., London, E.C.

Vol 33

Confidential

War Diary

of

1/8th Bn. Arg. & Suthd. Highrs.

From 1st to 31st Jan., 1918.

X 42

Vol 34

183/61

February 1918.

War Diary

— of —

8th A. & S. H.

X-43

Instructions regarding War Diaries and Intelligence Summaries are contained in F. S. Regs., Part II. and the Staff Manual respectively. Title pages will be prepared in manuscript.

WAR DIARY
or
INTELLIGENCE SUMMARY.
(Erase heading not required.)

Volume IV
Sheet 1.

Army Form C. 2118.

Place	Date	Hour	Summary of Events and Information	Officers K.	Officers W.	Officers M	O.R. K	O.R. W	O.R. M	Remarks and references to Appendices
	JAN. 1918									
FREMICOURT.	1		New Years Day, a Holiday. Officers joined for duty Capt. A. L. CAMERON posted to "A" Coy. Lt. J. K. McCALLUM " "B" " " G. B. McGEE. " "B" " " A. G. DAVIS. " "D"							
do.	2.		Company Training & Musketry.							
do.	3.		do. do.							
do.	4.		do. do.							
do.	5.		do. do.							
do.	6.		do. do.							
do.	7	11.30 a.m	The Battn. left MIDDLESEX CAMP at 11.30 a.m and proceeded to the LINE in front of DOIGNIES in the LOUVERVAL WOOD - BOURSIES Sector.							
DOIGNIES	8		Battalion in the Line.							
do.	9		" " "							
do.	10		" " "							
do.	11		" " "							
do.	12		" " "					1		
do.	13.		" " "					3		
do.	14		" " "							
do.	15	3p.m.	Battalion relieved in the Line by the 4th Seaforth Hrs. at 3p.m. & marched to FREMICOURT.							
FREMICOURT (Middlesex Camp)	16		Battalion rested. Capt. A. L. LOCKIE left for duty at BOULOGNE.							
do.	17		Battalion moved to BUCHANAN CAMP. at ACHIET-LE-PETIT.							
ACHIET-LE-PETIT	18		Training.							
do.	19		Training. - Lt. Col. J. R. McALPINE-DOWNIE joined & assumed command of the Battalion.							

(A7092). Wt. W12839/M1293. 75,0,0. 1/17. D. D. & L., Ltd. Forms/C.2118/14.

Army Form C. 2118.

WAR DIARY
or
INTELLIGENCE SUMMARY.
(Erase heading not required.)

Volume IV
Sheet 2.

Instructions regarding War Diaries and Intelligence Summaries are contained in F. S. Regs., Part II. and the Staff Manual respectively. Title pages will be prepared in manuscript.

Place	Date	Hour	Summary of Events and Information	Officers K.	Officers W.	Officers M.	O.R. K.	O.R. W.	O.R. M.	Remarks and references to Appendices
	JAN. 1918.									
CHIET-LE-PETIT.	20.		Training. DMD							
do.	21		do. DMD							
do.	22		do. DMD							
do.	23		do. DMD							
do.	24		do. DMD							
do.	25		Inspection by BRIGADE COMMANDER. DMD							
do.	26		Training. DMD							
do.	27		do. DMD							
do.	28		do. DMD							
do.	29		do. DMD							
do.	30		Training – Field Firing at range in L 22. DMD							
do.	31		Inspection by DIVISIONAL COMMANDER. – Presentation of Decorations. DMD							

Maclaurine-Downie
Lt. Col.
Comdg. 1/8th Bn. A. & S. Highlanders

(A7092). Wt W12839/M1293 75,0 0. 1/17. D. D. & L., Ltd. Forms/C.2118/14.

CHARLIE
CHAPLIN
CUBA
CUBA
DASH

CURLY
CUPID
HEAD
NEW TRENCH
CROOK
CROW
CUBA
COTE
30.5.17

13LA 363
20.5.17
CUPID
CORONA
CORONA SUPPORT
COLON

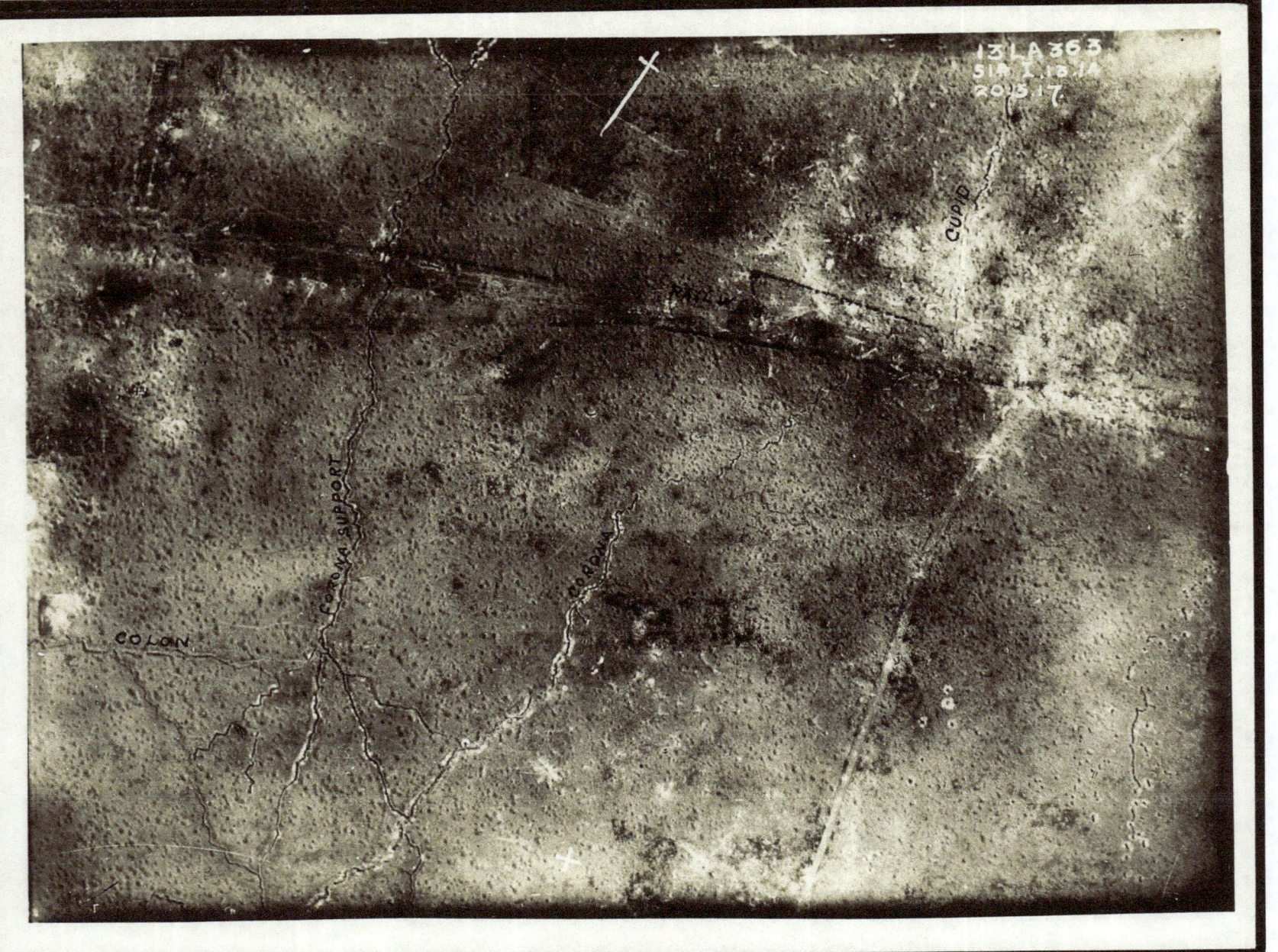

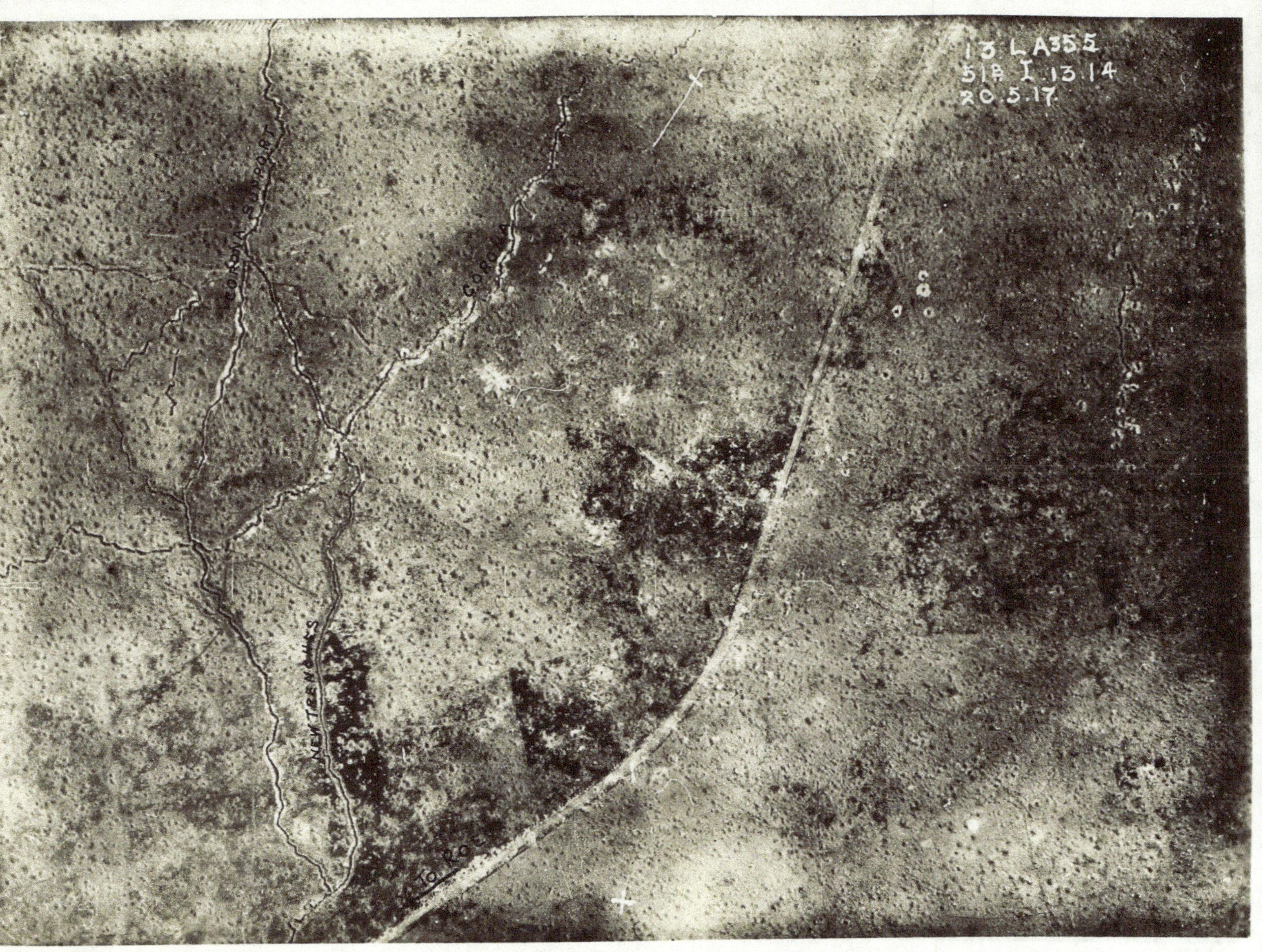
13 LA355
51B I.13.14
20.5.17
CORONA
NEW TRENCHES
CORONA SUPPORT

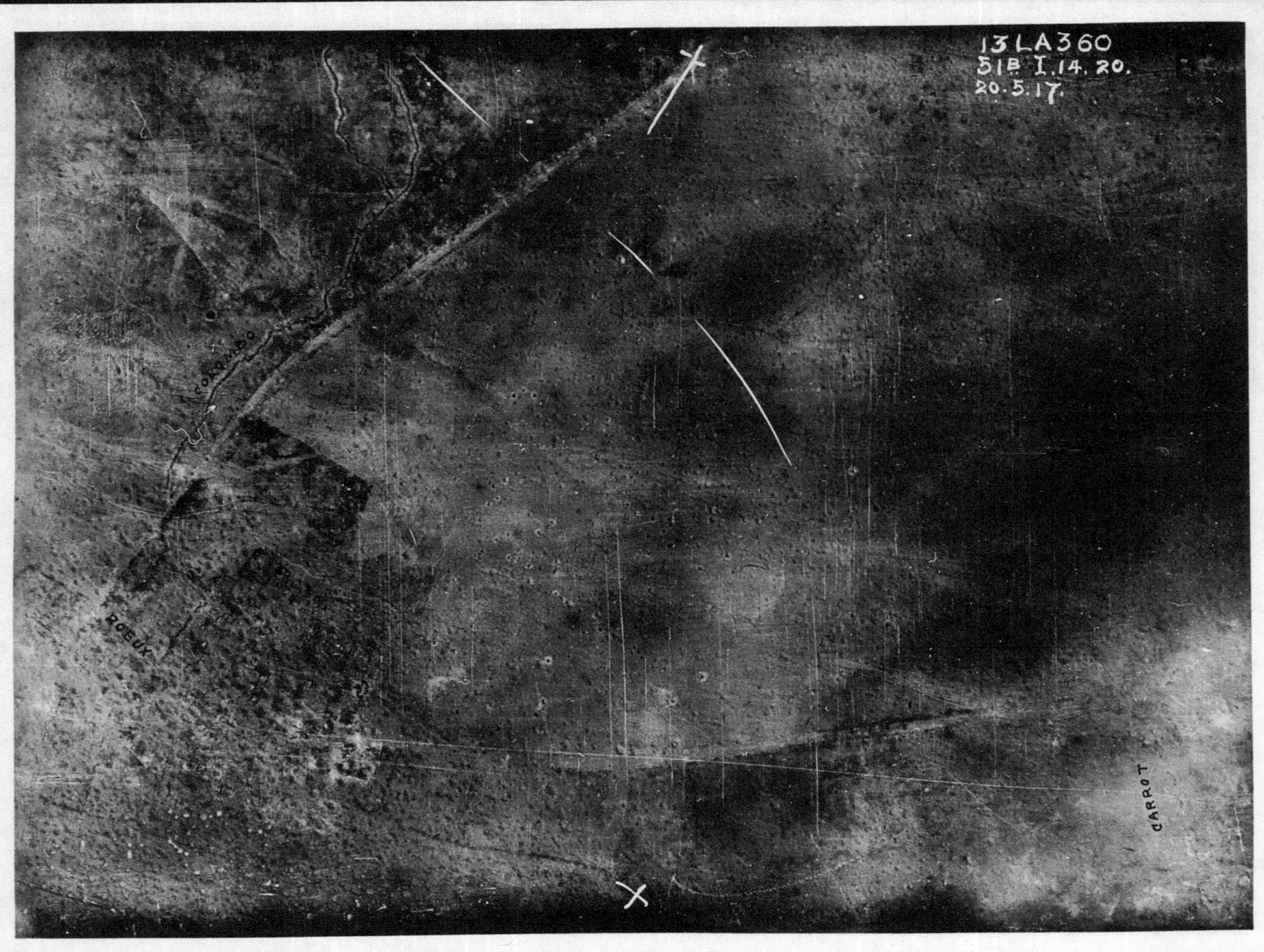
13LA360
51B. I.14.20.
20.5.17.
COLOMBO
ROEUX
CARROT

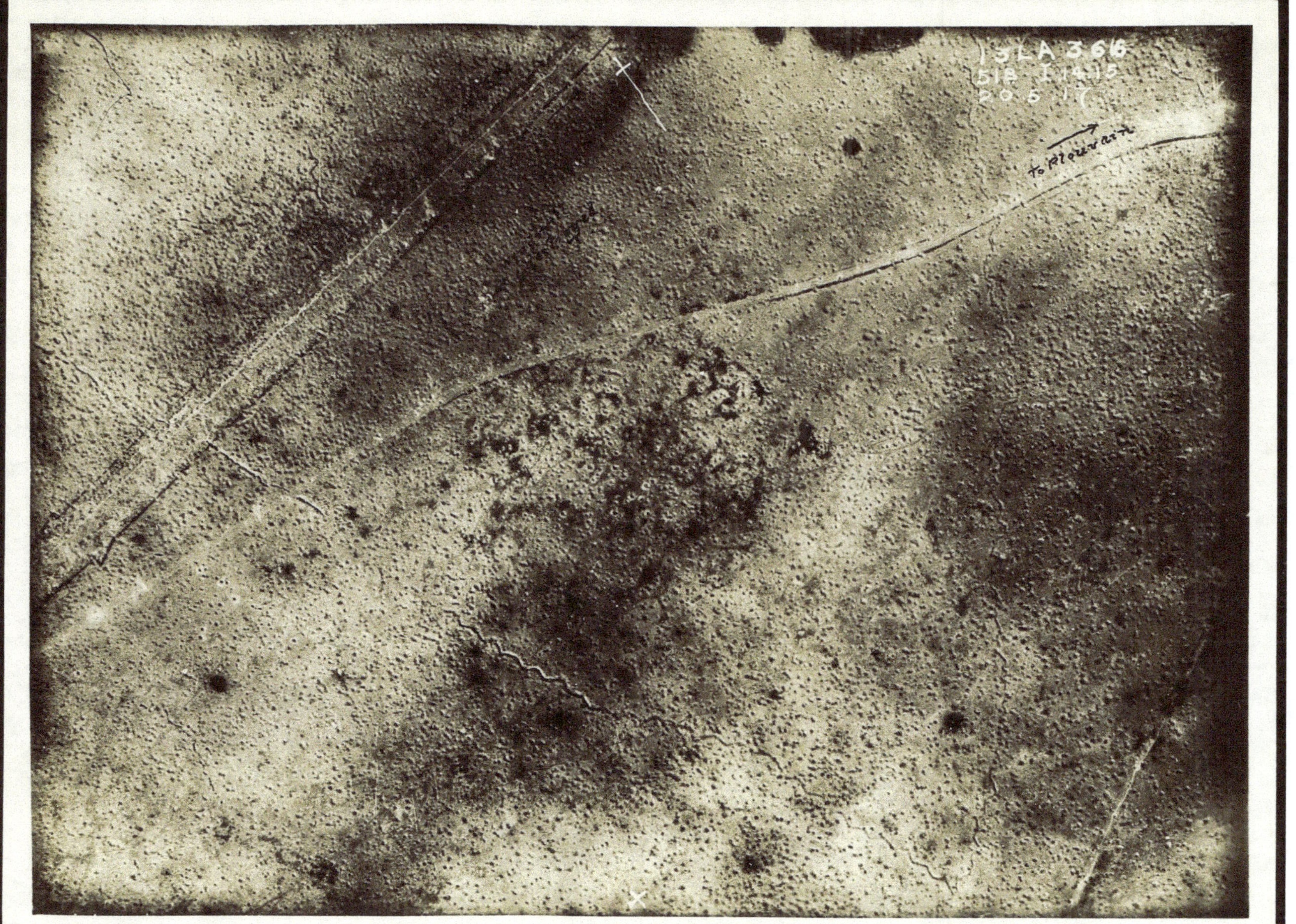
13LA366

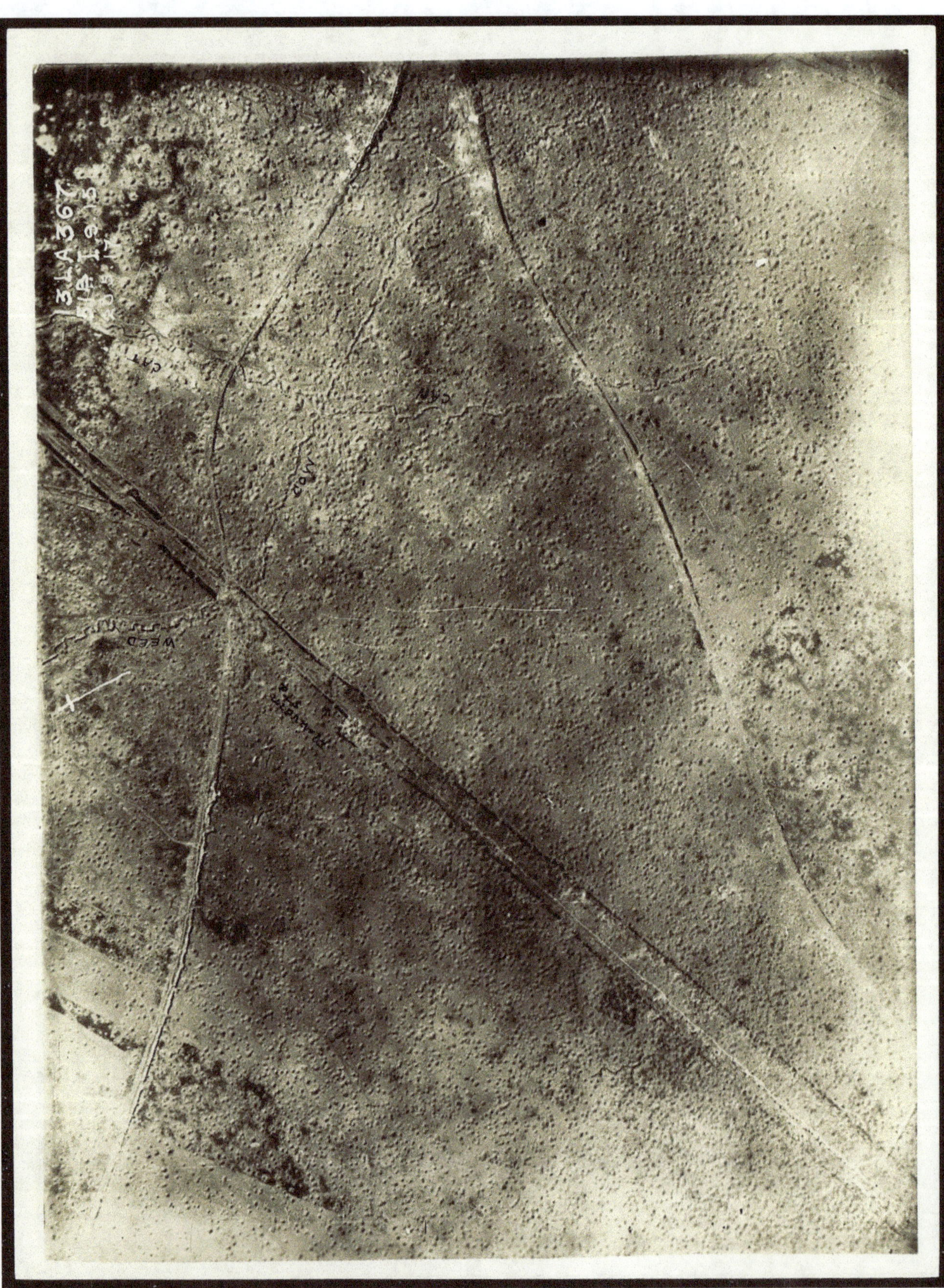

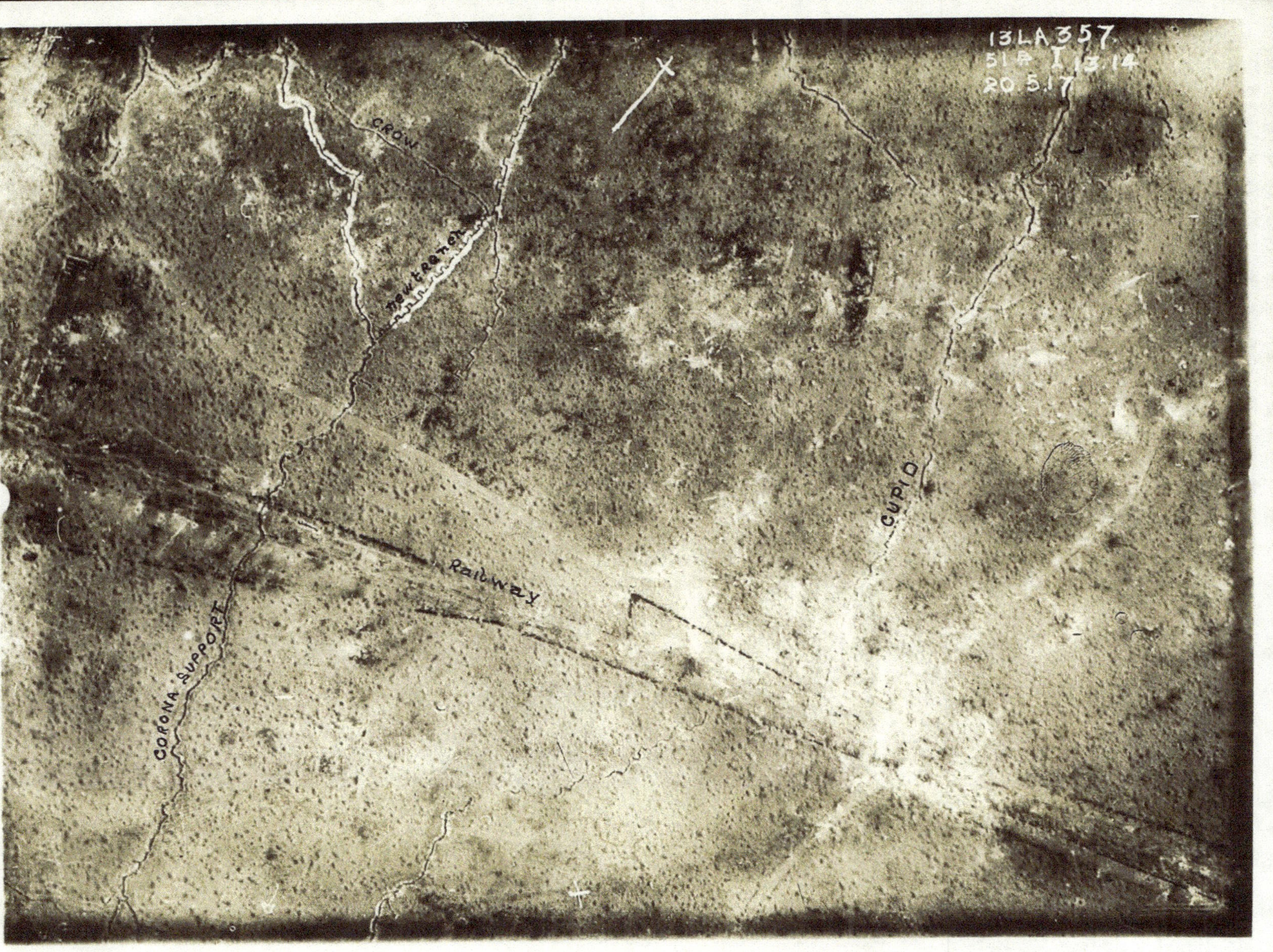
13LA357
51B I.13.14
20.5.17
CROW
new trench
CUPID
Railway
CORONA SUPPORT

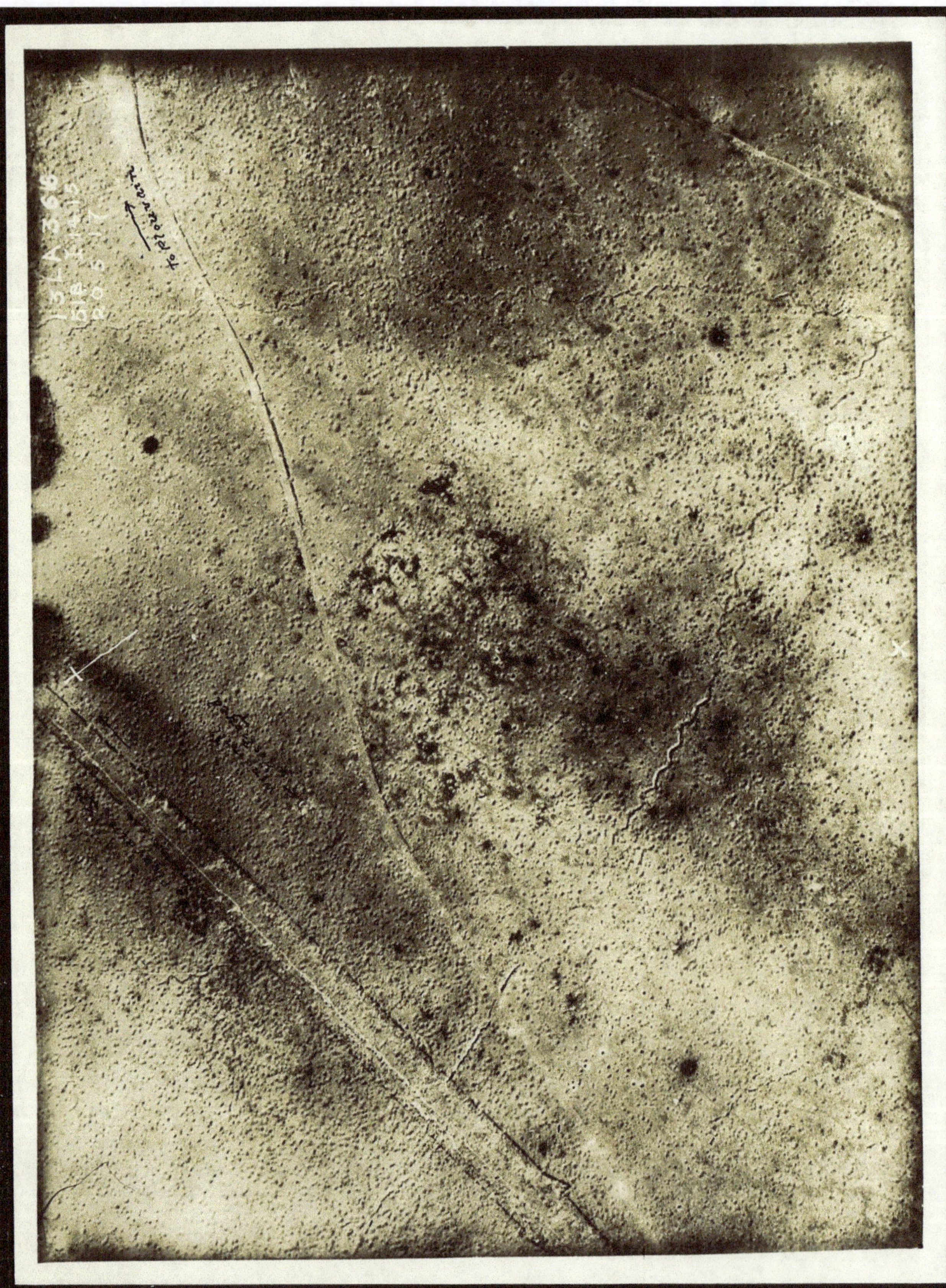

Instructions regarding War Diaries and Intelligence Summaries are contained in F. S. Regs., Part II. and the Staff Manual respectively. Title pages will be prepared in manuscript.

8TH A + S.H

WAR DIARY
or
~~INTELLIGENCE SUMMARY.~~
(Erase heading not required.)

VOLUME IV
Sheet 3.

Army Form C. 2118.

Place	Date	Hour	Summary of Events and Information	OFFRS K	OFFRS W	OFFRS M	O.R. K	O.R. W	O.R. M	Remarks and references to Appendices
BUCHANAN CAMP ACHIET-LE-PETIT.	FEB 1918 1		Training							
do	2		do.							
do	3		Church Parade - preparations for leaving 51st Division.							
do and LANGUEVOISIN	4		Left BUCHANAN Camp at 12 noon + proceeded by Bus to NESLE. Thence by march route to LANGUEVOISIN. Battalion billeted at 6 pm.					1*		*Self-inflicted
do	5		Cleaning up - also Musketry.							
do	6		Training. Musketry etc.							
do + VAUX	7		The Batt proceeded by March route leaving LANGUEVOISIN at 9.30 am arrived VAUX at 3.45 pm. + occupied billets							
VAUX.	8		The Batt came under orders of G.O.C. 183 Inf Bde + was engaged on work in Battle Zone.							
VAUX	9		Battalion worked in Battle Zone under R.E.							
VAUX.	10		Church parades - Orders issued for move into line							
VAUX	11		The Batt proceeded to line leaving VAUX at 3.15 pm. and relieved 2/6 + 2/7 Warwicks in front line							
PONTRUET	12		In the line							
do	13		do					4	1	
do	14		do							
do	15		do							
do	16		do							
do	17		do							
do	18		do					1		
do	19		do							
do + MARTEVILLE	20		The Battalion was relieved in the line by STRATHCONAS Horse and Royal Canadian Dragoons and marched to Huts in MARTEVILLE. Batt all billeted by 10 pm					1		
do	21		Cleaning up and resting							
do	22		The Battalion worked in the Battle Zone							
do	23		Ditto							

RLL ... Major 8 A&SH

(A7092). Wt. W12839/M1293. 75,0.0. 1/17. D. D. & L., Ltd. Forms/C.2118/14.

8th A & SH

Volume IV.
Sheet 4.

Army Form C. 2118.

WAR DIARY
or
~~INTELLIGENCE SUMMARY.~~
(Erase heading not required.)

Instructions regarding War Diaries and Intelligence Summaries are contained in F. S. Regs., Part II. and the Staff Manual respectively. Title pages will be prepared in manuscript.

Place	Date	Hour	Summary of Events and Information	Off[rs] K	Off[rs] W	Off[rs] M	OR K	OR W	OR M	Remarks and references to Appendices
	FEB 18									
MARTEVILLE.	24.		The Battalion worked in Battle Zone. DMP							
do	25		Ditto — G.O.C. 183 Inf Bde inspected Regt Transport DMP							
do	26		Ditto — DMP							
do	27		Ditto — DMP							
do	28		Ditto — Forwarded recommendations for Kings Birthday Dispatch to 51st Division DMP					3		

[illegible signature]

Major
Cmdg 8 A & S H

(A7092). Wt. W12839/M1293. 75,000. 1/17. D. D. & L., Ltd. Forms/C.2118/14.

"A" Form.

Army Form C. 2121.
(In pads of 100.)

MESSAGES AND SIGNALS.

No. of Message..............

Prefix........ Code........ m	Words.	Charge.	This message is on a/c of:	Recd. at .... m.
Office of Origin and Service Instructions.	Sent		.... *Service.*	Date..............
	At............m.			From ....
	To..............			
	By..............		(Signature of "Franking Officer.")	By..............

TO { H.Q 183 Inf Bde

Sender's Number.	Day of Month.	In reply to Number.	AAA
* A 4	6.		

Herewith War Diary for month of February

From

Place

Time

The above may be forwarded as now corrected.

(Z)

Major

Censor.

Signature of Addressor or person authorised to telegraph in his name.

* This line should be erased if not required.

(3796.) Wt. W492/M1647. 650,000 Pads. 5/17. H.W. & V., Ld. (E. 1187.)

1/8th Bn. Arg. & Suthd. Highlanders

Instructions regarding War Diaries and Intelligence Summaries are contained in F. S. Regs., Part II. and the Staff Manual respectively. Title pages will be prepared in manuscript.

WAR DIARY ~~or INTELLIGENCE SUMMARY.~~

(Erase heading not required.)

VOLUME IV

Sheet No 5.

Army Form C. 2118.

183/61

Place	Date 1918	Hour	Summary of Events and Information	Officers K	Officers W	Officers M	Other Ranks K	Other Ranks W	Other Ranks M	Remarks and references to Appendices
MARTEVILLE HUTS	March 1		Battalion working in Battle Zone. G McG							
do	2	3·30pm	Battalion marched to billets at BEAUVOIS. In Brigade Reserve. G McG							
BEAUVOIS	3		In Brigade Reserve. G McG							
do	4		do G McG							
do	5		do G McG							
do	6		do G McG							
do	7		do G McG							
do	8		do G McG							
do	9		do G McG							
do	10	4·45pm	Battalion marched to Trenches in FRESNOY-LE-PETIT area. (Ref. map. Sheet ST. QUENTIN 1:100,000.) G McG							
FRESNOY	11		In Trenches. G McG					1		
do	12		do G McG							
do	13		do G McG							
do	14		do G McG							
do	15		do G McG							
do	16		do G McG					1		
do	17		do G McG							

D. D. & L., London, E.C. (A8004) Wt. W1771/M2031 750,000 5/17 Sch. 52 Forms/C2118/14

www.ingramcontent.com/pod-product-compliance
Lightning Source LLC
Chambersburg PA
CBHW080905230426
43664CB00016B/2727